More Praise for *Leaders Make the Future*

"Bob Johansen's thesis that we, as business leaders, can create and guide our own future in a competitive and ever-changing marketplace has permeated throughout our organization at Scripps Networks Interactive. In *Leaders Make the Future* he takes his thesis to the next level, providing readers with a wise and thought-provoking guide to success in a changing world. It's going to be a must-read at our company."

—Kenneth W. Lowe, Chairman, President, and CEO, Scripps Networks Interactive, Inc.

"The first edition of *Leaders Make the Future* opened new vistas for visionary leaders and provided a road map for them. The second edition creates urgency to develop skill sets necessary to lead by describing the time compression of change and the resulting dynamic interdependencies of the complexity of the changes. These complexities not only require flexible and agile responses but also describe a world in which new measurements are required. These measurements can best be determined using a combination of learning from the social sciences combined with analytical applications or in a sense a set of social differential equations."

—Alfred A. Plamann, CEO, Unified Grocers, Inc.

"Bob Johansen focuses on how leaders can make decisions and perform when the pace of decision making and its consequences in our interdependent world have never been greater. *Leaders Make the Future* provides an analytical and operational framework for decision making in the VUCA soup."

—Thomas H. Glocer, former CEO, Thomson Reuters

"At EA University, we rock with the excitement and dangers of volatile and uncertain futures for our industry. Heck, for our whole world! We use Bob Johansen's concepts and future capabilities in preparing our high-potential leaders for this future. If there is uncertainty in your future, you will want your leaders reading this book."

—Andy Billings, Vice President, Profitable Creativity, EA University, Electronic Arts

"*Leaders Make the Future* is required reading for my students and essential reading for all interested in a better world and social profit. It is concise, readable, understandable, useful, necessary, replete with examples relevant to now and to tomorrow's world, and applicable to both career and daily life."

—Linda Golden, Marlene and Morton Meyerson Centennial Professor in Business, McCombs School of Business, University of Texas at Austin

"*Leaders Make the Future* applies the maker mind-set to leadership. The best leaders in the future will also be makers."

—Dale Dougherty, founder, *MAKE* magazine and Maker Faire

"Bob Johansen offers clear and inspiring guideposts to deal with profound leadership challenges that face us in the 21st century. Leaders take note: you will need both strategy and learning, expressed with great clarity. This book is an important call to action."
—**Willie Pietersen, Professor of the Practice of Management, Columbia Business School**

"Kudos to Bob Johansen for this revised edition of *Leaders Make the Future*! Not only can the leadership skills Bob outlines be applied toward producing effective leaders, but they are excellent for promoting happier, healthier ones too!"
—**Kelly Traver, MD, CEO and founder, Healthiest You**

"Having lived and worked with the future for almost forty years, the Institute for the Future's Bob Johansen returns to the present and shares his key insights on how leaders can move their organizations forward. If you want to thrive in the future—or even create your own—then reading this book will be time well spent."
—**Tom Kelley, General Manager, IDEO, and author of *The Ten Faces of Innovation***

"We find the unique perspective that Bob illustrates in this book incredibly important as we prepare our top leaders for the future."
—**David Small, Vice President, Global Talent Management and Leadership Institute, McDonald's Corporation**

"Bob Johansen has made *Leaders Make the Future* even better since anticipating the economic meltdown in 2008 and closely tracking events since then. By asking what skills leaders will need, working backward from future-shaping forces he and the Institute for the Future have identified, he offers a fresh and important call to action. The book is full of practical advice from watching Silicon Valley's booms, busts, and recoveries for more than three decades."
—**David Sibbet, President, The Grove Consultants International, and author of *Visual Meetings* and *Visual Teams***

"Johansen offers steps to strengthen our skills as well as insights to inspire us to build a better future. It is the must-read partner to his other recent book, *Get There Early*."
—**Jean McClung Halloran, Senior Vice President, Human Resources, Agilent Technologies**

Leaders Make the Future

Leaders Make the Future

Ten New Leadership Skills for an Uncertain World

BOB JOHANSEN

INSTITUTE FOR THE FUTURE

Second edition, Revised and Expanded

Foreword by John R. Ryan, President,
Center for Creative Leadership

Berrett–Koehler Publishers, Inc.
San Francisco
a BK Business book

Berrett-Koehler Publishers, Inc.
235 Montgomery Street, Suite 650
San Francisco, CA 94104-2916
Tel: (415) 288-0260   Fax: (415) 362-2512
www.bkconnection.com

Ordering Information
Quantity sales. Special discounts are available on quantity purchases by corporations, associations, and others. For details, contact the "Special Sales Department" at the Berrett-Koehler address above.
Individual sales. Berrett-Koehler publications are available through most bookstores. They can also be ordered directly from Berrett-Koehler: Tel: (800) 929-2929; Fax: (802) 864-7626; www.bkconnection.com
Orders for college textbook/course adoption use. Please contact Berrett-Koehler: Tel: (800) 929-2929; Fax: (802) 864-7626.
Orders by U.S. trade bookstores and wholesalers. Please contact Ingram Publisher Services, Tel: (800) 509-4887; Fax: (800) 838-1149; E-mail: customer.service@ ingrampublisherservices.com; or visit www.ingrampublisherservices.com/Ordering for details about electronic ordering.

Berrett-Koehler and the BK logo are registered trademarks of Berrett-Koehler Publishers, Inc.

Printed in the United States of America

Berrett-Koehler books are printed on long-lasting acid-free paper. When it is available, we choose paper that has been manufactured by environmentally responsible processes. These may include using trees grown in sustainable forests, incorporating recycled paper, minimizing chlorine in bleaching, or recycling the energy produced at the paper mill.

Library of Congress Cataloging-in-Publication Data

Johansen, Robert.
    Leaders make the future : ten new leadership skills for an uncertain world / Bob Johansen. — 2nd ed., rev. and expanded
        p.   cm.
    Includes bibliographical references and index.
    ISBN 978-1-60994-487-2 (hardcover)
    1. Leadership. 2. Executive ability. I. Title.
    HD57.7.J635   2012
    658.4'092—dc23   2012004912

Second edition
17   16   15   14   10 9 8 7 6 5 4

Project Management and book design: BookMatters; copyediting: Tanya Grove; proofreading: Nancy Evans; indexing: Leonard Rosenbaum. Cover design: Mayapriya Long, Bookwrights; cover image: Chris Harrison.

To Roy Amara
1925–2007

A leader who made the future with strength and humility
All the royalties from this book will go
to joint efforts by Institute for the Future and the Center for Creative
leadership to help prepare leaders to make a better future.

Contents

———

Please look inside the book jacket for a visual forecast map
of external future forces that will shape leaders in the future.

———

A futures context for the rest of the book and a taste of the
external future forces that will shape leaders—thinking ten years
ahead. Each core chapter will explore a leadership skill that will
be important in the future.

Ability to exploit your inner drive to build and grow things, as
well as connect with others in the making. Leaders need this
basic skill to make and remake organizations.

Ability to see through messes and contradictions to a future that
others cannot yet see. Leaders must be clear about what they are
making but flexible about how it gets made.

Figures

Foreword
to the Second Edition

My office at the Center for Creative Leadership (CCL) is overflowing with books. Volumes on strategy, history, science, talent, and numerous other topics crowd the shelves and pile up on tables. Colleagues are always free to borrow whatever they wish. There is one book, however, that is off limits: my first edition of *Leaders Make the Future*. Dog-eared and heavily underlined, crammed with notes in the margins, it has rarely been far from my thoughts since first reading it three years ago. In that book, Bob Johansen and the Institute for the Future perform an extraordinary service. They render the amorphous, unknowable future—that stormy VUCA horizon of volatility, uncertainty, complexity and ambiguity—a little less daunting. They do it by coaching us on the skills we must master to thrive in the unpredictable, opportunity-filled years to come. Well-researched, provocative, and wise, it's a superb piece of work. As one of that book's biggest fans, it is a pleasure to report to you some great news—this second edition is even more helpful to leaders at every level.

In the pages that follow, Bob offers an updated forecast for the future that carefully factors in the astounding global economic and socio-political tumult of the past few years. He digs ever deeper into the ten most important leadership skills for navigating our future, building on his previous work with fresh examples and insights about why these skills matter and how interconnected they all are. Then his book goes one giant leap further: it explores how we can nurture those skills in ourselves and in the women and men we are privileged to lead through immersive learning and leadership development.

We felt remarkably honored at CCL when Bob invited us to share our expertise with him—and with you—by collaborating on this second edition of *Leaders Make the Future.* To be honest, finding a way to make an excellent book better presented a real challenge. As we hope you will find, we believe we have hit on a way to do that. This new edition incorporates detailed instruction, based on more than forty years of research and client experience at CCL, on how to enact the skills highlighted in these pages. We are particularly proud of a new self-assessment at the end of the book. It will help you apply these ten core leadership capabilities directly to your own life and work.

After all, this book is intended to serve a highly practical and urgent purpose: the development of leaders who can take constructive action right now on behalf of their organizations and communities—and who are prepared to frame those actions in the context of the rapidly approaching future. Bob's work is strongly informed by deep thought and sophisticated models, but he has made sizeable and very effective efforts to translate that hard-won knowledge into accessible language. He strikes a conversational tone, shares compelling stories, imparts wisdom concisely for leaders in a hurry. Reading this book is an eye-opening, surprising, and ultimately inspiring experience, like rollicking dinner conversations with your most talented friends.

Its arrival is also remarkably well timed. Watching the Arab Spring unfold of late in the Middle East reminds us how prescient Bob's work is in assessing the dynamics of our VUCA World. He foresaw the rising influence of what Howard Rheingold first called "smart-mob organizing," through which social networks are used creatively and purposely to fuel change—foretelling events that unfolded in Tunisia, Egypt, and across the region. Frantic attempts by failing governments to quash social media interaction highlighted their hostility toward another emerging trend identified by Bob: "quiet transparency." The complete absence of that trait among many Arab leaders, from Mubarak to Gaddafi, factored crucially into their downfalls. The resulting new and highly uncertain era, not only in the Middle East but around the world, demands yet another skill highlighted by Bob—"commons creating," or the ability to develop shared assets, requiring collaborative leadership at all levels of the government, business, and social sectors.

In short, leaders at every level and anywhere in the world will benefit from this updated edition. For starters, senior executives in every organization should read it. If the upheaval of the past few years has taught us anything, it is that thriving in the future, as opposed to just trying to survive it, requires plenty of advance preparation. In this book, Bob does much of the spadework for us, providing a rare window into what awaits and advising us on how to plan for it. That is why his work is required reading for CCL's board and our senior management team. Precisely because this book grapples with the future, it is also an invaluable, affordable resource for a group that is customarily overlooked when training dollars are divvied up—young, emerging leaders. They will eventually take the reins of our organizations. The sooner they familiarize themselves with the skills needed to grow and sustain them in volatile times, the better.

Businesses of all sizes will find this book a valuable aid in crafting well-informed strategies. Certainly, it's no surprise that the Institute for the Future continues to work closely, as it has for years, with many top corporations. But it is perhaps government agencies, educational institutions, and nonprofits that will benefit even more. With resources tighter than ever, these organizations often do not have a lot of dollars to invest in long-term planning—and, yet, anticipating the future and making the necessary adjustments to their operations is crucial for sustaining their impact and fulfilling their missions over the long run. Indeed, we recently completed a ten-year strategy at CCL, relying heavily on the guidance in Bob's book. It was like having a savvy consultant in the room with us each step of the way.

It is always a pleasure to recommend an important book. It is even more delightful when the author is a person whom you admire greatly for his wisdom, focus, and humility. The second edition of *Leaders Make the Future* is that kind of book, and Bob Johansen is that kind of guy. Enjoy the journey as he leads you into a future of possibility.

John R. Ryan
President and CEO,
Center for Creative Leadership

Preface
to the Second Edition

The second-edition journey of *Leaders Make the Future* has three key elements:

1. A ten-year forecast of external future forces (updated from the first edition) that makes it obvious leaders will need new skills in order to thrive.[1]

2. The ten new leadership skills I believe will be required—given the external future forces of the next decade—with recent signals to bring each skill to life.

3. A new leadership development approach that emphasizes immersion in the future via both leadership development programs and personal learning adventures to develop your future leadership skills. This approach threads throughout the book, but becomes explicit in Chapter 11 on the use of this book in leadership development programs and Chapter 12 on developing your own future leadership skills. In addition, Berrett-Koehler is offering an online self-assessment at www.bkconnection.com/leaders-sa for both individual and group use.

The second edition is a serious re-making of the first edition, much more so than I expected when I began the rewrite. I have learned so much from my experiences with the first edition over the last three years. We are now three years into the ten-year forecast of external future forces affecting leadership that grounded the first edition of *Leaders Make the Future.* The core forecast is holding true: the VUCA World—Volatile, Uncertain, Complex, and Ambiguous—has gotten even more threatening over the last three years, but new opportunities to make the world a better place have also surfaced.[2]

Even if you cannot make peace with the VUCA World, you can make your way. I have included new examples of leaders who are making the future—in spite of the VUCA World.

The second edition is enhanced by the addition of leadership development insight and tools from the Center for Creative Leadership (CCL), which offers remarkable leadership development programs all around the world.

John Ryan, the president of CCL, was one of the early readers of *Leaders Make the Future,* and I was delighted to learn that he had selected the book for his own leadership team and board at CCL. I had not met John before, but his experience with the book led to a continuing exchange between CCL and Institute for the Future (IFTF) and to this second edition, which draws from and mixes the capabilities of both organizations.

At IFTF, we are focused on the future and looking back—in order to provoke insight and action in the present. CCL, in contrast, is grounded in the present with a focus on preparing leaders for the future. This second edition of *Leaders Make the Future* is a mix of the present looking ahead and the future looking back.

Sylvester Taylor from CCL worked with me to add a new self-assessment to help readers apply the future leadership skills to themselves. Sylvester and Pete Scisco worked closely with my colleague Deepa Mehta and me to work through how the leadership insights of IFTF and CCL could mix in synergistic ways. The models I share in Chapter 11 show the conceptual results of those discussions, but the second edition is spiced with CCL stories, tools, and references. Sylvester also worked with me to develop that online self-assessment on the Berrett-Koehler Web site. The online assessment can be used by individuals or groups, before or after leadership immersion experiences.

I am a ten-year forecaster, not a leadership development expert, so I am so glad to be able to add CCL's leadership development insight to my futures voice in *Leaders Make the Future.*

In this second edition, I've also incorporated many of the lessons I have learned in using the ten future leadership skills with an amazing variety of leaders over the last three years, including current or rising star leaders at Procter & Gamble, Tesco, Hallmark, Scripps Networks Interactive, Target, Kraft Foods, Walmart, Old Navy, Gap, UPS, McDonald's, Campbell's Soup, Johnson & Johnson, General Mills, Cargill, Givaudan, Syngenta, and Fairmont Hotels & Resorts. I am so thankful for these learning experiences.

We are now in the midst of a threshold decade: our natural, business, organizational, and social systems will reach tipping points of extreme challenge, and some of those systems are likely to break. However, such disruption can spark new opportunities. The Institute for the Future's 2011 Ten-Year Forecast points to the urgent need for rebalancing disruptive variables around the world, and the rebalancing must accelerate over the next decade. Rebalancing will require leaders to make better futures, using the skills that are described in this book.

Self-interest will not be enough: leaders will need to broaden their perspectives on winning to include the larger systems of which they are a part. Business leaders will still need to drive revenue, increase efficiency, and resolve conflicts, but traditional financial mandates won't be enough to succeed over the long term. Leaders must also embrace the shared assets and opportunities around them—not just the individual takeaways that will reward them or their companies alone. Leaders must both make money and make common cause with others to grow overall markets and economies.

This will be a very tough decade to be a leader, but it will also be a very exciting and meaningful time to lead, with the right set of skills and appropriate expectations. Rebalancing will be an unprecedented leadership challenge.

In some sense, we will all need to be our own leaders. Fortunately, virtual leadership tools in the emerging world of cloud computing are making new strategies for smart-mob organizing possible just at the time when it is becoming most necessary to work together in new ways and at great distances.

I believe that the more connected we are, the safer, freer, and more powerful we will be. But there will be frightening downsides: the more connected we are, the more dangerous it will become. Leaders will need to make new links and organize people for action—yet also protect against dangerous hyperconnectivity like we see in global financial spasms. It is good news that we are more connected than ever before, but leaders must now learn to lead in ways that make full use of the new connectivity of cloud-served supercomputing—while minimizing its considerable risks.

Chris Harrison's background cover art for *Leaders Make the Future* shows a real Internet traffic diagram. Leaders live in the web already, pulling the threads and weaving new patterns as they make and remake their organizations. In the cloud, the leadership resources will be even more extensive and more inspiring—even as the threats become more dire.

A forecast is a story from the future that provokes insight in the present. Nobody can predict the future, but you can make forecasts: plausible, internally consistent, and provocative views of what you think could happen. The best forecasts provoke insight and invoke action. This book uses forecasts to provoke insight about leadership. It draws from Institute for the Future forecasts, with a focus on the external future forces that will shape leadership over the next decade.

I have been focused on the future since 1968, when as a divinity school student I was a research assistant for a conference on religion and the future. I was the young "go-for" who did anything he was asked to do, including going to the airport to pick up the speakers— the world's leading futurists of the day. I listened with excitement as the future opened in front of me and the pioneers of forecasting that I had been reading showed up in human form. "That's what I want to do," I thought, and somehow, that's what I've been able to do and keep doing.

That same year (1968), Institute for the Future was founded by a group of engineers and mathematicians from RAND and Stanford Research Institute (now called SRI International) as an independent nonprofit think tank.

IFTF does an annual Ten-Year Forecast and has been doing so for almost forty years now. As best I can tell, IFTF is the only futures group ever to outlive its forecasts—and it has done so four times over. And, even though nobody can predict the future and prediction is not the purpose of forecasting, IFTF's forecasts have been remarkably accurate. Over the years I have been working with IFTF, 60–75% of the forecasted futures have actually happened.

I was the first full-time social scientist hired at IFTF in 1973. My graduate training was in sociology and world religions, and I've evolved into a forecaster focused on organizations, technology, and human values. My goal is to provide a futures lens to use on current models for leadership and executive development. These ten future leadership skills are not intended to replace existing leadership competency models but to challenge and stretch them.

In 2005, I wrote *Get There Early: Sensing the Future to Compete in the Present*, a do-it-yourself guide to how Institute for the Future uses foresight with leaders to kindle insight and action. The final section of the book suggested the need for the future leadership skills, which is explored further in *Leaders Make the Future*.[3] These two books are designed to complement each other.

My goal is to inspire leaders to make the world a better place. This book shares what I've learned about leadership, as well as my advice for future leaders, given the future external forces of the next decade. You do not have to believe in the value of the skills in this book to find them useful. In fact, they may be most useful if they provoke you to imagine your own future leadership skills.

This book is not an Institute for the Future consensus view of leadership. I do not presume to speak for all of my colleagues on this important topic, for they have rich leadership perspectives of their own. I have, however, been shaped by my experiences at IFTF and the many diverse organizations with whom we work.

The space between judging too soon (the classic mistake of problem solvers) and deciding too late (the classic mistake of academics) is a space that leaders of the future need to love—without staying there too long. Leaders must listen for the future, but make decisions in the present.

Hints of the future are all around us, if only we can learn to listen for them. At Institute for the Future, an event or happening in the present that gives indication of a future direction is called a "signal." For example, Maker Faire (to be discussed in more detail in Chapter 1: Maker Instinct), is a signal that the ancient do-it-yourself instinct is being reborn into something much bigger, transforming solo leadership into more of a do-it-ourselves leadership.[4]

All humans have at least a touch of what I call the maker instinct, but most leaders have a serious dose since they must make and remake the organizations they lead. The best leaders have always been tinkerers who imagine alternative structures and love to play around with them to see what new things they can create. Now, with amazing new tools and network connectivity, profoundly different organizations can be built. Leaders can make the future.

Each of the ten future leadership skills has links to the past and the present. As novelist William Gibson said, "The future is already here—it's just unevenly distributed."[5] The best way to learn about the future is to immerse yourself in it. Since the future is "already here," your challenge will be to find the best way to experience and learn from that unevenly distributed future. This book and the online self-assessment will help you engage with the future in ways that will enhance your leadership skills and impact.

Bob Johansen, Institute for the Future
Palo Alto, California
2011

INTRODUCTION

Listening for the Future

———

If a man take no thought of what is distant,
he will find sorrow near at hand.
CONFUCIUS

———

LISTENING FOR THE FUTURE is hard work. Leaders must learn how to listen through the noise of a VUCA World of Volatility, Uncertainty, Complexity, and Ambiguity.

But leaders can make a better future. We need not and should not passively accept any future as a given. Disciplined use of foresight can help leaders make better decisions today. There is short-term value in long-term thinking.

It is hard to think about the future, however, if you are overwhelmed by the present. Surprisingly, when the present becomes most overpowering, foresight becomes most useful. A global futures perspective can help leaders make a way through the chaos of the present. Looking to the future can help you decide what to do right now.

Many leaders today are overwhelmed by volatility, uncertainty, complexity, and ambiguity (VUCA). Some of their leadership behaviors are not constructive, and the prospects for leadership in the future are far from secure.

In these troubled times, many leaders are judging too soon and

1

judging too simplistically. Others are deciding too late and paying a price for their slowness or lack of courage. Some leaders react to the VUCA World with anger and disdain. Some pick a side and start to fight. And some leaders truly believe that the chaos will go away as things somehow get back to what they remember (often romantically) as normal. Such leadership responses are understandable, but they are also dysfunctional and dangerous.

When I listen for the future, I hear four overarching messages:

1. The VUCA World of Volatility, Uncertainty, Complexity, and Ambiguity will get worse in the future.[1] Solvable problems will still abound, but senior leaders will deal mostly with dilemmas, which have no solutions, yet leaders will have to make decisions and figure out how to win anyway. Many people are already living in a VUCA soup most of the time—especially people on the wrong side of the rich–poor gap.

While I was writing the first edition of this book in 2008, the VUCA world got a lot easier for me to explain as the markets around the world shook—and they are continuing to shake intermittently. Since the first edition, the VUCA World has gotten even more intense and obvious. More financial crises have shaken the markets, but so have a series of natural (or semi-natural) VUCA World events. On April 15, 2010, for example, I was in London talking about *Leaders Make the Future* with a group of innovation leaders from all around Europe. My morning keynote focused on the VUCA World and cloud computing. That afternoon, a cloud of volcanic ash descended upon London and closed British air space for the first time in history. I was grounded, with many others, in London for a week—at twelve-hour intervals, with no idea how long the shutdown would go on. Later that same week, the infamous BP oil spill erupted in the Gulf of Mexico. Two global VUCA events in one week.

If you are not confused by current events, you are not paying attention.

2. The VUCA World will have both danger and opportunity. Leaders will be buffeted, but they need not allow themselves to be overwhelmed, depressed, or immobilized. Some of those in authority positions today have turned nasty out of frustration. Leaders must do more than just respond to the whirl of events, though respond they must. Leaders can make their way in the midst of chaos. Some things can get better, even as other things get worse. You cannot listen for the future if you are deafened by the present or stuck in the past. Signals from the future are already here, all around us. There is also lots of meaningless noise, however, and leaders must learn to distinguish the signals from the noise.

We don't just live in the present. We are rooted in the past and we have chances to make the future. The VUCA World, even with all its threats, is loaded with opportunity.

3. Leaders must learn new skills in order to make a better future. Traditional leadership practices will not be enough to deal with startling external future forces. Leaders must have new skills to take advantage of VUCA opportunities—as well as the agility to sidestep the dangers.

This book introduces ten new leadership skills for the future: maker instinct, clarity, dilemma flipping, immersive learning ability, bio-empathy, constructive depolarization, quiet transparency, rapid prototyping, smart-mob organizing, and commons creating. When I completed the first edition, I assumed that others would suggest new leadership skills—beyond the ten I identified. To my surprise, in the hundreds of workshops we have done over the last three years, there were no obvious additional future leadership skills that were suggested to me. I am now confident that these ten future leadership skills cover most of the territory—even though the language to describe the skills may vary from organization to organization.

4. Something more is needed than traditional approaches to leadership development and executive training. In order to increase their own readiness and ability to make the future, leaders must immerse themselves in the future and practice their skills in a low-risk environment.

This will be a recurring theme in this book: immersion in the future. Leaders must immerse themselves in the future (through games and immersion experiences) and return to the present ready to make a better future.

Our societal ways of thinking about the future have shifted fundamentally. This artifact came from the 1964 World's Fair Futurama pavilion sponsored by General Motors. (See Figure 1.) Made of lightweight metal and designed so that it could be attached to your pocket or shirt, the motto reveals the prevailing public view of the future in 1964. In those days, thinking about the future was the mysterious territory of government, science, and very large companies such as General Motors. The future was distant and driven by technology and science. The future was created by others in positions of authority. The rest of us were supposed to accept the future with awe and applause, not create the future—except for small energetic pockets of activists that always felt they could make the future.

FIGURE 1. Badge from 1964 World's Fair Futurama pavilion sponsored by General Motors. *Source:* IFTF personal GM artifact, 2008.

Today, is anyone trusting GM—or any other large corporation for that matter—to create the future? I think not. We think GM will survive, and most of us hope they will succeed, but few are counting on GM to make the future. Today's consumers expect to make the future themselves and they don't like to be called "consumers." Consumption will be reimagined in the future world they are creating. Consumption won't go away, but it will be different and people won't be called consumers.

In 1964, the future looked so complicated that everyday people could only glimpse it if the big companies, powerful government agencies, and scientists allowed them to do so. The distant iconic leaders in this world were trusted to create the future for the rest of us.

In 2008, after discovering this 1964 vision of the future, my colleague Jason Tester, who designs artifacts from the future at IFTF (he calls this art human/future interface), hacked the original slogan "I have seen the future" and injected it with modern maker spirit. (See Figure 2.)

FIGURE 2. New version of an old slogan. *Source:* IFTF, *The Future of Making,* 2008. SR# 1154.

This artifact captures the spirit of futures thinking today. Big companies, government agencies, or universities are no longer trusted to create the future. "I am making the future" is a call to action, with an attitude.

The maker instinct is the most basic future leadership skill, and it energizes every other skill. All ten of the future leadership skills proposed in this book build on each other and work together. Clarity, for example, wraps a leader's vision in practical but inspirational language that motivates people through chaos. Commons Creating is the most ambitious, demanding, and important new leadership skill. Every leadership skill is linked to every other skill, and leaders need to decide which skills to emphasize when. Leadership teams need a mix of these future-inspired leadership skills.

On the map inside the book jacket is a summary of the external future forces that will shape leadership over the next decade. Leadership must change because of the external future forces we are facing.

The global rich–poor gap is the most basic and the most extreme future force—and the gap is growing dangerously. People who are poor already experience the VUCA World: their lives are volatile, uncertain, complex, and ambiguous every day. Realistically and sadly, it is hard to forecast a narrowing of this gap, but easy to imagine it getting wider.

In *Get There Early*, I wrote an entire chapter on "The VUCA World: Danger and Opportunity." VUCA is not new. There has been plenty of volatility, uncertainty, complexity, and ambiguity for leaders to deal with (or not) in the past. The need for leadership in the face of uncertainty is also not new. Life has always had its VUCA elements, and leaders have always lived VUCA lives. But I think the next ten years will be different.

What will be new in the years ahead is the scale and intensity of the VUCA World. Having spent forty years forecasting, I believe that the future world will be *more* volatile, *more* uncertain, *more* complex, and *more* ambiguous than we have ever experienced as a planet before.

In my nearly forty years of ten-year forecasting, the forecast inside the book jacket of *Leaders Make the Future* is the most frightening I have ever done. It is also, however, the most hopeful forecast I have ever done.

It bears repeating that nobody can predict the future. The purpose of forecasting is to provoke, not predict. I hope that this forecast provokes new insight about how to avoid the most dire aspects of this forecast. Many people, I hope, will dedicate themselves to proving this forecast wrong. There are many elements of this forecast that I hope will not occur. I hope that leaders will be smart enough to avoid them.

One of my jobs as a forecaster is to help people learn to be comfortable being uncomfortable—but certainly not passively comfortable. The most important value of forecasting is to help people learn to lead energetically even if they feel uneasy. As a forecaster, I am seek-

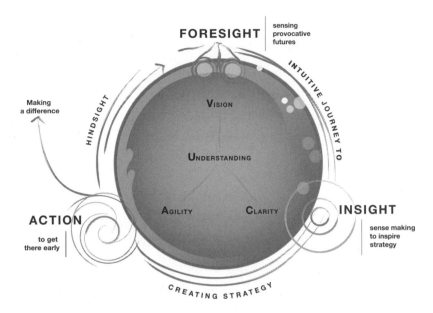

FORESIGHT
sensing
provocative
futures

INTUITIVE JOURNEY TO

Making
a difference

HINDSIGHT

VISION

UNDERSTANDING

AGILITY   CLARITY   INSIGHT

ACTION
to get
there early

sense making
to inspire
strategy

CREATING STRATEGY

FIGURE 3. The Foresight → Insight → Action Cycle. See *Get There Early* for more detail. *Source:* IFTF, 2007. SR# 1038.

ing to empower, not overwhelm. Discomfort will come with the territory for the next ten years—but the possibilities for positive action are everywhere.

Leaders must get used to an amplified VUCA World and learn to like it. If you are lucky enough to experience a future that is less chaotic, take it as a blessing and be happy that you are prepared to be surprised, since you are still likely to experience surprises later. For most leaders, very few experiences will be predictable or slow moving.

Figure 3 summarizes the Foresight to Insight to Action Cycle that I introduced in detail in *Get There Early*. Foresight provokes Insight; Insight seeds Action. The purpose of forecasting is to make better decisions in the present.

Notice the positive definition of VUCA inside the Foresight to Insight to Action Cycle. Leaders in the future will need to have Vision, Understanding, Clarity, and Agility. The VUCA World is not unyielding:

- Volatility yields to vision.
- Uncertainty yields to understanding.
- Complexity yields to clarity.
- Ambiguity yields to agility.

The biggest danger is getting caught off guard, but you can control that by preparing yourself and your organization. The best way to begin your preparation is to listen ten years ahead, but you must listen through the awful noise.

Ten Years Ahead: The Magic Time Frame

Making the future begins with listening. Even in a VUCA World, the directions of change are usually discernible—if you listen carefully. The large hot zones on the map (see inside book jacket) highlight the zones where change is most likely to erupt. At Institute for the Future, we've found that the sweet spot for forecasting is about ten years ahead. Ten years is far enough in the future to be beyond the planning horizon of most organizations, yet it is not so far out that it seems unbelievable or irrelevant. Ten years is also far enough ahead to see clear patterns that are not visible in the noise of the present.

Starting from Institute for the Future forecasts, this book looks ahead to explore the leadership skills that will be necessary to succeed in the future. This introduction gives a tour of the forecast. I recommend taking off the book jacket and leaving the map open as you read this Introduction.

As a forecaster, I can provoke you with foresight, but it is up to you to come up with your own insight and actions. Again, it doesn't matter if you agree with my forecast or not. In fact, some of the best forecasts are those that you don't like, those that make you squirm in your chair. Forecasting is about provocation, not prediction. Nobody can predict—especially in a VUCA World.

Each chapter is organized around a future leadership skill. Then links are made between the forecast and how it is provoking the need for that particular skill. Each of the ten future leadership skills corresponds to an iconic image that leads each chapter. These Zen-like images are intended to evoke the emotions of that particular skill. Artist and documentary filmmaker Anthony Weeks, who has worked with me for years to visualize the futures that we discuss in our workshops, has created the icons for each future leadership skill.

When you take off the book jacket and study the forecast, notice the look and feel of this map. It is an organic matrix that aptly represents the forecast for the next ten years in that we are moving into a world in which changes will unfold organically and also threaten nature. Engineering and mechanical thinking drove the last economic era; the next era will be driven by biology and what we are starting to refer to as the *global well-being economy*, which includes sick-care, wellness, and all the various aspects of well-being such as financial, social, physical, vocational, and spiritual. The forecast map is linked to nature in underlying metaphors and background graphics. This forecast sets a futures context for the rest of the book. These future forces will shape leaders and they will define leadership.

The book jacket forecast map summarizes on one page the external future forces that will be important for future leaders to consider. To the right of the map, you see the ten leadership abilities that are most important for this future world. The ten chapters that follow describe each of those skills, along with the abilities, competencies, and traits that will fit together to create a new leadership profile for the future. The book concludes with personal guidelines for future leaders, with a focus on what you can do to be more prepared for the future you intend to make.

Extreme imbalances in wealth are fundamental disruptors. For much of the world, hunger, safety, and subsistence are daily challenges. It is hard to do a ten-year forecast where the rich–poor gap gets smaller; it is easy to do a forecast where it gets larger. IFTF's annual Ten-Year Forecast for 2011–2021 said it this way:

> Resilience may be defined as the ability to adapt to changes in a socially positive way. While lack of education, exposure to violence and simply poor social skills all undermine resilience, the greatest threat to resilience is persistent poverty . . . worldwide the richest one percent earn as much as the bottom 57 percent.[2]

Two New Known Unknowns on the Map

The second edition ten-year forecast map includes two new central forces at the center of the map: digital natives and cloud-served supercomputing. I think of these future forces as known unknowns. Each force is known to some extent, but what we know is likely to be misleading compared to what we don't know. These two future forces are both obvious in some ways and wildly unpredictable in others. These two known unknowns will bend, shape, and stretch all ten of the future leadership skills. These two future forces were both implicit in the first edition, but I did not emphasize them enough.

The digital natives will be a disruptive force on a scale that we cannot yet imagine. I define a digital native as someone who is sixteen years old or younger in 2012. For those twenty-five or younger, the definition of a generation has shrunk to about six years, and it is still shrinking. Thus, the young people entering the workforce today (the twenty-somethings) are very connected via today's social media—but they are too old to be true digital natives. They should not be taken too seriously.

We know that whatever media ecology is present at the time a child becomes an adult will influence that person for the rest of his or her life. This is the first generation of young people to become adults in the emerging worlds of social media and cloud computing. We know how to assess and even predict demographics at a macro level, but we don't know how the brains and the behavior of the digital natives will be different—given their exposure to this unprecedented mix of new media. We know about demography—demographics are predictable in a macro sense—but we don't yet know just how the digital natives will be different nor how they will change the world.

Even though they were not digital natives, the 2011 protesters in Egypt give us an early hint of what the future may look like. Many of them had been educated but could not find jobs, so they had little hope. By 2021, everyone on the planet twenty-five years and younger will be a digital native. Unless we find a way to narrow the rich–poor gap over the next nine years, a significant portion of those digital natives will be hungry, hopeless, educated (formally or informally), and connected. This frightening forecast is a probability, not a possibility.

Digital Natives: The generation that will change the world. These are the key knowns and unknowns for leaders to consider:

KNOWNS

- This age cohort will be the first generation in history to become adults in the emerging world of social media.
- This generation has grown up with video gaming and the vivid user interfaces that gaming provides—as well as a lot of content that has been intensively violent and sexual.
- An access gap in technology still exists, but what used to be called the "digital divide" is no longer an either/or. No matter how poor you are, you already have some access to connectivity—and the access will certainly grow. Rich people will have better access to more advanced digital tools, but poor people will still be connected and increasingly so.
- Digital natives seem to filter information differently than older people, given their experiences growing up with more robust media.

UNKNOWNS

The brains of digital natives seem to work differently. Will their brains function differently from other generations—and if so, how? Will they have greater empathy due to their global connectivity, for example? Will cyber bullying be common among the digital natives? Will they lose some ability to concentrate and go deeply into subjects, or could these abilities actually improve? Nobody knows yet, though many people have strong opinions nonetheless. I am surprised that so many people I encounter are negative and even cynical about the digital natives. I myself am optimistic. At least, we should be open-minded about the potential positives they will bring to life, as well as the downsides.

- Will there be lingering impacts from early interactive exposure to overtly violent and sexual video games?

- How will the filtering skills of digital natives play out in terms of their ability to make sense out of complexity? What about their ability to think, to concentrate, and to write?

- Even digital natives who are hungry and hopeless will have increasingly good access to connectivity; we don't yet know how they will use it, but it is likely to be disruptive—perhaps violently so.

Cloud-served Supercomputing: The network will become the computer. Cloud-served supercomputing will provide a new infrastructure for innovation—and almost everything else. This disruptive shift in how we connect globally will enable and amplify what I think will be the biggest innovation opportunity in history.

We know that cloud computing will allow us to outsource IT, but we don't know what new forms of connections, collaboration, and commerce will arise. While transactions and early-stage social media dominate today's Internet, the currency of tomorrow's cloud will be reciprocity.

Reciprocity-Based Innovation, which I will discuss in more detail in Chapter 10: Commons Creating, will create new opportunities to give things away in intelligent ways, in the faith of getting even more in return. This give-to-get cloud logic will become more apparent and more practical for leaders over the next decade. Increasingly, the cloud will be the context within which leaders will make the future. The best leaders will get extremely skilled in choosing which medium—including in-person meetings—is good for what.

These are the key knowns and unknowns for leaders to consider with regard to cloud-served supercomputing:

KNOWNS

- Many current information technology functions will be outsourced to the cloud, but that's only the beginning—just the horseless-carriage stage of cloud computing.

- Cloud-served computing will mean that many more people will have access to supercomputing capabilities through a variety of access devices to reach shared resources in the cloud.

- People will carry cloud-based filters with them and these filters will guide their shopping and many other aspects of everyday life.

- Cloud-served supercomputing will mean that many more people will have access to connectivity that used to be available only to very large organizations.

UNKNOWNS

- What new models of connection, collaboration, and commerce will become possible through cloud-served supercomputing?

- How will cloud-based filters change the nature of brands, shopping, and advertising?

- Who will offer the best and the most popular trusted filters in the cloud?

- How will the digital natives develop new identities and new models of value exchange in the world of cloud-served supercomputing?

The columns on the map are the most important drivers, or future forces, that leaders should consider. The large circles are hot spots of both threat and opportunity. The small circles around the hot spots are signals that suggest the forecast is already coming to life. The small gray circles are signals that link to more than one hot spot.

Diasporas: New emerging economies. "Diaspora" is a very old word from the Torah that referred to the Jewish people who were separated from the Promised Land. These were people linked to a specific land but "set apart" from that land. The concept of a diaspora is particularly familiar to people who are Jewish or African American, or anyone who has studied the Old Testament. Diaspora is also a very useful concept for understanding the future, but future diasporas will be different. They will be less limited by geography and more amplified through virtual connectivity. Some will still retain deep historical traditions while others will be more modern.

The new diasporas will be values-linked social networks amplified by social media. Many kinds of diasporas will become important, including these:

- Climate-change diasporas, displaced by weather disruptions and linked by a common tragedy, like the massive Hurricane Katrina Diaspora. (See Figure 4.)

- Rural-to-urban diasporas will be common over the next decade, as we shift from being a primarily rural planet to a primarily urban one. Rural-to-urban diasporas are likely to be most dramatic in China, India, and Africa. Many, including children, may be left behind—creating other kinds of disruption and dysfunction.

- Cultural diasporas, such as offshore Chinese or offshore Indian people in the technology industry in Silicon Valley and other parts of the world. Of course, both China and India are so large that there are many different subsets of these diasporas. There are diasporas within diasporas.

- Corporate diasporas, such as alumni of McKinsey, P&G, IBM, or Apple. Companies that abide by the maxim "We're in it for the long run" include both current and former employees—as well as close friends of the family, suppliers, contractors, and others. You may no longer be an employee, but you can always be a member of the corporate diaspora.

- Bio-diasporas, which share biological traits, health conditions, or biometric markers. People with similar disease states, for example, form very strong support groups and are very effective users of the Internet, through sites such as patientslikeme.

- Financial diasporas, such as the Islamic financial communities that are creating new kinds of mortgages, bonds, insurance, and even currencies within the belief system or theology of the Islamic faith. Islamic finance is not new, but the Western world knew little about it until recently. The models for Islamic finance

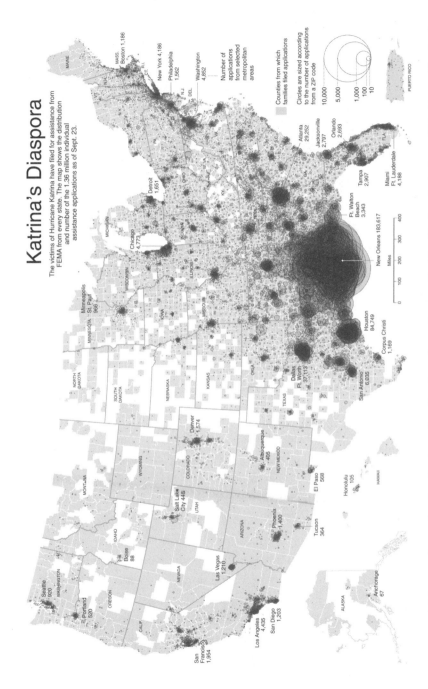

FIGURE 4. This map shows the distribution of applications for assistance filed by displaced victims of Hurricane Katrina.[3]

Source: Used with permission of *New York Times* Graphics, © 2005.

in a changing political and electronically connected world could change dramatically over the next decade.)

Some diasporas can be good, but other diasporas can be evil. Think of them as networks of people who may be physically separated but are bound tightly by shared values. In our forecasts at IFTF, we consider diasporas as even more important than traditional governmental or regional links in emerging economies. Indeed, in many parts of the developing world, diasporas are thoroughly integrated into both government and business practices. Within diasporas, innovations and ideas spread much more quickly because of common beliefs and high trust.

Diasporas often have a strong insider/outsider dynamic; members within a diaspora have a common bond. It can take longer for people on the outside—sometimes much longer—to build trust and a working relationship with diaspora members. Leaders must understand diasporas and be able to engage with them. In fact, most leaders themselves belong to at least one.

What diasporas help define who you are as a leader? With which ones can you easily identify? Which ones could amplify your leadership? Which ones threaten you or your vision of the future?

Civil Society: What will we choose to do together?[4] There are many different ways to mix business, government, nonprofit, and community interests all over the globe. On my first morning in China I vividly remember a newspaper article that referred casually to the "socialist market economy." That phrase popped off the page as I read it. I had thought of economies as being either socialist *or* market-driven. In China, the economy is both, mixing government and markets in ways that bewilder outsiders and sometimes even the Chinese people. What is the role of government? What is the role of markets? What roles do communities and individual people play? Today, some governments seem on the verge of collapse—for many different reasons, including financial. What will various societies choose to do together in the VUCA World of the future, the world that will be linked by cloud-served supercomputing?

Governments, markets, and people will interact in complex ways in the future—and many of those interactions will be through electronic connectivity. Networked connectivity can help to pull things together, and there will be many new opportunities to improve our civic infrastructure and our ability to cooperate. We are more connected than ever, but that does not mean we are automatically cohesive. The potential of connectivity, however, is extremely powerful. The more connected we are, the better we can work together—for broader benefit. The more connected we are, the more quickly disruptions can spread—as they did with global credit markets in 2008 or in the Arab Spring of 2011. Leaders in the future will have new opportunities to engage with the society around them using new infrastructures for cooperation. Competition and cooperation will need to coexist in ways that will vary from region to region, country to country, and even at times from city to city.

Corporations will play a major role in shaping the future. Although separate from government, there will be many ways in which they will need to work together. Corporations are often more technologically advanced and faster to change than governments. Still, we need at least some common infrastructure and shared services to succeed. Deciding what we choose to do together and what we leave to the marketplace will be key decisions for leaders in the future.

Food: The flashpoint for rich–poor conflict. Food and water are basic to life, and the next decade will be a critical period for food production and distribution. Global climate disruption is a force—actually a series of forces—with deep implications, but there are many more interacting variables to consider. Food is not just functional; it is deeply cultural. Over the next decade, food and water will be scarce in many parts of the world, and food safety will be a continuing challenge for all. Without healthy food, little else matters.

Distribution of food will be just as important as producing it. People are spread out and food must get to them. Where food comes from is becoming an important part of how it is valued. Food from some places may not be safe, or at least may not be perceived as safe. Food and water—and specifically the shortage of food and water—

will be flashpoints for conflicts, which will often be between rich and poor. Tragically, the rich–poor gap is likely to be a gap between the healthy and sick or the well fed and hungry.

Ecosystems: Navigation of life. The lack of response to global climate disruption aptly demonstrates the shortsightedness of governments that do not take into account the larger context of life—looking generations ahead.

In the world of today, profit is measured by narrow economic criteria like quarterly returns. Profitability over time will take place in the larger context of sustainability. Global climate disruption is a wake-up call: it is important to think not only years ahead but generations ahead. Natural ecosystems are both robust and fragile. While many businesses are still struggling to adapt to this demand, most governments are even further behind. Environmental regulations at Walmart, for example, have become stricter than those of the U.S. government. This is remarkable and admirable behavior by Walmart, but what does it say about the U.S. government?

Global climate disruption will be a storm cloud over the next decade and beyond. Many climate models suggest that the majority of serious negative effects will happen beyond ten years from now (some are even more frightening), but the decisions we make in the next decade will have long-term impacts. Ten years may seem long to most companies and government agencies, but it is a short time in the context of climate cycles. Global climate change can only be seen with a decade-to-decade view. Leaders will need to think about these larger ecosystem issues as an important part of everyday decisions. Humans are having profound impacts on the earth. Leaders in the next decade will not just be leading organizations; they will be leading life and influencing the climate for generations ahead. Leaders in the present have a chance to make the world more sustainable in the future.

Amplified Individuals: Extending the human body. In the next decade, there is real potential for many people to live for longer—with better health—than ever before. Of course, there is also the health gap that sadly mirrors the rich–poor gap. While many will struggle to live at all, others will be healthier than normal and a few may enjoy much longer life spans. Minds, bodies, and networks will all be connected in novel and powerful ways to create extended individuals who are amplified in ways we can only begin to imagine. Leaders will control new tools of human amplification, but individuals who may not have the same agenda or values will challenge them.

The Baby Boom generation will lead the way in body extensions as they wrestle with and resist the process of their own aging. This is the generation of people who said when they were young: "Don't trust anyone over thirty." As they age, I half expect that one of their leaders will coin a new generational motto: "Don't trust anyone under sixty." The Boomers will want to extend their lives and experiment with life—as they have at each life stage. The Boomers will have a new medical tool kit with which to experiment, at least for those who have the financial resources to do so.

Amplified individuals will create amplified organizations. Our global connectivity is growing dramatically, which is creating new ways to organize ourselves. Think of a leader not just as an individual but as a node on many different networks. The best leaders will not be isolated; they will be ravenous networkers with active links all around the world.

In the future, economies of scale (in which bigger is almost always better) will give way to economies of organization (in which you are what you can organize).

Leadership is all about engagement, and networked media provide several ways in which leaders can engage to make better futures. The most connected leaders will be the best leaders. The most healthy leaders will be the best leaders. In fact, ten years from now, it will be rare to see top leaders who are overweight or live unhealthy lifestyles. This is a big shift from the past, when many top leaders ate too much, drank too much, traveled too much, and exercised too little.

These external forces will appear in each of the next ten chapters on leadership skills for the future. They provide a context for assessing what skills will be most important in the future.

Although the rest of the book will focus on future leadership skills, I want to first acknowledge what I see as enduring leadership principles that will still apply in the VUCA World of the future.

Enduring Leadership Principles

When we do ten-year forecasting at Institute for the Future, we always look back as well as forward. For a ten-year forecast, we generally look at least fifty years back. Almost nothing happens that is truly new. Almost everything that happens was tried and failed years before. For a recent forecast on green health, for example, my colleague Rod Falcon and his Health Horizons team at IFTF actually looked two hundred years back as well as ten years ahead. This is the largest time span I have ever seen in a forecast and it was completely appropriate—given the long history of linking nature and health. There is an argument to look one to two hundred years back whenever you do a ten-year forecast, since major societal shifts often take place within those time frames—rather than the quarterly myopia that guides so many of today's business decisions. Many people ask me, "How can you do ten-year forecasting when we cannot even do one- or two-year forecasting?" I respond that, surprisingly, it is actually easier to do ten-year forecasting than one-year forecasting. The patterns of change are much clearer through a ten-year lens, with a good sense of the historical context around that view.

When I became president of Institute for the Future in 1996, I began a list of leadership principles. I had studied leadership but had not been a leader myself on this scale. Being the president was much tougher than I expected. I realize now that many of the challenges were inside my head and I was not ready for them. I was frequently frustrated and occasionally downright discouraged. I had physical reactions, such as headaches, almost every afternoon. I had emotional reactions, such as unexpected tears at awkward times. These symptoms convinced me that I needed to make changes in how I was living and how I was leading. This eight-year immersion experience taught me that being a leader is much harder than studying leadership. Being president during a very difficult time gave me firsthand experience that added greatly to my understanding of leadership and where it needs to go in the future.

This book focuses on the new leadership demands, but not everything about leaders in the future will be new. In its research, for example, the Center for Creative Leadership (CCL) finds that personal and early career experiences play a formative role in igniting any or all of the future leadership skills. Experience allows leaders to deepen and broaden skills as well as apply and transmit the skills.

Here are some enduring leadership principles that I admire greatly and that influenced the ten future leadership skills that I'm about to describe.

Get There Early: The ability to anticipate when to move in order to get there early—but not too early. As I described in my *Get There Early* book, I take this principle literally: I run my life early as a conscious strategy that I believe improves my performance and decreases my stress.

Physical and Mental Exercise: The ability to stay healthy in an unhealthy world. In my experience, physical exercise and healthy living are vital to leadership. More information is available to those who want to lead a healthy lifestyle now than in the past, and it is more obviously needed, but it takes personal and mental discipline as well. Leaders must develop physical and emotional energies that work for them as individuals as well as inspire those around them.

Active Attention: The ability to filter out noise and distraction, combined with a strong ability to stay centered—even when overwhelmed with stimuli. No leader could absorb everything, even in the old days before the Internet. All leaders must filter and learn how to see patterns as they emerge. The difficulty in screening increases dramatically as data sources multiply, making generational differences more apparent in the future. Young digital natives are better able to filter and have skills such as "continuous partial attention" that will be critical for people in leadership roles.[5] Filtering has always been important for leaders, but in the data-everywhere world of tomorrow, it will also be much more difficult.

Readiness Discipline: The ability to anticipate, prepare, and practice. You cannot control the VUCA World, but you can be prepared. Leadership has always benefitted from preparedness, but the demand for it will be much greater in a world of increasing uncertainty. Surprises are inevitable. Leaders can, however, consider a wide range of alternative scenarios and practice how they might respond. Readiness discipline will be explored in more detail in Chapter 4: Immersive Learning Ability. Leaders cannot predict but they can prepare.

Urgent Patience: The ability to know when to challenge and when to comfort. Bill Walsh, who coached the San Francisco 49ers when they were a great team, saw this as a key leadership trait: to discern when people are overloaded (and be patient with them in those times) and when they are overly confident (and press them with appropriate urgency). When Bill Walsh retired, he had an office in the same park as IFTF adjacent to Stanford. I got to interview him about his approach to leadership. He kept coming back to what he called "urgent patience." Leaders can be both urgent and patient, depending on what is needed at the time. The most important role of a leader, he said, was to listen, sense, and apply this strategy. When things get too tense, pull back to help relieve the pressure. When things get too relaxed, up the urgency.

Story Telling and Listening: The ability to discover and tell engaging stories that help people imagine a future. Great leaders are usually great storytellers. While problems can be summarized in a formula or an algorithm, it takes a story to communicate a dilemma. The future will be loaded with dilemmas, so it will take lots of stories to help make sense out of them. Many of these will be mysteries, and some will be thrillers, and they will be told by leaders through a wild mix of media.

Humble Strength: The ability to act with courage and clear intent in an authentic, engaging, and self-effacing way. This leadership skill will be more difficult to achieve in a fragmented multimedia world.

Thinking about the long-term future certainly seeds humility. This enduring strength will be explored in more detail in Chapter 7: Quiet Transparency. This book is dedicated to former IFTF president Roy Amara, who is my personal model for humble strength. He was understated but powerful.

Synchronicity: The ability to find meaning in coincidence. Leaders need to see patterns before others see them. The ability to see links between personal experience and future possibilities will be essential. Great leaders have always had this ability, but in the future the underlying patterns are likely to be more difficult to discern. When I was in divinity school, I found Carl Jung's notion of synchronicity to be one of the most profound concepts I encountered. In fact, the concept of synchronicity is in the same space as the concept of god. Meaningful coincidence is so important for leaders: they must listen and sense the patterns, sense the links.

These enduring principles have shaped my understanding of leadership in the future. They are my grounding and you will see my roots coming out in the future leadership skills, even though the future world will be very different. This book focuses on anticipating those differences.

My new colleague at IFTF, Liisa Välikangas, argues that in addition to leadership and strategy, we need resilience in our organizations:

> The burden of leadership is such that it is wise to bet on resilience, not on leadership alone. Build resilience into the organization. It is necessary because of the likelihood that leadership actions will be delayed, wrong, inadequate, or just missing. (Perhaps the wrong person was indeed in charge!) Building resilience into the organization improves the company's chances to survive the moments of weak leadership and to get through the (eventually inevitable) strategy shifts. Resilience is what organizations can fall on, when leadership fails.[6]

Liisa is broadening the call for leadership. It is not just the top leaders who need to be resilient in order to win in the VUCA World, it is all of us. We all need to be leaders. All leaders have innate personal skills that they should leverage, but there is so much more to learn. This book is about changes in how leaders will need to lead, drawing from the past, but listening for the future. Leaders can make the future, but not by themselves and not without new skills. Enduring leadership principles will morph into future skills. These ten future leadership skills will give you the resources to be resilient in the face of the VUCA World.

Leaders Make the Future introduces ten new leadership skills that will be necessary to respond to external future forces. I struggled with what to call these characteristics of leadership. Competencies? Abilities? Traits? Styles? I decided to call them skills—since I am convinced that they can be learned—and I want to emphasize those areas where leaders can improve themselves. I understand, however, that some people consider "skills" to be more narrow than other terms I might have used. For me, however, I mean skills in the broadest sense.

This book will unfold the ten new leadership skills in a definite order, moving from instinctive to transformative. Each of the ten core chapters will describe a future leadership skill that any leader or prospective leader can either develop personally or partner with someone else to perform. The core chapters will help leaders answer these questions:

Chapter 1: How can you draw out your inner *maker instinct* and apply it to your leadership? Future leaders—working with others—will need both a can-do and a can-make spirit.

Chapter 2: How can you communicate with *clarity* in confusing times, so you are simple without being simplistic?

Chapter 3: How can you improve your skills at *dilemma flipping* so that you succeed with challenges that cannot be solved and won't go away?

Chapter 4: Do you have an *immersive learning ability* so that you can learn by immersing yourself in new physical and virtual worlds that will take you out of your comfort zone?

Chapter 5: Do you have enough *bio-empathy* to learn from nature and use that wisdom to inform your leadership?

Chapter 6: How can you *constructively depolarize* conflict in order to calm and improve tense situations where people cannot agree?

Chapter 7: How do you lead with a *quiet transparency* so you are open and authentic—but not self-advertising?

Chapter 8: How can you do *rapid prototyping* that allows you to fail early, fail often, and fail cheaply—while learning along the way?

Chapter 9: How can you *organize smart mobs* using a range of media, choosing the best medium for each communication challenge?

Chapter 10: How can you *create commons* or shared assets within which both cooperation and competition may occur?

1

Maker Instinct

Ability to exploit your inner drive to build and grow things,
as well as connect with others in the making.

YOU HAVE NO CHOICE about whether or not to have maker instinct; everyone has it. You can choose, however, whether or not to let your maker instinct lie dormant or express itself. Leaders can choose whether or not to encourage people in their organizations to express their maker instinct.

The instinct to make is built into our language and ways of seeing the world. Ponder this long—but still only partial—list of maker idioms in daily use all around us:

- Making sense
- Making time
- Making money
- Making ends meet
- Making peace
- Making love

- Making war
- Making hay
- Making work
- Making waves
- Making every effort
- Making music
- Making fun
- Making light of things
- Making blood run cold
- Making certain

- Making contact
- Making clear
- Making a fool out of someone
- Making friends
- Making concessions
- Making calm
- Making common cause with
- Making history
- Make my day

The maker instinct is everywhere. The challenge is to turn the universal urge to *make* into a leadership skill, to synchronize the maker instinct of leaders with maker instinct of others. Many people don't realize their own maker instinct and potential. It must be recognized, valued, and nurtured if it is to become a leadership skill for the future. The maker instinct is key to making the future.

Beyond do-it-*yourself*, leaders need to nurture do-it-*ourselves*. The maker instinct must be amplified by connectivity.

When I go into a new company, I like to ask leaders about their hobbies. If they have complex, exotic, time-consuming hobbies, it may mean that their maker instinct is not being fully expressed at work. Perhaps the organization is operating at a routine level that does not demand deep engagement and does not tap the maker instinct of its leaders.

I remember meeting one top engineering executive for a very large corporation who rebuilt old steam engines in his spare time. Building steam engines is a great hobby, but this executive was overdosing: he had fields (literally fields) of steam engines that he was in the process of rebuilding. As I learned more about his company and his role, I realized that his corporate culture did not tap into the maker instinct. Rather, the leaders in that company tended to do what they had to do at work, then go home to do what they wanted to do. They had created a culture of discipline focused on good management, but they were not tapping the maker instinct and channeling it into leadership. This company was emphasizing management at the expense of leadership. Employees expressed their maker instinct at home, often through exotic time-consuming hobbies.

I'm certainly not against hobbies, but I am against leadership roles that focus on telling people what to do, and following the rules, rather than requiring people to get personally involved in *how* things work and how they could be improved.

Another example: some public speakers like to arrive, give a speech, and leave. They have no interest in the group process that was unfolding before they arrived and will continue after they depart. On the other hand, makers *like* to see how ideas develop and unfold—and they like to be able to influence how that happens. Leaders need to get involved in the messiness of group process to understand the context and underlying relationships. The speak-and-run approach may be considered leadership on the speaking agent circuit, but that's not group leadership. The best speakers strive to figure out how things work and what a group needs, not just give their usual talk and go.

The maker instinct is basic and precedes all other skills that will be needed for future leadership. The roots of the maker instinct run deep. Go to any beach in the world and you see kids digging in the sand. Why do they dig holes and build sand castles? These young makers are honing their maker instinct. My guess is that most successful leaders were very ambitious excavators when they were kids. Leaders are makers by definition. Leaders make organizations with an energy similar to the one kids employ to make castles in the sand. Leaders create the circumstances under which high-performing organizations become possible.

The leaders of the future will be less controlling than those of the past. They will be more engaged with others, since connectivity will be required to make the future. Everyone is part of a network. Leaders are nodes, and the best ones are hubs that form, nurture, and grow networks that stretch far beyond themselves.

My dad was a maker. To relax, he would go to the basement by himself, where he always had several projects in progress. He read *Popular Mechanics*, a magazine that aroused the maker instinct in readers every month with outrageous but inspiring projects like gliders you could pull behind a car. Dad had a large Shopsmith multi-purpose woodworking machine—a frightening contraption that loomed behind our furnace. I learned as a child that this awe-inspiring machine was dangerous and that I should stay away unless I myself learned how to become a maker. It was not easy for me to learn woodworking skills, and I never became nearly as good as my dad. However, thanks to his wisdom as a Cub Scout leader, I still have a serving tray that I made at a Cub Scout meeting using discarded records from a local radio station and imprinting circular patterns on them with a spinning wire brush. Actually each of us Cub Scouts spent only a short time pressing scratchy circles into the disc. When we returned the next week, my dad had almost finished each project—except for the last few circles and crimping the edges. I still feel like I made that tray—thanks to my Dad. He made it easy for me to satisfy my early urge to make, giving me lots of advice while he watched over me so I didn't get hurt. The lurking Shopsmith in our basement, like the maker instinct itself, was both attractive and imposing.

My dad was a solo maker, working alone in our basement. In the future, solo makers will still be around, but networks of makers will be much more powerful. The maker instinct is solitary, but leaders will need to connect their maker energy to others in order to fuel change. Makers have always been interested in sharing what they make with others and the new media tools will facilitate this urge.

My mom had a maker instinct as well. She loved to sew and then to knit. She made clothes for my sister and me, though I didn't appreciate them until I got older. At our church, my mom and grandmother would go to sewing circles where people would talk as they sewed or knitted. Late in her life, my grandmother became part of the Leisure League at church, a group that made clothing for people in developing countries. She loved the making, but the fact that others valued her products and found them useful gave meaning to her making.

Making things was a big part of my grandmother's identity at each stage of her life, even as the things that she made changed. Everyone has a maker instinct, but it can play out in many different ways with different people. The maker instinct is widespread, but it will be even more so in the future.

MAKE: Magazine is a modern reinvention of *Popular Mechanics* and the other maker magazines of that era. Its founder, Dale Dougherty, is well aware of the historical roots of his magazine and what he refers to as the "maker mindset." In honor of those roots, *MAKE* the magazine is exactly the same size in its paper version as *Popular Mechanics, Popular Science,* and the other do-it-yourself magazines that were popular thirty years ago. Makers tend to respect their roots, and many makers have deep roots.

The annual Maker Faire now draws more than 100,000 people to the San Mateo Expo Center to share what they've made and admire what others have made. The Maker Faire continues to spin off other maker efforts, such as TechShop and Instructables. TechShop (http://techshop.ws/) is a kind of monthly membership club for makers.

Instructables, recently acquired by Autodesk, is an online sharing medium for makers. It has an elegantly simple interface to allow makers to explain how they make things and how others can do what they did.[1]

Maker instinct is kind of a DNA imprint that we all carry in our own ways. *MAKE: Magazine,* the Maker Faire, TechShop, and Instructables are profound signals that indicate a very important direction for the future. The rebirth of the maker instinct will remake the future of leading.

Maker Instinct Defined

The maker instinct is an inner drive to build and grow things. The maker instinct is deeply human and organic, even though the things that people make are often machines or mechanical. Certainly, the maker instinct can be expressed in growing and farming as well as making stuff. The key here is the instinct to make, not what is made.

Leaders with maker instinct have a constant desire to improve the organizations around them. Both managers and leaders ask how things work, but leaders have an urge to make things work *better.*

When I was a Little League Baseball manager for my son's team, my maker instinct urged me to juggle the lineup to try out different batting orders for maximum effect. Actually, it was for what I thought was maximum effect but, in the case of my baseball managing skills, I was usually wrong. Still, my maker instinct persisted.

The popular Kevin Costner movie *Field of Dreams* is a romantic baseball fantasy around a maker theme: "If you build it, they will come." He made a baseball field in the middle of an Iowa cornfield and a miracle happened. True, the Costner character was idealistic and unrealistic, but he also had an overwhelming maker urge that just had to be expressed. I suspect that everyone who watched that movie feels that he was right to follow the maker urge.

Makers like to be hands-on and see things from the inside. The *MAKE: Magazine* motto is "If you can't open it, you don't own it." *Open* means transparent and accessible, but it also means able to be altered, customized, or personalized. Think about how that maxim has major implications for today's manufacturers, many of whom do not want you to open their products and will void your warranty if you do. Of course, the specifics of how consumers are allowed to "open" a product are critical. The Toyota Scion, for example, is designed to be customized, but that doesn't mean that everything about the Scion is open. Manufacturers must decide what they can open, while still owning what they can own that gives them an advantage. This is not an either/or choice. The clear direction of change, however, is from more closed to more open. This does not mean, however, that intellectual property will go away. It will be a very messy process of change over the next decade and beyond.

Leaders will grow, regrow, and reimagine their own organizations again and again. The maker instinct fuels that growth. Leaders will make the future in the context of the external future forces of the next decade.

Maker Instinct Meets the Future

In the future, personal empowerment will mean that customization and personalization will be desired and often demanded. Even global products will need to feel local, or at least not feel foreign. Grassroots economic systems like eBay will make bottom-up financial transactions possible. Smart networking will create results that will not be predictable but will be profound.

DIASPORAS OF MAKERS WILL GROW

At the 2008 Maker Faire, IFTF gave visitors inexpensive video recorders and asked them to go out and gather stories from the makers. They brought back accounts of the maker instinct at work. For example, a twenty-foot-high electric giraffe named Russell created quite a stir rolling around the fair. Russell cost its maker $20,000 plus lots of time to build it—but it was a priceless family experience for the makers. Colorful cupcakes, each one accommodating a single rider, rolled around the grounds in wandering paths. Two liquid sculptors dropped Mentos candies into Diet Coke bottles to create patterns of spray.

Computer giant and master maker Steve Wozniak spoke at the second Maker Faire and commented that the spirit of Maker Faire reminded him of the early days of the personal computer. Many of today's makers are out to create new products or services, but others are just out to have a good time. Makers are coming together in new ways that are likely to have profound impacts on leadership in the future.

Nowhere is the maker instinct burning more than in the world of design and digital art. As the demand to create increases, companies are making a move toward more accessible products. Autodesk, Inc. sells engineering and design software—very expensive software for very specialized engineers and designers. Over the past thirty years, this international company has built a customer base of 12 million. In 2009, Autodesk launched Sketchbook, a $1.99 iPhone and iPad application that attracted 7 million new global users in only two years. Autodesk anticipated the growth of the maker instinct and was able to respond with software that reached a much larger community of makers—professional and amateur.

Maker communities, as showcased at the Maker Faire, are often diasporas linked by strong, shared values and sometimes a common place—physical or virtual—where its members feel at home. Many of these communities are bound together by ideals about how their work should be practiced, or where their craft was born. Maker diasporas believe passionately in what they are making and how it is made. They often want to spread their word and share their truth. The annual Maker Faire is a vibrant gathering of makers shouting out to a wide array of other makers and celebrants of all ages. Although showing off is part of it, far more is going on.

Sometimes there is a strong bond among makers that stretches back in time and forward. Leaders share stories that keep maker traditions alive and draw in new members. Makers have the skills to make the world a better place, but they often don't know it. They just build what gives them pleasure, but leaders will know how to tap that maker energy as a force for change.

Shared energy is what diasporas are all about. The maker instinct will feed right into diasporic energy that will be amplified by social media. As these new groundswells of grassroots innovation disrupt traditional patterns, however, traditional organizations are likely to be confused about what to do. For example, both Mentos and Coca-Cola threatened to sue the artists whom they claimed were misusing their products by dropping Mentos into Diet Coke and creating massive displays of fizz. A short while later, both companies realized that lawsuits were unlikely to be successful and were likely to be unpopular with consumers. With some consternation but great consumer insight, both companies dropped their lawsuits and decided to sponsor the artists. Makers learn from those who use their products and services, and they learn even more when they encourage people to use them in ways that the manufacturer never imagined.

Solo makers, like my dad in our basement, are evolving into networked artisans through gatherings like the Maker Faire. Makers love to show and tell. Instructables allows makers to meet virtually and share projects. The original banner on the Instructables home page refers to itself as "The World's Largest Show and Tell."[1] Maker messages will circulate very rapidly within and among maker diasporas. Products will be turned into stories, and the stories will spread like viruses on maker blogs and a wild mix of other social media.

MAKERS WILL CREATE SHARED SPACES

One leadership dilemma that I will discuss in more detail in Chapter 10: Commons Creating is how to intelligently give things away without putting your own organization at a disadvantage. Your competitors don't necessarily need to lose in order for you to win. Open-source logic teaches that it can be good to give away ideas if there is a good chance that you will get back even better ideas in return. This logic is counterintuitive for many leaders, but those who tap into the maker instinct understand this concept much more readily than those whose maker instincts were repressed in large corporations. Makers easily access the wisdom they have learned from their hobbies and from others to help them with the demands of their jobs. Makers tend to like giving things away.

At the 2008 Maker Faire, for example, Jimmy Smith from Team FredNet talked about the Google Lunar X Prize, which was awarded to the team that could land a rover on the surface of the moon. FredNet used only off-the-shelf products. They shared their activities with everyone, including their competitors. Thus a new zone was created within which competitors could pool their resources in order to achieve the ultra-ambitious goal of landing a rover on the moon. This logic challenges traditional assumptions about competition. You divulge information to competitors? Yes, in pursuit of the prize there is sharing, but competition continues beyond that base of information.

Corporations used to think of research and development (R&D) as something that happens inside big laboratories and gradually gets released to the people who use the products. In the future, much of the innovation will come from backyards, basements, and kitchens of those guided by their own maker instinct—in both developed and (especially) developing worlds. At the edges of traditional R&D—and even far beyond the edges—corporate-mandated methods are giving way to maker-inspired grassroots innovation. Central corporate R&D will still exist, but it will be more open and network savvy. Threadless, for example, is a T-shirt maker that holds a design competition in which consumers compete and vote on the designs. Those that get the highest ratings get manufactured. The Threadless model may be extreme, but it suggests the direction of change. Makers can be the inspiration for future products.

MAKERS AND THE TOOLS OF WARFARE

When I started out as a forecaster in the early 1970s, many leading-edge information technologies were developed within the Advanced Research Projects Agency (ARPA), which created the ARPAnet, the precursor to the Internet. Gradually, innovations that were classified as military secrets made their way to public use in everyday life. In just the thirty-five-year period of my career, this pattern has reversed. Now, the leading-edge tools are coming from consumer electronics, video gaming, and makers. Even the tools of war are coming from everyday products adapted with a mix of maker ingenuity and anger. The most sophisticated roadside bombs used in insurgent warfare, for example, come from consumer electronic and cell phone technologies—not from sophisticated, big technology innovation developed inside massive defense establishments. Insurgent makers are everywhere—on the battlefield and behind the scenes. Gradually, these innovations make their way back to the military industrial complex. The maker instinct will have both positive and negative results. In a world of asymmetric warfare, innovation happens from the bottom up—fueled by their own kind of destructive maker energy. Enemies (and potential collaborators) can come together any place and any time. Terrorist networks tend to be organizationally sophisticated, and they know how to make their own weapons. The maker instinct is often very strong within dangerous mobs, and it is likely to grow in the future. Access to tools has improved for the bad guys as well as for the good guys, and sometimes it will be difficult to tell which is which. Makers, alas, can be thieves, vandals, or killers—even as the positive energy of events like the Maker Faire continues to grow.

MAKERS IN THE MARKETPLACE

Global climate disruption and an ecosystem that is clearly at risk will continue to be concerns in the next decade. Meanwhile, a new generation of makers is coming of age. Stimulated by the first round of ecological thinking in the late '60s and early '70s, schools provided students with a strong dose of environmental education. These next generation makers are more likely to be eco-motivated and guided by a new mantra to reduce, reuse, and *remake*. Remaking will be even more important for this new generation of eco-makers than making. Their exchanges will grow into marketplaces for goods and services.

Etsy.com, for example, is an online marketplace for makers to buy and sell. Swapthing.com is a sort of eBay for people who want to trade rather than buy. Both Etsy and SwapThing are indicative of this new generation of makers who want to reuse more and consume less. They salvage what they can and redesign existing products for new applications. They suggest that there are alternatives to just buying more stuff. Green aspirations will translate into a bottom-up economy of makers who are skeptical about big corporations and planned obsolescence. Maker gatherings already tend to be green, and they are likely to get much greener in the future. People want green energy, and corporations are made of people. These makers are likely to seed shifts within large corporations as well as within communities. They will swap, build, and rebuild.

MAKERS IN THE FOOD WEB

Food has always been an interesting medium for expressing the maker instinct. The best kitchens are designed for makers, with as much elegance and creativity as the cook (aka maker) would like. In the always-busy world of the future, the desire to prepare meals will be tempered by time. Although people want to be involved in making food for themselves and their families, they won't have hours to invest in cooking. Expect food retailers to respond with approaches to cooking that will allow people to participate in meal preparation, thus providing the psychological satisfaction of making their own food, without requiring the time to do so from scratch.

Founded by some of the team from *Wired* magazine, TCHO is a high-tech chocolate company in San Francisco, based on the idea of chocolate as a creative medium, with many different customization options. Customers are involved in creating their own chocolate without having to make it themselves. Consider how the maker instinct plays out at TCHO, based on how they describe themselves in these selections from their home page. Makers are often obsessed, very obsessed. Their customers can benefit from that obsession, as is clear from their principles:

TCHO is where technology meets chocolate; where Silicon Valley start-up meets San Francisco food culture.

TCHO is an innovative method for you to discover the chocolate you like best.

TCHO is scrappy and high-tech—recycling and refurbishing legacy chocolate equipment and mating it with the latest process control, information, and communications systems.

TCHO's social mission is the next step beyond Fair Trade—helping farmers by transferring knowledge of how to grow and ferment better beans so they can escape commodity production to become premium producers.

TCHO encourages our customers to help us develop our products, as we launch limited-run, "beta editions" available on our website.

TCHO creates new rituals for sharing chocolate.[2]

These TCHO principles reflect an emerging style of maker culture as it transforms into a sophisticated business. Notice the mix of maker instinct, leadership style, and professional expression. That's leadership with a maker attitude. Expect more efforts like this that allow the maker instinct to be played out in the experience of food.

FIGURE 5. Chef Homaro Cantu. *Source:* Used with permission of Cantu Designs.

MAKERS MEET LIGHTWEIGHT MANUFACTURING

Lightweight manufacturing will magnify the importance of makers of the future. Within the next ten years, desktop manufacturing will allow us to "print" other products similar to the way we print ink on paper now. For example, Chicago chef Homaro Cantu offers edible menus so that customers can taste dishes before ordering them. Using special flavor-printing techniques, Cantu blends his own mixtures of fruits, meats, fish, and vegetables in a form that can be printed on paper and eaten. (See Figure 5.)

"You can make an ink-jet printer do just about anything," says Cantu. He hopes that his idea may find its way into popular media. "Just imagine going through a magazine and looking at an ad for pizza. You wonder what it tastes like, so you rip a page out and eat it," says the chef who is working at perfecting the flavors and has applied for a patent on the technique.[3]

Homaro Cantu is an edgy hybrid maker with both information technology and cooking skills. Recently he brought edible menus to a workshop we conducted in London—they were tasty, even if not an alternative to lunch. He also showed that with the right kind of printer one could send sushi through the Internet. The next generation of makers will have a new tool set available, resulting in creations that at this point are hard to imagine. Desktop manufacturing will allow us to "print" food, 3-D objects, and other products we have yet to conceive. If you can print sushi and send it through the Internet, what will makers make next? Cantu is already working on an effort to do 3-D printing of food.

A Leader with Strong Maker Instinct

Founding publisher of *MAKE: Magazine* and creator of the Maker Faire, Dale Dougherty is a leader of makers with a very strong maker instinct himself. Through the Maker Faire he is giving everyone the chance to meet the makers. He calls it a "world's fair by and for the people. It's not like institutions. It's not big companies bringing stuff. It's really individuals just saying, here's what *I* do!"[4] (See Figure 6.) Big companies can still play a role, however. For example, they often sponsor areas of the fair where makers show off what they have done with standard products. "Hacking" used to be a negative term, but the makers are recasting it. Manufacturers create products, but makers can add new life to them and even repurpose them for very different applications, if manufacturers are smart enough to listen and learn from this kind of grassroots innovation. Makers will reimagine products even if the manufacturers resist.

Physical places like TechShop will combine with virtual resources like Instructables to produce a powerful new mix of media for making.

Applying his maker instinct, his leadership instinct, and his instinct to teach, Dougherty has established the remarkable event now known as the Maker Faire. I expect more of these fairs and similar events as

FIGURE 6. Poster for Maker Faire. *Source:* Used with permission of O'Reilly Media, Inc.

the maker instinct spreads do-it-ourselves wisdom throughout our business and social cultures.

Maker Instinct Summary

Leaders with a high maker instinct are able to approach their leadership with the commitment of a job and the playful energy of a hobby. The leaders of the future will kindle this maker energy in themselves and in others. They will make the future and connect with others in the making. Makers don't always know the answer, but they're working on it. Often, makers are more interested in the process of making than in what gets made at the end. For many makers, they do not want to be done making.

In times of great uncertainty, the maker instinct releases power. When leaders feel overwhelmed, they can become passive. It is much better to make something than it is to sit back and wring your hands. Leading is making.

2

Clarity

Ability to see through messes and contradictions to a future
that others cannot yet see. Leaders must be clear about
what they are making but flexible about how it gets made.

ON DECEMBER 17, 2007, I was at the end of a twenty-hour
British Airways trip from San Francisco to Milan, via London. Just
before we landed, the flight attendant asked me to put away my laptop, so I stood the computer on its side under the seat in front of me,
right up against the seat frame, which was not my usual habit. I was so
tired from the trip that I had lost the ability to think clearly.[1] When
we landed in Milan, I got caught up in the race for customs and left
my MacBook behind. I didn't realize I had lost it until later that night
in my hotel room when I was unpacking. What a shock! Still, I naively
thought I would get it back quickly. I was at a very nice hotel and the
concierge had a transcendent presence that assured me he could solve

any problem elegantly. I slept pretty well, almost expecting that my laptop would be returned to me at the hotel the next morning. "Here you are, sir. Sorry for the inconvenience," the concierge would say as he delivered my laptop in a Four Seasons envelope.

No such luck. I kept calling the lost and found at Heathrow Airport (the hub airport) and waiting for a response. Finally, after twenty-two days, I connected with a very nice person who said she would "take one last look" in what I imagined was a large pile of lost stuff. She returned saying there *was* a white Mac laptop in the pile. Did I know the serial number? I didn't, but I could describe the colorful stickers on the machine from a recent IFTF game experience. "You are *so* lucky," she said. My laptop arrived two days later, unharmed. I was indeed lucky.

Routines lay the groundwork for clarity when life breaks down around us. Breaking my routine impaired my clarity of mind. In times of stress, clarity can blur quickly. Leaders can only make the future if they are clear about where they are in the present, so they will need standard practices as a base to build upon. Clarity will be particularly important since volatility, uncertainty, complexity, and ambiguity will naturally lead to confusion. When people are confused—as I was at the end of twenty hours of traveling—they have an urgent need for clarity, even if there is no clarity. Routines help us manage chaos with clarity, as long as the routines don't become too rigid. We need great clarity about direction but great flexibility about the details.

Clarity is important for companies and for individuals. British Airways had an opportunity to deepen its relationship with me by helping me find my lost computer. Indeed, it should have been relatively easy for them, since they knew exactly where I was sitting and should have been able to connect the lost computer to me—based on where it was found. Unfortunately, the British Airways employees I interacted with did not have clarity about their customer relationship with me. A lost computer could have been an opportunity to build a positive customer relationship; I really needed their help and I was already positively inclined toward them as an airline—based on my earlier experiences with them. They should have a clear process to retrieve lost items and a commitment to returning them, although if they have such a process I certainly did not experience it. Instead, they made no apparent effort to get it back to me.[2] It seems that many airlines view lost luggage as a nuisance, not an opportunity to bond with customers. A lost computer may be a nuisance to an airline, but it is critical for the customer who lost it.

Compare my experience with British Airways to the professional baseball park Safeco Field in Seattle, where the operations staff prides itself on returning lost items. They have a return rate of 80 percent for items left at the stadium, an area much bigger than an airplane. The Safeco Field operations staff has found that when a lost item is returned, the person is at first very surprised and then becomes a dedicated fan for life. A company can view a lost item as a burden, or as an opportunity to grow a strong customer relationship.

Clarity like this is key for companies and for leaders. Although it has always been an enduring leadership trait, clarity will have new importance in the VUCA World. The VUCA World lacks clarity, by definition, yet people yearn for it nonetheless. For example, the Bush administration's reasons for going into Iraq were very clear in advance, but their assessment regarding weapons of mass destruction was later proven to be inaccurate. Bush won a second term even after his decisions that led to the Iraq War were extensively debated and eventually exposed as flawed. In spite of this exposure, the electorate decided that George Bush was clear and decisive, but John Kerry was not. For the voters, the fact that Bush was clear appears to have been even more important than the fact that he was wrong. It may also be that certainty was perceived as clarity.

Certainty is a feeling of absolute knowing and a kind of clarity—but it is different:

- Clarity includes curiosity about other points of view; certainty does not.
- Clarity includes knowing what it is you don't know; certainty does not.
- Clarity is expressed in narratives and stories; certainty is expressed in rules and absolute *shalls*.
- Clarity is resilient, while certainty is brittle.

Both the urge for certainty and the quest for clarity will become increasingly apparent in the world of the future, even more apparent than they are today. Politicians will have a particularly difficult time being both clear and accurate—given the complexities that we will all be facing and the public demand for clarity. Some situations are *just not clear,* but it is hard for politicians to say that without recourse from an electorate trying to make sense out of an often-senseless world. When people are confused, they are attracted to clarity—even if it's wrong. Certainty feels even better than clarity, since there is no doubt. In the short run, politicians are rewarded for certainty, even if it turns out in the long run that they were both certain and wrong. At the moment in Washington, DC, I see more certainty than clarity.

In CCL's leadership development practice, clarity is part of a leader's journey toward vision and purpose, and, ultimately, it produces direction. Individual clarity leads to organizational clarity.

In 1987, CCL undertook an Innovation Assessment based on 120 interviews of research and development scientists, uncovering characteristics that stimulate and obstruct creativity within organizations. Their model, called the Diamond Model for Creative Climates, emerged out of this study that CCL now uses to guide its work with organizations. Goal clarity, or Clear Goals, lies in the center of the model, as seen in Figure 7. The model accounts for "long-term goals of the organization, a clear shared vision, and the short-term goals and actions employees are expected to take."[3] Supporting goal clarity are attributes such as organizational encouragement, challenges, work group supports, and freedom. The lesson: our best work happens when we combine all four.

Clarity Defined

Clarity in leadership is the ability to

- See through messes and contradictions
- Make things as clear as they can be and communicate that clarity (In other words, make things clear—but not artificially clear.)

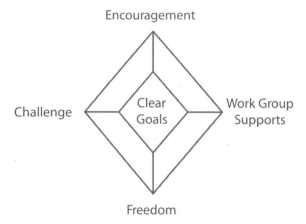

FIGURE 7. Keys to Creativity and Innovation Diamond Model for Creative Climates. *Source:* CCL, 2010.

• See futures that others cannot yet see
• Find a viable direction in the midst of confusion
• See hope on the other side of trouble

As volatility, uncertainty, complexity, and ambiguity increase, there will be many people wanting to be led out of the mess. In a VUCA World, many people will be so confused that they will be grasping for clarity. Especially in a VUCA World, clarity will be a prerequisite for compelling leadership. As the world gets more confusing, it will become harder to have legitimate clarity, to see through the mess to a better future. False clarity will abound.

The best leaders are seers, sensors, and listeners. They seek clarity from many sources, even as they hone their own inner clarity. The future will be loaded with contradictions, but leaders with clarity will need to see through those contradictions and have the ability to discern what to do and where to go—when neither is apparent.

In order to grapple with complex questions, leaders will need to resist the temptation to oversimplify. One of the most difficult dilemmas for leaders will be to provide clarity without false hope.

Clarity requires inner strength and discipline—even when you are exhausted. Clarity requires great self-knowledge, so leaders will have to look within and sort out what is most important to them. That can be very difficult when you are worried or upset.

When I was preparing for a trip to a dangerous part of the world recently, I found myself worrying about my own safety and dreading the trip. A friend suggested that, when I began worrying about the trip, I should focus on the purpose of the trip—not the things that could go wrong. I tried to do all I could to prepare and take reasonable safety precautions, but then focus on the purpose of the trip. Why was I going? I was indeed very excited about the mission of the trip, but my clarity got blurred when I started to worry. We each need our own ways of fueling our own inner clarity and quelling the fears that can eat away at it.

An inner purpose is an important element of clarity, but it is not enough. Clarity must be communicated. One leader's clarity may make others uncomfortable or may even lead to polarization. Still, if all sides are clear, the disagreements will at least be authentic, and people want authenticity in their leaders.

Clarity requires external engagement. Leaders must express themselves clearly in ways that inspire others to follow and must be able to make sharp statements about the future with an enthusiasm that attracts others.

Clarity in the VUCA World requires flexibility. The best leaders will be clear about their long-term intentions but very flexible about how to get there. Clarity sets the parameters within which creativity can occur. As with jazz, the structure sets the limits within which improvisation is encouraged.

Years ago, my family went rafting on the Middle Fork of the Salmon River in Idaho. Our guide taught us to concentrate on the water that flowed through these world-class rapids, rather than on the rocks we wanted to avoid. I also learned that the very act of paddling provides stability and some sense of direction—though certainly not control. When you find yourself in extreme rapids, you must be clear about where you are going and keep paddling, no matter what.

Clarity in a business context is a precise statement of your strategy, sometimes called strategic intent. It lays out where you are going and how you intend to get there. Strategy thought leaders Gary Hamel and C. K. Prahalad talked about strategic intent as "an ambitious and compelling... dream that energizes... that provides the emotional and intellectual energy for the journey... to the future."[4] They go on to describe how an effective strategic intent should not only indicate direction, but also relay a sense of discovery and even destiny.

Willie Pietersen from Columbia Business School, a former CEO himself, emphasizes clarity when he talks about his notion of a Winning Proposition: what does a company do better than its competitors to give value to its customers as well as maintain successful financial performance? "If strategy is about winning," he says, "we need to be clear about the measures of success. In business, success means winning against the competition for value creation on two fronts: greater value for customers and greater profits for your company and its shareholders."[5] Pietersen says the Winning Proposition should be expressed in a concise phrase that is honed to bring clarity.

The Winning Proposition should be both clear and inspirational. The best ones demonstrate a very clear future intent, but they should also stretch everyone in the organization beyond the present toward a desired future state. The Winning Proposition provides great flexibility for people to pursue the dream in varied ways. Consider the clarity in these statements from four very different big brand companies.

Global branding agency Ogilvy & Mather: "The brand of choice for those who value brands."[6]

Southwest Airlines: "On-time airline performance that rivals the cost of automobile travel, with a touch of fun."[7]

Consumer products leader Procter & Gamble: "... improve the lives of the world's consumers, now and for generations to come."[8]

Agribusiness leader Syngenta: "Bringing plant potential to life."[9] (See Figure 8.)

All of these companies are leaders in their industries. Each has a strong future orientation that is clearly articulated. A Winning Proposition does not guarantee success, but it positions companies

FIGURE 8. Syngenta's Winning Proposition. *Source:* Used with permission of Syngenta.

very well for the uncertainties of the future. Even in a VUCA World, these companies are very clear about where they are going, yet very flexible about how they might get there.

Challenges to Clarity

The next ten years look more complex to me than any future time period that I have studied in my career as a ten-year forecaster. There are so many variables at play, with such high stakes on a global scale. Absolute clarity will rarely be possible, particularly in this next decade, but leaders can choose to be either *less* clear or *more* clear.

Leadership clarity in the VUCA World will be elusive and some will see it before others. Nassir Ghaemi is a professor of psychiatry at Tufts University School of Medicine and director of the Mood Disorders Program. His new book suggests that mood disorders may actually help people find leadership clarity in VUCA times: "When times are good and the ship of state only needs to sail straight, mentally healthy people function well as political leaders. But in times of crisis and tumult, those who are mentally abnormal, even ill, become the greatest leaders. . . . Mildly depressed people . . . tend to see the world more clearly, as it is."[10]

On the subject of Winston Churchill, Ghaemi says, "The depressive leader saw the events of his day with a clarity and realism lacking in saner, more stable men."[11]

Making the future in a VUCA World will require an ability to restart, reframe, and see things that others do not yet see. Being normal may be a disadvantage in abnormal times. Leaders need to embrace the chaos, and those who are more familiar with chaos are likely to have an advantage.

CLARITY INSIDE AND OUTSIDE DIASPORAS

Clarity is not absolute—it varies depending on your point of view. Many things seem very clear from within a diaspora. Members share values and have similar worldviews. To those attempting to look in, however, diasporas can appear opaque or even threatening. Because diasporas tend to be so inwardly focused, they are often difficult for others to understand. It is tempting for outsiders to oversimplify, which is the first step down the slippery slope toward stereotyping.

A stereotype is false clarity—an oversimplified label that puts a person or a group in a box. A stereotype presents an illusion of understanding but is actually more likely to result in dangerous misconceptions and estrangement for both the person who is stereotyping and the one being stereotyped.

Diasporas have different social identities. Social identity is important in our understanding of leadership and clarity because it plays a role in how we lead, how we respond to other people, and how other people respond to us. Social identity theory tells us that we may, oftentimes unintentionally or subconsciously, use social identity to categorize people into groups based on a shared belief, that we may identify with certain groups, and that we may compare the groups we belong to with other groups.

Of course, one's identity is seldom static and often represents a mosaic of life choices and circumstances. Often the first step in understanding the role of social identity is to understand our own unique identity. CCL defines identity as made up of three overarching components: given identity (such as birthplace or age), chosen identity (such as occupation or interests), and core identity (attributes that make you unique). Through a unique process of identity mapping, CCL allows leaders to increase their understanding of their own social identities and those of others, and how to lead effectively despite social differences.

CCL author Kelly Hannum concludes, "The idea is not to try to erase those differences, but to work in the context of those differences with acceptance and respect. Individuals can maintain their group identity and also value the contributions of other individuals from different groups. And the more that happens, the better it is for the organization as a whole."[12]

Some diasporas define themselves as profoundly different from the rest of the world, and some are exclusive and do not want contact with outsiders. Some diasporas may only want clarity for themselves.

Expect to see more diasporas with great power in the next ten years. Clarity in this complicated world of many different and some-times-competing diasporas, however, will be elusive.

CLARITY IN BATTLE

Since 9/11, I have facilitated a series of workshops with business executives, nonprofit administrators, and military leaders at the Army War College in Carlisle, Pennsylvania and at West Point. We meet to compare approaches to strategy and leadership in our various fields of practice. We meet to learn from each other. It is at the Army War College (the Army's graduate school) that I learned about clarity in the world of warfare. They call it "commander's intent."

> The commander's intent describes the desired end state. It is a concise expression of the purpose of the operation and must be understood two echelons below the issuing commander.... It is the single unifying focus for all subordinate elements.... Its purpose is to focus subordinates on the desired end state.[13]

Commander's intent calls for a leader to be very clear about the end state desired but very flexible about how the soldiers in the field actually get to that clear end state.

Television viewers got an inside view of commander's intent when they watched the PBS ten-part series called *Carrier,* filmed aboard the USS *Nimitz.*[14] This documentary shows everyday life on a giant modern aircraft carrier. It shows how young people—many of whom came from troubled backgrounds and would have had difficulty landing jobs at most companies—have risen to the challenges presented on this very large and dangerous ship. Military personnel have principles and they have their commander's intent—which varies depending on the mission. Within the parameters of their commander's intent, individual crew members have freedom to improvise—and improvise they do, as *Carrier* reveals with great insight and humor. At the individual level, life on board leaves room for flexibility and personalization, while as a whole the crew moves ahead with clarity and purpose.

The military concept of commander's intent was confusing to me at first. Commander's intent is very different from command and control. The modern Army still has a hierarchy, but it is no longer governed by command and control—since nobody can control in a VUCA World. Rather, commander's intent sets the direction and desired end state.

My advice for leaders in the VUCA World is this: *Be very clear about where you are going but very flexible about how you get there.*

CLARITY IN FOOD SAFETY

My IFTF colleague Lyn Jeffery is a cultural anthropologist who has been doing research in China for many years. Fascinated with their culture and practices, she views people in China through the lens of the future. What do these practices say, Lyn asks, about possible threats and opportunities?

In her studies of Chinese families a few years ago, she saw that many of them—for the first time—were buying vegetables wrapped in plastic instead of buying them in the traditional open market setting with all the produce on display. As a good anthropologist is taught, Lyn tried to figure why these consumers had changed their behavior. Gradually it became clear to her that these rural Chinese families were becoming concerned about the safety of their own food and no longer felt they could trust the food in the open market. They wondered if the efforts to control food quality were good enough and believed, perhaps incorrectly, that plastic-wrapped food was safer than produce purchased from open bins.

This ethnographic research was an early indicator of what has grown into a widespread concern about food safety—particularly the safety of food from China. More and more people now want to know where their food came from, how it was grown, and what happened to it before it got to them at the point of purchase. People want transparency with regard to their food, so they can have more confidence that what they are eating is at least safe. In the world of food, transparency is clarity.

In the simpler world of the past, the branding of food was all about look, feel, and taste. Does it look appetizing? Does it feel ripe? Does it taste good? As we grow up, we are all taught how to make those choices—although the guidance regarding what is good to eat varies dramatically from culture to culture.

Now, the stakes seem higher. How do we make safe food choices from a food web that is increasingly suspect? Manufacturers need to assure consumers with credible clarity that their food is safe.

Leaders with Great Clarity

Leadership clarity is certainly not a new concept, even though the context of the future will make clarity much more difficult to achieve. Martin Luther King Jr. is a classic example of clarity, and his lessons are still very relevant today. Dr. King had a very effective way of making the future with great clarity.

I went to divinity school in Chester, Pennsylvania, at Crozer Theological Seminary, where Dr. King also attended divinity school, and I was there when he was killed in 1968. To honor his legacy, the school designed a course that replicated the intellectual influences that Dr. King experienced in divinity school. Dr. Ken Smith, a Christian Ethics professor who had been one of Dr. King's mentors, taught the course, and I was fortunate to be one of his students.

Martin Luther King Jr. was very clear in his overall leadership direction, even though he was very flexible about his tactics. His clarity focused on human justice—wherever those issues arose. While he is known for his groundbreaking work on civil rights, he also took controversial stances on what he saw as related issues, such as the war in Vietnam and the budding ecology movement around the first Earth Day. Many said that Dr. King had lost focus and should concentrate on civil rights. He talked about that vision in his famous "I've been to the mountaintop" speech just before he was killed.[15]

His vision was very clear for his followers, but his social change strategy evolved considerably as the civil rights movement took hold and other social issues joined the mix. His clarity focused on human justice (not just civil rights), while his tactics varied considerably in response to the challenges and opportunities of the time.

Nobel Prize–winner Muhammad Yunus is a current leader with clarity about social justice. Yunus developed the principles and practices of microfinance to help impoverished people help themselves. His approach is local, personal, and integrated with local communities. His model focuses on microcredit that allows someone with little or no resources to start a business, which creates an upward cycle of receiving income, investing more into the business, making a profit, and repaying the loan. He works with and grows social capital with small loans, primarily to women in local communities.

Expressing his clarity about social justice, Yunus says, "One day our grandchildren will go to the museums to see what poverty was."[16]

Clarity in Summary

Leaders must have clarity to be successful in the VUCA World. The best leaders will understand why people crave easy answers, but they won't fall into the easy answers trap. Leaders must develop clarity while tempering certainty. Clear-eyed leaders will experience hopelessness on occasion, but they won't accept it; they will see through it and be determined to make it otherwise. Leaders will immerse themselves in the VUCA World and—even if they become disoriented for a while—make a way to clarity as they make the future.

3

Dilemma Flipping

Ability to turn dilemmas—
which, unlike problems, cannot be solved—
into advantages and opportunities.

———

The test of a first-rate intelligence is to hold two opposing ideas
in mind at the same time and still retain the ability to function.
One should . . . be able to see that things are hopeless
yet be determined to make them otherwise.

F. SCOTT FITZGERALD

———

HOLDING "TWO OPPOSING IDEAS" in mind will be even more
important in the future than it was when Fitzgerald made this observation in 1936. In fact, there will sometimes be more than two opposing ideas—all of which have some validity.

The dilemmas of the future will be more grating, more gnawing,
and more likely to induce feelings of hopelessness. Leaders must
be able to flip dilemmas around and find the hidden opportunities.
Leaders must avoid oversimplifying or pretending that dilemmas are
problems that can be solved. Dilemma flipping is a skill that leaders will need in order to win in a world dominated by problems that
nobody can solve. Top leaders will deal mostly with dilemmas. There
will still be plenty of problems to solve, but people who work for the
leaders will solve them. Top leaders will rarely get the satisfaction of
solving a problem.

Many people will find the VUCA World depressing and hopeless.
Certainly, we all have those moments—and looking ahead ten years
may spark more of them—but the lesson for future leaders: nurture
the ability to engage with your own hopelessness, learn how to wade
through it to the other side, and flip it in a more positive direction.
Dilemma flippers have the ability to make their way through hopelessness into hope.

My definition of a dilemma is a problem that cannot be solved
and will not go away. The traditional definition of a dilemma was
the choice between two equally bad options (often referred to as a
"Hobson's Choice"), but that is a limited definition. Dilemmas are
often embedded with hope, even if the hope is hidden.

The challenge for leaders is to flip a dilemma into an opportunity.
At Walt Disney World in Orlando, for example, standing in lines is a
dilemma. Nobody likes to stand in line, but neither does Disney want
long down times when there is nobody ready to ride. They have made
a number of attempts to flip the waiting dilemma, including video
entertainment and indicators about how long the wait will be from a
particular point. An interesting prototype was Pal Mickey, a stuffed
Mickey Mouse doll that entertained the kids and had a sensor in its
nose that could pick up signals and tell the guest where lines were

shorter. Theme parks will never solve the queuing dilemma, but they can make it a much better experience. Pal Mickey was a step.

Leaders in the corporate context can surely relate to the F. Scott Fitzgerald quote about holding opposing ideas in tension. One such dilemma we see in business is balancing global scale and local customization. On the one hand, products and services need to be scalable in order to be on a growth path in terms of efficiency and return on investment. On the other hand, consumers in the next decade will increasingly desire products and services that feel local, even personalized.

Leaders who exhibit dilemma flipping will find an opportunity in this tension, to explore new models of markets. Perhaps they will tap the market power of diasporas, or engage with the Maker movement to offer products and services that are designed to be redesigned. Either way, these seemingly competing forces of global scale and local customization are not going away, and may even harbor great opportunity.

A common family dilemma in today's world: balance of work and private life is impossible to achieve. This is not a problem that can be solved. Rather, the intersection of the two is a territory that can only be navigated with assistance and intelligent choices. My wife is a lawyer who is always subject to the schedule of judges, and she rarely has control over her own calendar. My schedule has some flexibility, but I often have events scheduled months in advance and I don't have much slack in my calendar. Whenever we'd plan a vacation, one of us would come up with a fully legitimate reason why the trip was not feasible. It took a while for us to realize that this was not a problem, but a dilemma, which we flipped by finding an available place close to home that we both liked and was accessible on a last-minute basis. We traded off the possibility of more distant vacation sites, but we could take off spontaneously when time windows did appear. We have not solved this work/life challenge; we're just navigating it as best we can. And, occasionally, we get a last-minute special retreat we hadn't counted on—which makes it more delightful.

Another family dilemma that we had as our two kids were growing up was that there was no activity that we all liked to do, or even that both of our kids liked to do simultaneously. As they got older, this situation got worse, and we never seemed in sync for a family vacation. Our resolution—not a solution—was to take separate vacations where one parent would go with one kid. It turned out it was much easier to find something that one parent and one kid wanted to do than it was to find something that all four of us wanted to do and could schedule. We flipped the dilemma of finding something for all four of us to coming up with two activities, so that everyone was happier.

Leaders of the future will need to thrive in the world of modern dilemmas. Often, there will be more than two choices and they may not be equally bad. The good news is that dilemmas can present new opportunities to create win-win strategies, beyond the I win–you lose models common to the world of problem solving.

The dilemmas of the future that I find most interesting for leaders to understand have the following characteristics:

- Unsolvable
- Recurrent
- Complex and messy
- Threatening
- Confusing
- Puzzling
- Potentially positive.[1]

Dilemma Flipping Defined

Dilemma flipping is reimagining an unsolvable challenge as an opportunity, or perhaps as both a threat *and* an opportunity. Dilemma flipping is the ability to put together a viable strategy when faced with a challenge that cannot be solved in traditional ways. But first one must distinguish between a problem (that can be solved) and a dilemma (that cannot).

The classic optical illusion from gestalt therapy of the duck and the rabbit (see Figure 9) demonstrates the notion of a dilemma visually.

FIGURE 9. Optical Illusion. Source: http://en .wikipedia.org/wiki/Optical_illusion.

This image is neither a duck nor a rabbit: it is both a duck *and* a rabbit, depending on how you look at it. Leaders need to develop their own skills and see how the same challenge can be perceived in different ways. The VUCA World is a world of "and" not "or." Expect to see a duck and a rabbit in everything, as well as a tiger, a snake, and maybe something you don't even recognize but know that it is there. As you look at this image and flip back and forth between the rabbit and the duck, notice how your brain feels. This is a feeling that future leaders must learn to like.

Dilemma flipping is not a trait that is always associated with American leaders. Henry Kissinger, a former U.S. Secretary of State, observed:

> You Americans, you're all engineers. You think that all the world's problems are puzzles that can be solved with money and material. You are wrong. All the world's great problems are not problems at all. They are dilemmas, and dilemmas cannot be solved. They can only be survived.[2]

I find Kissinger's view a bit pessimistic because I think many dilemmas can be flipped, but Henry Kissinger was dealing with some very tough dilemmas. I agree that many American leaders I have worked with do tend to be problem solvers. They consider all the options, reduce them to two as quickly as possible, pick the best solution, and run in that direction, expecting to be evaluated by how fast they run.

On August 8, 2011, right after the credit downgrade by Standard & Poors, President Barack Obama went on television in an attempt to reassure the markets and the people of the world. After outlining the economic VUCA World all around us, President Obama said, "But here's the good news: Our problems are eminently solvable. And we know what we have to do to solve them."[3]

Leaders must set appropriate expectations. Promising to solve problems that turn out to be dilemmas (unsolvable problems) is very frustrating for everyone. I do not believe that the economy is a problem that can be solved. Certainly, the economy can be improved and possibly managed, but not solved. President Obama, in this speech, was expressing certainty in promising a solution when he should have been expressing clarity of direction in terms of what can be done to make the economy better. Of course, the tension for any politician is that many people who elect them are demanding certainty, even when there is none.

If nothing else, the economic tensions of recent years have shown that nobody truly understands the global economy—in spite of the fact that some claim that they do. The global economy is indeed a VUCA environment that cannot be solved or controlled. Leaders must start from this sobering realization and then come up with a way to make the economy better—without overpromising.

It is very dangerous to suggest that you can solve a problem that cannot be solved, that you understand something that cannot be understood. On the other hand—in most cases—you can figure out a way to make things better even if you cannot solve them.

A "flip" turns a dilemma around. It is a move from hand wringing to opportunity analysis. Dilemmas often seem overwhelming but are rich in potential, even if the opportunities are masked.

Dilemma flipping is not completely new. Consider the truth in these old adages: Is the glass half empty or half full? When life gives you lemons, make lemonade. Indeed, leadership has always been related to the ability to see something good where others see only limitations. In the future it will be much harder to find the silver linings—but they will be there. For example, employees in network-style organizations want to feel involved. Leaders must create a climate that delivers a feeling of involvement while also exerting strong leadership when that is needed. The demand for involvement will always be there, but the opportunities for leadership will be difficult to see and even more difficult to grasp.

Strategist Roger Martin encourages leaders to develop an "opposable mind," the ability to engage constructively in the tension between opposing ideas and not be forced into premature choice or resolution. New ideas often emerge from conflict but may not need to be resolved. Martin's work on what he calls "integrative management" is inspirational for many leaders and highlights how the best of today's leaders strategize in a VUCA World.[4]

Global dilemmas abound. For example, more than 90 percent of the world's population lacks regular access to food, clean water, and shelter. While policymakers strive to increase access, build large-scale infrastructure improvements, secure necessary funds through municipal financing, and strengthen policies, there is a growing movement by designers, engineers, architects, academics, and social entrepreneurs to fill the gap between availability and possibility. By partnering with non-governmental organizations (commonly called NGOs), individuals, and institutions, designers are proactively developing low-cost solutions to flip the everyday dilemmas faced by much of the world's population. They are not solving problems, but they certainly are improving the situation.

A partnership between organizations in Cambodia, technology companies, Honda, Massachusetts General Hospital, Harvard Medical School, and the Internet Village Motoman Network (see Figure 10) provides "telemedicine clinics," consisting of a nurse, a motorcycle, a solar-powered computer, a satellite, and a mobile access point connecting patients in rural Cambodia to physicians in Boston, Massachusetts. This program allows doctors to treat patients without being physically present, carried out by a local nurse. This service has expanded to

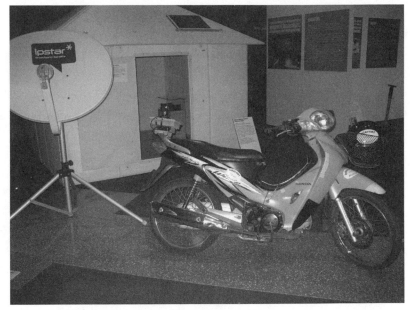

FIGURE 10. Internet Village Motoman Network, Cambodia. *Source:* Flickr User hoyasmeg (James Emery).

other parts of Asia, South America, and Africa. It is an example of flipping the dilemma of access to health care in remote areas.

But many people do not have an "opposable mind" and cannot live with great levels of uncertainty. They crave answers, even if there are none.

Dilemmas in the Future

If you look at the ten-year forecast inside the book jacket, you will see dilemmas everywhere. Consider these:

DIASPORA DILEMMAS

Diasporas are complex, living, social networks that require nurturing and deep understanding as dynamic, organic, and extremely important phenomena. Diasporas are complex. Bonded by common values, diasporas help their members make sense out of the world around them and often guide members in very explicit ways.

Most leaders belong to at least one diaspora themselves; some leaders belong to many. Leaders need the ability to work across diasporas, however. We all need to move beyond the comfort of our own clan.

Dealing with a diaspora is tricky if you do not belong to it, and especially if you are a member of a competing one. Some are formed in response to a dominant group. They often have sharp distinctions between insiders and outsiders and sometimes the former distrusts the latter. Some people are part of many different diasporas, which mix and overlap.

Diasporas not only raise dilemmas, they *are* dilemmas. They are too complicated to understand completely. You cannot think of them as static market segments; they are dynamic. You may be able to gain insight about one, but you will not be able to control it. Diasporas cannot be "solved" and they will not go away. In fact, they will grow in reach and power as they become more amplified by electronic media.

For example, corporate diasporas pose both a threat and an opportunity. Even as recently as ten years ago, most of our client companies did not stay in touch with their alumni. Their goal was to keep employees for as long as possible, but when they left, it was as if they had died. Losing an employee is a major cost for companies, since it is expensive to replace them. This negative, however, can be flipped into a positive. A former employee can become a new client.

Companies like McKinsey saw this opportunity early. They realized that when consultants left the firm there was a good chance that they would become clients of McKinsey. The more star consultants that McKinsey creates, the more those star consultants will seed other companies. Losing an employee to gain a client can be a great trade-off.

Now, a wide range of companies has active former employee networks, such as the Apple Alumni Association and the IBM Alumni Network. SelectMinds, for example, is a corporate social network company that supports large corporations who want to stay connected to former employees and others who are part of a corporate diaspora.[5] Of course, such organizations are a mixed blessing for many companies. They require constant nurturing and they can generate both positive and negative buzz. Still, sustaining the corporate diaspora is, in the long run, something that most companies should choose to do.

DILEMMAS OF WAR

VUCA World warfare is packed with dilemmas. Warfare was always awful, but VUCA warfare is so bad that this ugly acronym for volatility, uncertainty, complexity, and ambiguity seems appropriate.

When I first visited the Army War College the week before 9/11, it felt like a sleepy liberal arts college that just happened to study warfare. The week after 9/11, the campus became an armed camp and they started referring to themselves informally as VUCA University.

Traditional warfare rewarded problem solvers. When one large state went to war with another large state, there were clear rules of engagement. In a conflict where terror is a primary tactic and the enemy could be anyone, anytime, anyplace, there are no rules that are generally accepted. In fact, the various participants have different rules for engagement and different standards regarding what is appropriate and what is humane. To engage in such warfare is to engage with dilemmas. Hopelessness abounds. Creative courses of action appear, but they are often hidden in fear or grief.

Over the next decade, network-based warriors will seek to disrupt social, economic, and political systems through meme warfare. Memes are trigger thoughts that can spread rapidly. Rigid responses to this kind of threat can cripple the systems they are intending to protect. Resilient strategies that include great flexibility and ability to absorb disruption will work best. Economic markets, for example, are dependent on trust. Meme warfare would seek to undermine trust and spread a sense of worry and concern. It is hard to imagine how this could be flipped into an opportunity, but it is easy to imagine how it could disrupt markets.

An important part of this resilience will be leaders who can engage with dilemmas and try to flip them into opportunities. For example, many local people in Iraq viewed American soldiers with skepticism, but there was always the possibility that skepticism could be turned around and built into trust—at least on a person-to-person basis.

A BOOMER-FUELED DILEMMA

As some humans struggle even to survive, other humans over the next decade will strive to become more than human, healthier than normal. In this context of crisis and reinvention, new dilemmas will arise for individuals and institutions.

The technologies of health are blossoming in new ways, just as the Baby Boomers are reaching what used to be called "retirement age." Most Boomers, however, don't want to retire even if they could afford it—and most of them cannot. (See Figure 11.) A subset of this group is the richest cohort of retirees in history, which is doubly interesting since most of them won't actually retire. Instead, the Boomers will reshape the later years in life and reinvent retirement, just as they have had great influence on so many other social institutions as they have aged.

I expect a Boomer term to replace the word "retirement" within the next decade. My favorite candidate at this point is "refirement," but "redirection" and "regeneration" also capture some of the new concepts of aging. Many of the Boomers seem to view death as an option they are not planning to take. This mindset will create a rich market for death-avoidance techniques and technologies—at any price. A series of dilemmas will arise out of this vibrant yet futile quest:

- How can the best health care be delivered when there are limited resources to do it? Do just the rich get to live longer and in more comfortable ways?

- How will performance-enhancing drugs be handled in the workplace, where drugs of some kinds are not allowed? In sports, performance-enhancing drugs are typically outlawed, but what about in offices? In the next decade, new drugs could allow longer work hours on less sleep, for example. Do leaders allow such drugs? Might some leaders require them?

- How do leaders encourage healthy lifestyles without invad-ing the privacy of workers? For example, if a rising star leader *looks* overweight (looking overweight does not necessarily mean

THE NEXT 20 YEARS

FIGURE 11. A Boomers Forecast. *Source:* IFTF, *Boomers: The Next 20 Years,* 2007. SR# 1053.

someone is at an unhealthy weight that might affect performance), is that enough to discourage a promotion? Can a leader require healthy behavior, since physical health does contribute positively to leadership performance?

Problems Disguised as Dilemmas

If you are lucky, you will experience situations that look to you like dilemmas, yet when you flip them you will find a solution on the other side. Don't expect this kind of luck in the VUCA World of the future, but enjoy it when it happens.

For example, my ninety-something mom once called me to report that her ceiling fan had stopped working. In order to diagnose what was wrong, the fan company needed the serial number of the fan's motor. To find the serial number I would need to climb up to the ceiling and look on top of the fan. I climbed cautiously up a ladder to the ceiling fan, only to discover that the fan's motor was so close to the ceiling that when I tried to squeeze my head in the small space between the fan and the ceiling, the sticker with the serial number was too close to my face to read the numbers. Hmm . . . I thought: how could I fit my head in that tiny space so I could read the number? Use a mirror? Try tilting the fan so I could read the serial number? This puzzle seemed like an everyday household dilemma to me and I was ready to stretch my creativity to get that number.

About that time, my mom asked quietly, "Could you remove the sticker?" My mom, in her own humble way, had flipped the dilemma I was working on by reframing it as a problem that could be solved.

In the VUCA World, we will increasingly face dilemmas, or what CCL calls "turbulence." Board Chairman of CCL Ingar Skaug asks how we can use turbulence as a positive, creative force for change and offers a recipe for dilemma flipping that lies in the collaboration between innovation and leadership. In order to navigate change effectively and for the better, a "flexible, creative leadership style is needed in order to span country and cultural boundaries, promote collaboration and respond to an ever-shifting environment."[6] Skaug's research finds that complex challenges can "begin to crack and shift" when we see them differently (dilemma flipping). Here are some techniques to do that:

1. Standing in different places: I can change my point of view by turning the problem upside down.

2. Using lenses from other domains: if I am a scientist, I may visualize the dilemma from the point of view of a policymaker.

3. Ask powerful questions: I can immerse myself in possible scenarios and "what ifs."

4. Foster new knowledge: I can spend time with others who are impacted by this dilemma and understand their point of view.

5. Create an innovation journal: It can be a public or private way to think through my questions.

6. Change the pace of attention: I can change the speed at which I approach this dilemma.

An historic example of a problem disguised as a dilemma comes from World War II. General George Patton, during the Allied invasion of German-occupied France, came upon his staff as it was plotting strategy. Patton's staff leaders were depressed by the hopelessness of the current troop placements they were analyzing, which showed that the Allied Forces were completely encircled by German troops. Patton looked at the same hopeless troop configurations and said something like: "They've got us surrounded again, poor bastards."[7] Patton saw that by surrounding the Allied Forces, the Germans had thinned their resources so that U.S. troops could break through the German circle and gain an advantage. He saw where the enemy was strong, but he also saw where his own leaders were weak: their point of view was limited. Where Patton's staff interpreted the situation as hopeless, Patton saw it as an opportunity for a new kind of attack. He flipped the dilemma they were facing by seeing the same data in a very different way. Patton didn't win the war right there (that is, he didn't solve the World War II Problem), but he certainly improved that battle situation. Being surrounded is only hopeless if you stay where you are.

Dilemma flipping is an everyday skill. The world of today can be a practice ground for the future. Unfortunately, many dilemmas in the future will not be able to be flipped into solvable problems—such as reading the serial number on the fan—but they usually can be flipped in a way that makes the situation better.

Problem solving works when the parameters of a situation are clear and there is a problem that can be solved. Many future leaders will never experience a mature industry that is predictable and slow moving.

A Dilemma-Flipping Leader

Shortly after A.G. Lafley became the CEO of Procter & Gamble (P&G) in 2000, he visited the Institute for the Future and expressed a concern: research and development (R&D) was very important to P&G, but it was also quite expensive and not productive enough. While P&G is known for its marketing and advertising, it also has a massive commitment to science. P&G is known for hiring great scientists who create the base innovations for its products.

When I began working with P&G in 1977, my first assignment was to help them assess how the ARPAnet (the predecessor to the Internet) could be used to improve the R&D productivity of the "invisible college" of P&G scientists worldwide. "Invisible college," a term commonly used at the time in the literature of sociology of science, refers to the notion of scientists linked across physical distance. P&G had researchers around the world, but their emphasis was on the invisible college of scientists *within* P&G. Now P&G reaches far beyond their internal scientists to seek out and improve product ideas. In those days, when scientists joined P&G or most other large science-based companies, they more or less withdrew from the open scientific communities in the universities in which they were trained. Now P&G scientists participate much more actively in the external world of science.

In 1977, IFTF was doing pilot tests of group communications media in use by defense contractors on the ARPAnet, who were the only people allowed to use the network in those early pre-Internet days. Within P&G's community of scientists, we were able to prototype a similar medium that eventually grew into a very large network. In fact, P&G is the only organization I know that created a group communications environment (akin to what we would call social media today) in the late 1970s, before it adopted e-mail.

P&G had a big dilemma in the year 2000: it had a very large R&D infrastructure that was a major overhead cost. Ideas were being generated, but not with the frequency or impact that Lafley wanted. Of course, P&G wanted to own or at least benefit from the new ideas it developed, but it also wanted to benefit from outside ideas. A. G. Lafley looked around at the decaying structure of research laboratories across industries around the world and asked if there was a better way. He valued the importance of science in P&G businesses. His dilemma was how to keep R&D a priority while moving into a new model of how it was conducted.

He explored many different models, including those common in

Silicon Valley. Gradually, as his ideas about the future of R&D took shape and as Gil Cloyd became his Chief Technology Officer, the Connect + Develop strategy emerged. Connect + Develop is essentially an open model for innovation in science and product development. Instead of viewing science as something that happens inside P&G and moves to the outside only in the form of finished products, P&G reframed the R&D dilemma as an open network challenge. Of course there would be new issues of intellectual property and ownership in this new environment, but there would also be a much wider range of resources from which P&G could draw.

I was surprised in 2006 when P&G published its strategy about Connect + Develop.[8] I knew about the P&G strategy, but assumed that I knew it under nondisclosure. At the time that I started working with P&G, it was very secretive and its R&D productivity was concentrated within the company. Now, with Connect + Develop, Lafley has reframed the community of scientists to include those outside P&G. By leveraging the external world of science, companies can innovate faster with less internal investment. This model of R&D still requires investment, but it is able to cast a much wider net for opportunities and resources.

A. G. Lafley did not *solve* the problems of cost, productivity, and intellectual property issues of R&D, but he did reimagine what was possible. His clear and public challenge to P&G was to derive half of the company's new product ideas from the outside world. This goal has now been achieved and publicly celebrated.[9] This new approach to R&D has increased its productivity for P&G. Lafley flipped the traditional notion of R&D into a much more open-source and flexible network model. A. G. Lafley and Roger Martin are now finishing a new book based on Lafley's experiences at P&G, and I am looking forward to how they share the lessons learned for leaders.

I wish there were a hundred examples of dilemma-flipping leaders like A. G. Lafley, but I have not been able to find them. The ability to thrive in the space between judging too soon and deciding too late is rare. Dilemma flippers must love the process of puzzling—not *just* the outcome. You cannot, however, enjoy the process so much that you don't make decisions and act. Even in a world of dilemmas, leaders must decide.

Dilemma Flipping Summary

Dilemma flipping begins with a mind reset. As Winston Churchill once said, "The empires of the future are the empires of the mind."[10] The fact that Churchill struggled with depression means that the empires of his mind were used to dilemmas and disruption. Indeed, dilemma flipping is an ability that lives in an empire of a leader's mind—your own mind.

Dealing with dilemmas requires an ability to sense, frame, and reframe a situation. Reframing is stepping back, checking assumptions, and considering other ways of looking at a situation to see what's really going on—and what *could* be going on.

Making the future starts with listening and making sense. Of course, with some dilemmas, there is little rational sense to be made. The best leaders will stay alert, be sensitive to their environments, and keep an open mind about what they are sensing and what it could mean. Often, leaders will not understand exactly what is going on in the present, but they will have to decide on a direction of change anyway.

At IFTF, we have found that foresight is a particularly good way to provoke insight about dilemmas—even if you don't agree with a particular forecast. The big-picture view of a forecast frames what could be possible. Once you discern what's going on and what *could* happen if you intervene with the right action at the right time, you are more likely to see your way through a dilemma. Often, the path will not be clear until you stop thinking and start doing. Getting there early gives you time to sort things out, to reflect, and to plan your strategy.

To improve your own dilemma-flipping abilities, try these three steps.

- First, if you are not sure if you are dealing with a problem or a dilemma, it is better to assume it is a dilemma. If it turns out to be a problem you can solve, just solve it. If, on the other hand, you mistake a dilemma for a problem, you may be in deep trouble by the time you realize your mistake. If others expect you to come up with a solution and you don't, it is hard to recast the situation as one that you cannot solve after all. Often the lack of distinguishing problems from dilemmas gets classified by the popular media as "flip-flopping."[11] Mistaking a dilemma for a problem can lead to this perception—perhaps with good reason. Don't promise a solution if you are not sure you are dealing with a solvable problem.

- Second, immerse yourself in the dilemma (as I will discuss in more detail in Chapters 4, 11, and 12). Immersion allows you to listen to and learn about what is going on within the frame of the dilemma—without jumping to a conclusion. Immersion also allows you to look for patterns and ways of making some sense out of what is going on. This is the space that leaders in the future must learn to love, but which problem solvers will have an urge to pass through as quickly as possible.

- Finally, explore ways to flip the dilemma in a more positive direction. Dilemmas don't go away, but a leader can learn to reframe them and then reimagine the apparent contradictions in a way that leads to new opportunities that others don't yet see.

Leaders of the future must revel in the space between judging too soon and deciding too late, leaning toward action.[12] Judging too soon is the classic mistake of the problem solver, who has an urgent inner drive to solve. It is also a common error of people who *know* the answer before they fully hear the question. Many people with fundamentalist leanings, for example, are very comfortable judging others. Fundamentalism can be comforting psychologically, but it can be dysfunctional socially—especially if a group moves over the threshold of self-righteousness from being confident they are right to knowing everyone else is wrong.[13] Careful reflection is critical in the decision-making process so that you don't judge prematurely and risk judging incorrectly.

Dilemmas require that you live with uncertainty for a while before you decide what to do. Deciding too late is the classic mistake of those who love to study but have trouble getting around to deciding what to do with their research results. Deciding too late is also a challenge for the passively agnostic person who gets stuck in questioning mode. Leaders need to lean toward action, since leaders—unlike many academics or agnostics—are decision makers and must decide, even in the face of dilemmas. Leaders cannot just lean back and ponder the dilemma indefinitely. They must ponder for a while, but they cannot *just* ponder. Leaders still have to decide how to make the future.

4

Immersive Learning Ability

Ability to immerse yourself in unfamiliar environments,
to learn from them in a first-person way.

IN 1997, DR. SCOTT DYE had both of his own healthy knees "inspected" without anesthetic (that is, cut open and probed for pain sensitivity by an orthopedic colleague). Dr. Dye immersed himself in pain so that he could answer the following question very personally and very specifically: what are the sources of pain his patients are experiencing in their knees? This is a dramatic—and painful—example of immersive learning ability.

If you are trying to help people relieve their knee pain, the best way to learn about that pain is to experience it yourself. Dr. Dye is an associate clinical professor of orthopedic surgery at UCSF who runs the San Francisco Knee Clinic. Dr. Dye describes his pain-seeking immersive learning experience with charming academic understatement in a medical journal article:

> Penetration of the unanesthetized anterior synovium and fat pad region during the initial examination of the right knee produced severe pain that elicited involuntary verbal exclamations from the subject [Dr. Dye himself] and nearly resulted in the cessation of the study. Further documentation of this sensory finding in the left knee was thought to be unnecessary.[1]

Based on his own immersive learning experience, Dr. Dye came up with a familiar analogy to share what he had felt with his patients. He likened the pain to what you feel when you bite your cheek. The swelling after the bite makes it very difficult to avoid reinjuring the cheek and it hurts terribly when you bite down on the sore.

To learn how to help people with knee pain, Dr. Dye immersed himself in that pain and documented his experience—to the point of "involuntary verbal exclamation"—and he figured out a way to communicate that experience to his patients. As a result, he redesigned treatment for knee pain and is now a leader in the field of knee pain relief. Where other physicians focus on replacement knees, Dr. Dye focuses on knee pain and how to relieve it.

Thankfully, there are ways to do immersive learning that don't require getting your knees cut open without anesthetic. Variants of simulation and gaming are the best low-risk ways of learning in the VUCA World, and they are practical ways for leaders to experience the future before it happens.

Growing up playing video games could be very helpful for prospective leaders since serious gamers have the chance to immerse themselves in dilemmas and learn advanced social networking skills. Gaming and simulation are low-risk and high-return learning media, if used in a constructive fashion. But today's video games have a bad reputation, particularly among parents. Games provide mind expansion and leadership skill development, even as they allow for exposure to overt violence and sexuality.

Grand Theft Auto has been widely criticized for its over-the-top violence and random sexuality. Serious players, however, can play this game with less violence, even though it seems impossible to play it without any violence at all. The medium of gaming is extremely rich, but the games themselves provide the content and context. Grand Theft Auto also has amazing visual virtual reality rendering of the cityscapes and provides so many options that there are infinite ways to play. The stories embedded in the game may not be that compelling, but the patterns of play can be remarkably complex and dilemma ridden. Gaming allows players to experience alternative worlds in a low-risk way.

I believe—although I'm sure that many parents will be skeptical—that serious gamers will have an edge when they apply for leadership positions in the future. The key is whether or not they have learned the skills of dilemma engagement and social networking that many online games teach implicitly. For example, academic gaming researchers Constance Steinkuehler and Sean Duncan studied World of Warcraft players and found that they were developing very sophisticated mathematical models as part of their strategies for play and were also learning the basics of scientific thinking—in spite of what they and their parents thought they were doing. At least *some* serious gamers are "practicing scientific habits of mind in virtual worlds."[2] There is hope for worried parents of serious gamers.

Games can help you learn how to succeed in the real world by providing you with a low-risk practice field. Games can help you practice so that you don't choke when the pressure is on. Sian Bielock explores why people often fail at routine tasks in her new book called *Choke: What the Secrets of the Brain Reveal About Getting It Right When You Have To.*[3] Through the use of fMRI (functional magnetic resonance imaging of the brain), she has shown that the prefrontal cortex of our brains can get in the way, causing us to overthink routine tasks and choke when trying a short putt in golf or a free throw in basketball, or example. The good news is that practice—developing a routine—can help. Experience at performing under pressure helps you develop new ways of coping with pressure and coming through. Gaming gives you a low-risk environment to practice your skills.

Immersive learning can also happen in the world of new media and the practices that have grown up around them, such as social networking, social bookmarking, instant messaging, and tagging. Immersive online environments can be a safe place to practice leadership skills. Leaders don't have to adopt every model they come across, but it is important that they explore and understand what they can and cannot do. At least, leaders should encourage others to explore online social worlds so they have some organizational intelligence. Reacting with fear or disdain to new technologies and media (and the ecosystem of social and cultural practices that surround them) is precisely what a leader should not do. Engagement with gaming environments and encouraging (not just accepting) similar immersion among those being led will be an important dimension of leadership. Social networks are necessary to succeed.

Game playing style is also a critical element in what gets learned. Parents often ask me what to do about their children's desire to play video games. I recommend that they learn to play video games with their children. Video games provide great opportunities for reverse mentoring where the kids teach the parents. The parents can also teach and demonstrate their values in their styles of play. Think of video games as dangerous but interesting urban neighborhoods. You can either forbid your children from going there or go there with them to help them develop their own safe practices. I recommend the latter. Learn from your kids, as you hope they will learn from you.

Immersive learning ability is more than the willingness to use online immersions, simulation, and gaming. It can be simply going into a world that is *different* for you.

I once did a keynote talk in Orlando, Florida, for an industrial cleaning products company. I came in the evening before and was invited to go out with the top leadership team. Usually this sort of dinner would be at an upscale restaurant. This time, however, we gathered in front of our hotel and boarded vans to a local $40 per night motel where this company's industrial cleaning products were being used. On the way, we stopped at a fast food restaurant that also used their products.

When we arrived at the motel, we huddled in the parking lot with the lead sales person for that account and were herded into the laundry room to see how their cleaning products were used with soiled sheets and towels. Then we were each given a cleaning cart and taught how to clean authentically dirty motel rooms that had been "rented" for the occasion by the company who manufactures the cleaning products. I was taught, along with the top executives and the CEO of the company, how to use each of the products to clean very dirty rooms. Our assignment during this immersion was to finish one room every twenty minutes—the time budgeted per room for the people who do it every day. It is very difficult to clean a dirty motel room in twenty minutes, I learned. The motel was happy to rent the rooms for this purpose, but (I am relieved to say) they did send people back to re-clean the rooms after we were done. Cleaning motel rooms, I learned, is very hard work!

I stay in hotel rooms often, but I had never cleaned one. This simple immersion experience changed the way I look at and experience hotel rooms. I learned how hard it is to follow the correct cleaning instructions, especially those regarding sanitation and disinfecting. I learned how hard it is to do a good job cleaning a hotel room in twenty minutes. I learned how dirty some people leave their hotel rooms. I've always left tips in my hotel rooms for cleaning people, but having experienced just a taste of their everyday lives, I now leave a much larger tip.

My learning was less important for the company, however, than was the learning of the top executives who cleaned rooms alongside me. Will they make better business decisions because of this experience? I think so. Executives need to be able to put themselves in the shoes of the people using their products. These executives don't usually stay in $40-per-night motels, and they certainly don't clean them.

This outing provided valuable information about the product. For example, the directions for use of the cleaning products were just not clear. The cleaning staff at that motel was made up mostly of people whose first language was not English. The directions for the cleaning products should have been in the language with which they were most comfortable—or better yet, in a very clear visual format that works across languages.

Immersive learning experiences can change your life in tangible ways. It is always a good idea to immerse yourself in the world of the people who use your products.

The best immersive learning involves making fun out of the experience. So often in corporate settings, the fun is extracted from learning. Fun, however, is a giant motivator. Making fun can lead to learning.

The Center for Creative Leadership builds immersive learning into what they call Feedback-Intensive Programs (FIP). These learning adventures are personalized and designed to stretch the learning by immersing him or her in situations that are dramatically different:

> Every phase of a well-designed FIP has multiple sources of challenge. Assessment and feedback, by their very nature, provide one source of intense challenge: that of looking inward, the discomfort of being observed and rated by others, the fear of having weaknesses exposed, and the ultimate test of goal achievement and behavior change. Structured experiences in the classroom, which take participants beyond their comfort zone, also provide challenge and present participants opportunities to consider the value of beliefs, approaches, or perspectives offered by others.[4]

Challenging assignments are immersions that create opportunities for learning. The best learning assignments are both challenging and at least somewhat protected from risk. For example, John Ryan, the president of CCL, likes to assign rising star leaders at CCL the task of organizing United Way campaigns. These campaigns are important and the results are measurable, but they also have limited risk for CCL and for the learner. They are high profile assignments and wonderful learning opportunities. For many companies, unfortunately, the United Way campaign is a hassle to endure, rather than an opportunity for immersive learning.

CCL launched a Leadership Beyond Boundaries global initiative to democratize leadership development and unlock human potential across traditional borders. Boundaries exist and, in some cases, boundaries are becoming harder to span. On the other hand, new forms of connectivity are becoming possible. The program promotes capacity development and enables social innovations to emerge. Through this effort, CCL forms strategic partnerships with non-governmental organizations, educational institutions, government agencies, and community organizations to offer leadership development training mainly in disadvantaged communities in developing countries.

CCL facilitators immerse leaders by providing them access to the tools, techniques, and process of leadership development that the center has modeled over the past forty years. By working closely with communities and imparting strategic guidance, CCL directly contributes in strengthening capacity development and institutional innovation in communities that need it the most. For example, CCL partnered with faculty from the Caribbean Health Leadership Institute, training the trainers to lead at this multi-disciplinary public health initiative. The customized curriculum included on-site and remote instruction, materials, and assistance in disseminating the acquired knowledge to other leaders across the twelve participating nations. This process established a robust framework of interconnections, thereby creating a unique commons for shared public health research, education, and information in the Caribbean. It was learning through immersion.

Immersive Learning Ability Defined

Immersion is close-up engagement in a world that is different from your own, whether it is a virtual world or just a world with which you are not familiar. Immersive learning ability sounds kind of fuzzy for a future leadership skill, but—depending on where you immerse yourself—experiences like these are likely to be both vivid and deeply memorable.

I use the term immersive broadly to include a wide range of first-person learning environments:

SIMULATIONS OF REALITY

Some aspects of the real world can be modeled so that they can be experienced in a low-risk way. Direct simulation of the real world is very difficult to achieve in most situations but is sometimes possible;

and the attempt to mimic can be worthwhile even if the result only approximates reality. Simple realities can be duplicated, but the more complex the reality, the harder it is to simulate. Some simulations are designed to be more difficult than reality, so that it will be easier for participants in the real world than it was in the game. In the world of leadership, full-scale simulations of reality are rare because the real-life choices leaders make are so difficult to replicate.

ALTERNATE-REALITY GAMES

Individuals, small groups, or massive numbers of players can engage in hypothetical worlds, either in digital environments or in physical space. An alternate-reality game is not necessarily a simulation of anything real, but it is a compelling immersive environment with challenges—again, a low-risk world where people can learn in a first-person way. In these games, people "play" themselves in an unusual and often playful setting. Jane McGonigal, one of the world's leading game designers who is now at IFTF, calls this "real-play," not role-play—since you play yourself.[5] Alternate-reality games combine elements of games with the real world to create a different setting. Jane also uses the term "gameful" experiences to describe learning environments that have gamelike elements—even if they are not full-scale simulations or games. Jane defines games as "obstacles that we volunteer to overcome." She has concluded that games give players "superpowers" such as these:

- Urgent optimism
- A sense of social fabric
- Blissful productivity
- An experience of epic meaning[6]

3-D IMMERSIVE ENVIRONMENTS

People can become other people in an online setting. There is no story and no game in these worlds other than what the players themselves create. For example, young people who have forms of autism have used 3-D immersive environments like *Second Life* to practice social skills. Expect to see many more 3-D immersive environments in the future that extend the early experiences of *Second Life*.

ROLE-PLAY SIMULATION GAMES

Learners play roles in interactive simulations that draw from real-world experiences, giving them a taste of new situations and a chance to practice possible responses. Role-plays can be either more or less realistic and can allow leaders to learn for themselves without being themselves.

IMMERSIVE SCENARIOS

A scenario is a story brought to life in order to animate a forecast and engage with the users. For example, digital stories are short visual scenarios that can bring aspects of a forecast to life during a presentation. A text scenario may be more like a story from the future, while a physical one could be more like an artifact. Immersive learning or gameful scenarios allow participants to actually live in the scenario, rather than just read or watch it.

MENTORING, REVERSE MENTORING, OR SHADOWING

Learners can immerse themselves for a period of time in the life of another person from whom they want to learn. For example, some corporations have used reverse mentoring to help male managers get a taste of what female managers experience, to help white managers understand what managers of color experience, or to help older managers know what it's like for someone recently hired. In Europe, this practice is called a *secondment,* and it is often done in the early stages of someone's career.

AD HOC IMMERSIVE EXPERIENCES

The goal of such an experience is to help someone see the world from another point of view, as I did when I cleaned motel rooms. Think anthropology light, since the goal is similar to what anthropologists would call ethnography: a researcher becomes immersed in a culture to qualitatively understand it. Whereas an anthropologist goes deep for an extended time, an ad hoc immersive experience is just a quick taste—but it is a firsthand and potentially useful taste nonetheless. Ad hoc immersion experiences are similar to simulations, but they are much less ambitious since no imaginary world is created. Special body suits have been designed with weights and awkward padding, for example, to give young people a sense of what it feels like to be inside an older body. Other special suits have been designed to give men some sense of what is like to have a menstrual cycle or to begin to understand what it is like to be pregnant in the later stages.

THEATRICAL IMPROVISATION

Actors bring a future possibility to life in a vivid way while learners watch. These experiences can be more or less elaborate and vary on the degree of learner involvement. When the actors can engage with the learners, the learning opportunities are most profound. On several occasions, I have used actors in prototype homes or stores of the future to show how consumers might use them. For example, in a CEO Forum sponsored by P&G at Cambridge Business School in 2000, we used actors to show how consumers might behave. In this case, we felt it would be difficult to get the CEOs to role-play, but using actors was a more realistic demonstration than giving a presentation.

IMMERSIVE CASE STUDIES

A real-world situation is described in an engaging way so that learners can become involved with the case. Case studies have a long history and much current practice in business schools (with many different approaches), so most people have become comfortable with them as a learning method. Case studies are engaging for the students who write them, but less so for the readers. They can be presented, however, in very engaging ways by skilled professors. You can read case studies and they are better than abstract anecdotes, but you can't experience them unless you have some kind of immersion experience as well.[7] The term "immersive case studies" is used by Steve Jones of United Parcel Service (UPS), who uses it to describe how the company uses immersive learning to prepare its drivers and executives.

Immersion in the Future

Immersion is the learning medium of choice for the world of the future. You must experience something in order to learn it well, to learn it viscerally. It is much easier to make a future if you've had at least a taste of it. Finding your own clarity about options is much easier if you dive into possible future worlds.

IMMERSION DURING CRISIS SITUATIONS

Climate disruption diasporas, or large numbers of people who are forced to move by a storm or other natural disruption, are likely to become more common in the future. The Hurricane Katrina diaspora, for example, resulted in first an exodus of people from New Orleans and then their multiple migrations across the United States. Katrina's many tragedies became shared life-changing experiences that created strong social bonds. The Katrina diaspora was abruptly separated from New Orleans. Many wanted to return but could not. Now, gradually, New Orleans is being rebuilt and the Katrina diaspora is taking on new shapes and forms. The post-Katrina world is now loaded with immersion experiences for residents and relief workers alike—and often together.

Relief workers went to New Orleans for years after the storm to help rebuild. There was so much work and it was likely to go on for such a long time that churches and government agencies set up temporary housing for them. For the volunteers, rebuilding New Orleans was and still is a life-changing experience, an immersion in a broken world that is gradually coming back together. It was a chance to make a difference in a disaster that caused a feeling of helplessness for many.

In the aftermath of Katrina, Procter & Gamble sent in large trucks with washers and dryers and gave people Tide detergent so they could wash their clothes right on the truck, giving many survivors their first opportunity to have clean clothes in a long time in very hot and sticky weather. This was a startling concept: an immersion experience in a branded laundry detergent. In the context of the extreme

FIGURE 12. Tide's Mobile Laundromat for Hurricane Katrina survivors.[5]
Source: "Loads of Hope" used with permission of Tide.

needs after Katrina, laundry detergent—something ordinarily taken for granted—took on dramatic new value (See Figure 12). P&G will be regarded positively for being very responsive to this disaster, but a secondary benefit to the company was a chance to introduce the brand experience to thousands of people who were then likely to buy Tide after the crisis was over. Brand loyalty toward Tide within the Katrina diaspora spread quickly, as ideas always do within diasporas. P&G has continued this link to Katrina survivors—and can respond to other disasters when they occur—as part of the Tide brand.

FINANCIAL IMMERSIONS

Financial planning is not one of my strong skill sets. I've had two recent immersion experiences in my own finances that are helping me prepare for my next phase of life.

IFTF uses TIAA/CREF, the pension planning organization for many universities and nonprofits. As I approached sixty, TIAA/CREF assigned a planner to me. She works mostly with people my age or older from Stanford and SRI International, as well as other nonprofits. As part of this program, she basically immersed me in my own finances. She used a simulation to play out alternative scenarios for the coming years, based on my priorities and things that could happen outside of my control. She placed my family and me in our own future world—actually several possible future worlds—and helped us make choices. Because things keep changing, we update that plan every year.

In parallel, our family broker at Stifel Nicholas invited me to their offices, where the company uses immersion experiences as a way of helping people approaching retirement to consider their options. They also create a hypothetical world to help you explore your options. Actually going to another city is part of the experience—to get you out of your home and away from your usual ways of thinking.

Personal finances are important, but until this trip I just could not bring myself to spend much time thinking things through. This immersion experience got me out of my normal space and into a new one that provided information and prompted more informed action on my part.

IMMERSION IN CIVIC ISSUES

The probability of a major earthquake in California over the next ten years is very high. Earthquake preparedness, however, is something that is difficult to promote—unless there has been a major earthquake recently. American Red Cross Bay Area is using a fascinating approach that is essentially an immersion experience in the impacts of an earthquake. A vivid and greatly enlarged photograph of the San Francisco Ferry Building in flames and falling is positioned on one side of the back of a large flatbed truck which is parked right in front of the Ferry Building. For an instant, passersby see the image of the collapsing Ferry Building, and it looks real. The message from the Red Cross Bay Area is simple: What do we have to do to get your attention? Be prepared. On the other side of the truck is a similar photograph of Market Street. This immersion experience is memorable, but takes no effort on the part of the participants other than walking by and looking, and it is compact enough that it can go right out in the midst of people.

Another interesting example of this kind of street theater immersion is the work of Justin "Projekt" Rowley in San Francisco, who uses tape on lampposts to designate the future sea level in the South of Market area after the effects of global warming have taken effect. Of course, the future sea level is debatable, but the tape is striking and it certainly gets conversations going among people walking down the street—which is the point of this kind of immersive street art. The result is a vivid immersion experience in this topic and this art, just by walking by and looking.

Future of California

As the state of California faced budgetary crises, social divisions, and environmental challenges, IFTF partnered with the California Institute for Telecommunications and Information Technology (Calit2) and the Center for Information Technology Research in the Interest of Society (CITRIS) to develop scenarios for the state of California as part of a future of California project called "California Dreaming: Imaging New Futures for the State." The four alternative scenarios allow citizens, policymakers, and communities to immerse themselves in alternative futures for California. Scenarios of transformation, growth, collapse, and constraint provoke dialogue about the state's largest issues: health, education, food, water and energy, work, governance and equity, and migration. The hope is that immersion into futures pro and con will engage individuals and policymakers to see the future in an interconnected, multifaceted way—and thus, allow for better decision making today.

IMMERSION IN THE FUTURE

Institute for the Future has had a long-term interest in immersion experiences as a way of evaluating and trying out alternative scenarios. Just before IFTF was founded in 1968, two of our founders, Olaf Helmer and Ted Gordon, designed a board game called Futures,

FIGURE 13. Superstruct, a simulation game for
forecasting the future. *Source:* IFTF, Superstruct,
2008. SR# 1176.

which created a cross-impact matrix of future events and their interactions. In 1979, we made a game called Spinoff, which immersed
people in a multimedia world where they had to choose among face-
to-face, audio, video, and computer-based teleconferencing (what
would now be called social media) to resolve a crisis simulation.[8]

Gaming has become a platform for forecasting. IFTF's resident
game designer, Jane McGonigal, with Ten-Year Forecast leaders
Kathi Vian and Jamais Cascio, created an immersion experience that
contributed to the annual Ten-Year Forecast for 2009–2019. The first
simulation of this kind was called Superstruct (for superstructure,
within which planning and choices for action are made) and was
played in the fall of 2008 over a two-month period. (See Figure 13.) It
allowed thousands of people to participate in the Ten-Year Forecasting process.[9]

A Ten-Year Forecast can include a commons on which a wide variety of organizations can build. As the future gets more complex, there
will be new challenges to create commons for base forecasting and
frameworks for choice making. Superstruct is a kind of commons, a
platform for forecasting and exchanging information about forecasts.
It is also a place to try out new ideas about the future. Within the

game, participants can fast-forward ten years in their own lives to imagine a range of options. What external challenges will they face? What kind of person and what kind of leader do they want to become?

Superstruct is a real-play game, taking a step beyond role-play games by inviting participants to be themselves in a future world where they can grow their own skills and explore new social possibilities.

Based on the experiences with Superstruct, IFTF has created Foresight Engine as a crowd-sourced gaming platform developed by Jane McGonigal. In its first incarnation, Foresight Engine was used as the platform for a game designed for the Institute of Electrical and Electronics Engineers (IEEE) to consider the future of the smart grid—bringing together 600 players from thirty countries over twenty-four hours. The game relies on idea sharing by way of short, 140-character submissions, and the most popular ideas rise to the top of the scoreboard.

Most recently in 2011, after a series of earthquakes in Christchurch, New Zealand, 850 played a game within Foresight Engine that resulted in over 9,000 ideas for the future of this post-disaster city.

Games like these build on a tradition of socially constructive gaming that began to blossom with SimCity, the very successful Will Wright game that presents players with social dilemmas for which there are no clear solutions. Players are immersed in decisions that are like those faced by city planners and others who create shared public spaces. SimCity is one of the early pioneering efforts to simulate the real world in such a way that players can learn in a low-risk manner. Leadership in the future will require new strategies and tactics. You will still have to learn as you go, but gaming can help you do some learning *before* you go.

Games like Superstruct and SimCity are win-win games, as compared to zero sum games where—in order for one player to win—another player needs to lose. In a VUCA World, the search for win-win solutions is vital. Growing the market, for example, may be far more valuable than just growing market share. Winning does not necessarily imply that others are losing.

IMMERSION BEFORE AND AFTER BATTLE

Doug Campbell, the chief war-gaming puppet master at the Army War College, likes to say, "Simulation builds calluses." Indeed, the essence of military pedagogy is simulation and other forms of immersion; and immersion is the essence of the learning transformation that the army and other military agencies have gone through since the Vietnam War. The big incentive to learn in immersive worlds is that you can practice without the risk of getting hurt physically. You can even experience being killed without having to die. Games are an excellent way to learn about war in a low-risk setting, to develop your own leadership style, and to grow those calluses before you get into battle.

Anne Lilly Cone, a former consumer insights leader at Procter & Gamble, points out that, beyond calluses, immersion experiences build muscle. They give leaders a chance to experiment and learn in realistic but not real settings.

War games are often designed to make the simulation harder than the real world, so that when a soldier is actually in a battle, it is easier than expected. In the Iraq and Afghanistan wars, soldiers were taught with immersion experiences through war games at the army's National Training Center (NTC) in the Mojave Desert for two weeks, twenty-four hours a day, in the world's largest video gaming parlor (about the size of Rhode Island). Almost everyone loses when they go to the NTC and many people are killed, without having to die.

Simulation has obvious benefits in training people for war, but it also seems to be useful to help people recover from war. Simulation is being tested as part of what is sometimes called "immersion therapy" for Iraq veterans returning with post-traumatic stress disorder. The Virtual Iraq reality game is modeled on an earlier game called Virtual Vietnam as well as a current video game called Full Spectrum Warrior. Virtual Iraq re-immerses veterans in the frightening world of war that they are trying to return from both physically and psychologically. Working with trained therapists in a safe environment, soldiers are able to relive those awful moments that they cannot get past when they return to life off the battlefield. For many of these returned soldiers, their minds have been *dis*ordered by ugly experiences and they must *re*order when they return. The idea is to revisit the negative experiences and learn how to isolate those cues from a psychological chain of negative reactions. Immersion experiences, coupled with therapy, can help traumatized soldiers to come to grips at their own pace in a low-risk virtual world. One of the therapists testing the new game summarizes the challenge: "Because numbness and avoidance are symptoms of PTSD, you're asking the person to do in treatment the very thing their mind is avoiding doing. That's quite a dilemma."[10]

A CEO'S IMMERSION EXPERIENCE WITH A SHOPPER

Immersion experiences are important for leaders so they can see the world as others see it. On a recent occasion, I went on an immersive shopping experience with the CEO of a larger consumer products company. A market research company paired us anonymously with a young single mom living on an annual income of $50,000 in the upscale peninsula region of the Bay Area. The CEO was surprised to see that the mom did not choose any of his company's products, but he got a firsthand sense as to *why* when he went around the store with the mom and her three restless kids. A $50,000 income still seems like a lot of money to many people, but not for a single mom in San Mateo. Things are changing so fast that leaders need to immerse themselves in the currents frequently to grasp the points of view of people who are most important to them.

IMMERSION IN AMPLIFIED ORGANIZATIONS

Alegent Health in Omaha, Nebraska, has created a "Decision Accelerator" space in one of its buildings. From the outside, it looks like a typical suburban office building. Inside, however, it is very different. Alegent wanted to get people out of their normal constraints, amplify their everyday ways of thinking, and break patterns of thought. Everything in the Decision Accelerator is flexible. The furniture is movable so that it can be reconfigured easily, and most things are on wheels. Also in the space are facilitators and artists who can help to visualize the ideas. The vision is both to speed up decisions and reframe those decisions in ways that might be more productive for Alegent and for its community.

The Decision Accelerator is an immersion in a different kind of decision making. By going there, a group is saying that it is open to ideas that are out of the ordinary, and perhaps better. The Accelerator stretches thinking and presses for something better—but leaves it up to the groups to make those changes. It immerses groups in a different space to provoke alternate ways of thinking and speed up the overall process in a way that leads to improved results.

A Leader with Strong Immersive Learning Ability

Doug Campbell is the lead gamer at the Army War College, a place where games of war—and peace—happen all the time. A former cavalryman, Campbell carries battle scars with him: he walks with a limp and is missing a finger. He is a crusty, down-to-earth, friendly genius who loves gaming. I've been in a number of simulations with him, and he is incredibly engaged and animated. I was at the Army War College when he conducted a two-week global crisis simulation. During the entire time, Professor Campbell had a headset on to follow the play of the game, while also navigating his real-life duties, including talking to me periodically. I was not his priority during the game, nor should I have been, but he was still able to multiprocess in multiple realities with remarkable grace. He was staying one step ahead of the game players, but not too far ahead. As the gamemaster, he was continuously resetting the parameters of the game to stretch the players to their limits while not overwhelming them completely.

Doug Campbell's war gaming includes a range of different experiences, such as NATO war gaming in Europe. At the Army War College, he makes the immersion as much like the real world as possible while also stretching the scenario ten years ahead in the world of warfare. He has an amazing ability to do that, like a good trainer stretches an athlete before a game. Sometimes he gives demonstration immersion experiences to business executives, nonprofit leaders, and military commanders. At one of these sessions, he allowed us to play an abbreviated version of the global crisis simulation. It was an experience that provided us all with an immersion in the awkward sticky choices and trade-offs that must be made in the world of insurgent warfare.

Immersive Learning Summary

Immersive learning provides a safe environment within which to practice active attention, the ability to listen and filter, and to see patterns while staying centered—even when overwhelmed with stimuli. Leadership in the VUCA World will require active attention. Leaders can't absorb everything, so they must filter out extraneous information and learn how to recognize patterns as they are emerging. The difficulties of signal/noise filtering are increasing dramatically as data sources multiply.

Generational differences will be important, and leaders who have grown up in the digital age will have better skills for active and continuous partial attention.

Another requirement for immersive learning ability is open-mindedness beyond what many top executives can muster. Once leaders get toward the top of organizations, they get more and more insulated from what is really going on. Leaders need to step outside their protected roles to step inside very different experiences from which they can learn. Ideally, an immersive learning environment will be more difficult than what the leader will experience in the real world. Leaders should seek out immersive learning opportunities— especially experiences that make them uncomfortable in constructive ways. If you make the future in an imaginary world, it will be much easier to do in the real world.

5

Bio-empathy

Ability to see things from nature's point of view;
to understand, respect, and learn from its patterns.

———

A significant part of the pleasure of eating is in one's accurate
consciousness of the lives and the world from which the food comes.
WENDELL BERRY

———

EATING IS EVERYONE'S EVERYDAY LINK with nature. If we
eat with consciousness about where our food comes from, we have the
potential to empathize more deeply with natural processes. Eating
with awareness is one form of bio-empathy, the ability to learn from
nature. Bio-empathy applies to many different forms of leadership in

many different ways. Bio-empathy is leadership through a natural filter. What are the underlying patterns of nature that could inform how leaders lead? Nature can help us make sense of the VUCA World, if only we humans can understand its lessons.

In Virginia's Shenandoah Valley, three generations of the Salatin family have run Polyface Farm since 1961 using the following principles, which do a great job of expressing bio-empathy in practice:

- **Transparency**: Anyone is welcome to visit the farm anytime. No trade secrets, no locked doors, every corner is camera-accessible.

- **Grass-based**: Pastured livestock and poultry, moved frequently to new "salad bars," offer landscape healing and nutritional superiority.[1]

- **Individuality**: Plants and animals should be provided a habitat that allows them to express their physiological distinctiveness. Respecting and honoring the "pigness" of the pig is a foundation for societal health.

- **Community**: We do not ship food. We should all seek food closer to home, in our food shed, our own bioregion. This means enjoying seasonality and reacquainting ourselves with our home kitchens.

- **Nature's template**: Mimicking natural patterns on a commercial domestic scale ensure moral and ethical boundaries to human cleverness. Cows are herbivores, not omnivores; that is why we've never fed them dead cows like the United States Department of Agriculture encouraged (the alleged cause of mad cows).

- **Earthworms**: We're really in the earthworm enhancement business. Stimulating soil biota is our first priority. Soil health creates healthy food.[2]

These are not rules; they are principles. The name of the farm comes from the practice of polyculture, which is growing two or more crops on the same piece of land. The Salatins are makers dedicated to farming the perennial prairie on which they live in a way that learns from nature.

They use unique temporary fencing, for example, that allows the animals to move around the farm, so that other animals can follow them in cycle and do what they do best. Essentially they put them in the context of a farm governed by natural principles and empathy for nature. They have lowered their purchased food dramatically and, by rotating the grazing areas, various animal species play varied natural roles. They are able to work with nature to produce very tasty, very healthy products.

Scott Dye, the orthopedist who had his knee cut open without anesthetic in order to understand knee pain, demonstrates another kind of bio-empathy. (See Chapter 4.) Many orthopedists seem to view knee pain as a mechanical problem. Their typical fix is to replace the knee. Mechanical knees are impressive, but not nearly as impressive as the real thing. An artificial knee can't really do all the same things in the same way; rather, it provides a limited functional alternative to the natural knee.

Dr. Dye has a different way of thinking: he thinks about the knee biologically, not mechanically, and focuses on knee pain. "From this new biologic perspective, it clinically matters little what structural factors may be present in a given joint . . . if the pain-free condition of tissue homeostasis is safely achieved and maintained."[3] What he learned under the knife led him to a much greater empathy for his patients, but also an appreciation for the amazing design and wonder of the human knee. He does not rebuild a knee—unless all the other approaches fail.

The term bio-empathy may take some readers over their California new-age thinking threshold, but I hope you will bear with me. I'm convinced that the next big global economic driver will come from biology and the life sciences. Much of that economic energy will be applied to the global well-being economy—which not only includes care for the ill but also health, wellness, and well-being.

Engineering and control-oriented thinking will still be important, particularly in mature markets with stable technologies where control is possible. The next big wave of change, however, will grow from biological and organic ways of thinking. Bio-empathy is simply the attempt by leaders to stay in touch with and learn from the natural cycles that are all around us. How would your business decisions change if you looked at your company as an ecosystem—not a machine?

Bio-empathy comes easily to a life scientist, but one can learn it through wilderness camping or just being out in nature. Familiarity with the outdoors and with outdoor living is a big plus for bio-empathy building.

The Presiding Bishop of the Episcopal Church, Katharine Jefferts Schori, is an example of a person with high bio-empathy, in a very different field from Scott Dye or Polyface Farm. Before she was ordained, the bishop was an oceanographer for the National Marine Fisheries Service. In addition, she was a science teacher and researcher at Oregon State University. She has spoken from the pulpit about her personal tendency to demand scientific evidence before believing the truth of anything, while at the same time acknowledging areas of mystery, of the unknown. Also a pilot, Bishop Schori uses examples in her teaching and preaching about the power of the wind or spirit, comparing it to Hebrew Scriptures and the New Testament. She often uses biological metaphors in conversation. To promote environmentalism and social justice, she explains the connectivity of everything:

Scientists are teaching us that everything in the universe is connected, not just complex human and mechanical systems. A remarkable experiment a number of years ago showed this in a new way. If you take a pair of electrons with opposite spins, and send them off in different directions, and then change the spin of one of them, the spin of the other also changes—instantaneously. We're beginning to understand that everything in the universe is connected, even at the most elemental level.[4]

Bishop Schori challenges people to examine the rhythms and tendencies in nature, and to look for resonances in their own lives.

Bio-empathy Defined

Bio-empathy requires seeing things from nature's point of view. Respect for nature is basic to this perspective, with a long-term view of what is needed for life to go on for generations beyond the present.

Bio-empathy also depends upon a knack for natural thinking and a leadership resilience that draws from nature's ways.

One characteristic of bio-empathy is being able to see the big picture of ecological systems, not just the components. Some people begin to understand ecosystems through immersion in the natural world by camping or going on a safari. Even in the everyday business world, leaders are often challenged by multiple interrelated variables, nonlinear relationships, and change cycles that seem to have a life of their own.

You don't need to escape from corporate capitalism and return to the natural world to have strong bio-empathy. Bio-empathy is about seeing human activity as nested within environmental stability and vice versa. Our human systems live within natural systems. Bio-empathy is about respecting the inevitable ecological consequences of one's actions and seeing these new parameters not as barriers but as opportunities. The Eastgate Centre in Harare, Zimbabwe, for example, uses the airflow principles of termite mounds to regulate temperature without conventional heating or air conditioning. Bio-empathy gives leaders new ways of making the future.

Bio-empathy in the Future

In the background visual on the map inside the book jacket is a natural pattern of cells to demonstrate how nature will always be in the background. However, the issues of nature—both challenges and opportunities—will come to the foreground over the next decade. Biology and the life sciences will shape business performance. Gradually, humans are facing up to their part in abusing the earth and are sincerely looking for ways to make things better from nature's point of view. The dilemma is how to get greener while allowing corporations to make money and be sustainable along with the environment.

BIO-EMPATHY & ENVIRONMENTAL COOPERATION

The Global Environmental Management Initiative (GEMI) is an industry association for environmental, health, and safety leaders in a wide range of organizations across industries. GEMI worked with Institute for the Future to do a forecast of external future forces affecting sustainability. (See Figure 14.) The forecast map we created looks at sustainability through seven different lenses: people, regions, built environments, nature, markets, business, and energy.[5] With so much activity around it right now, even the term "sustainability" has come to be used in many different ways. The starting place for GEMI was to sort out the various options and put them all on one page for comparison, looking across functions and across industries.

This kind of forecasting is useful because it maps the territory of external future forces. Like any map, the GEMI/IFTF forecast map does not tell people where to go, but it does provide a context for leadership in sustainability. Organizations and individual leaders can place themselves in the stories of the map and consider their roles in the context of the external future forces. The forecast map gives leaders a big-picture typology of the options and the forces that they are likely to encounter on the way to their goal.

GEMI leaders tend to be focused on the technical aspects of environment, health, and safety. Sustainability has now been elevated to a topic for discussion at the most senior levels of a firm. The GEMI map gives a framework for these conversations, as well as some specific suggestions of hot zones where organizations can have the biggest impacts.

IFTF has also worked with Business for Social Responsibility (BSR) to create a series of cross-industry scenarios to explore how sustainability concern and business strategy can be brought together in creative ways. There are many new models for business strategy that incorporate concern for sustainability, but there is a lot to learn and the pressures to learn are urgent. Bio-empathy must be expressed in business models that are economically sustainable as well as good for the environment.

Bio-empathy also has a prominent presence in the exponential growth of alternative energy sources, technological change, and sustainable design. In 2003, Alex Steffen and Institute for the Future's Jamais Cascio cofounded the nonprofit, award-winning online magazine *Worldchanging*. Based on the principles of sustainability and social innovation, *it* advocates "bright green environmentalism," a term coined by Alex Steffen that refers to the dominant role of new

FIGURE 14. GEMI map. *Source:* IFTF, Map of Future
Forces Affecting Sustainability, 2007. SR# 1073.

design and technologies in catalyzing global ecological sustainability. *Worldchanging* captures the global ethos of techno-social foresight in order to draw sustainable insights and seek practical solutions. Many of its ideas, solutions, and inventions are documented in the book *Worldchanging: A User's Guide for the 21st Century.*

BIO-EMPATHY AND RECOVERY FROM WAR

The families of soldiers serving in Iraq and Afghanistan are learning from immersion experiences in nature to help them cope with the side effects of war. Operation Purple is a camp for kids of soldiers who are in Iraq. Sponsored by the Sierra Club, the entire premise of the camp is built on healing through nature. This camping experience is a "leap away from the worries of war."[6] The kids learn how to work through stressful challenges in a low-risk and supportive environment with others who are going through the same things. These children get to see, touch, and feel the military equipment that their parents are using in Iraq. For example, they feel how heavy a bullet-proof vest really is, so they have the sense that their parents do have *some* protection. They practice finding adults they can turn to when their parents are not there or not able to help and also build their own resilience in a natural outdoor setting.[7]

ECOSYSTEM EMPATHY

Ecosystems are lives in balance, at least on the good days when they *are* in balance. Ecosystems are not problems to be solved or machines that can be controlled; they are life systems that need to be nurtured as delicate dilemmas of life.

Over the next decade, the issues that are likely to dominate are food, energy, and water, or FEW, as they are coming to be called.[8] All three of them interrelate and all are laced with dilemmas.

There is great potential here to flip these dilemmas into new ways of thinking about priorities. For example, I was speaking recently at the University of Texas business school in Austin as part of a course called "Marketing for Social Profit." That course title is an interesting flip, where "profit" is applied much more broadly but is still very much within the tradition of the profit motive.[9] Social profit is economic return that also includes positive social impacts and usually involves creating shared assets.

What we call the "Blue Economy" on the forecast map inside the book jacket symbolizes water, which will be the focal point of economic development and environmental debate as we struggle with collapsing fisheries, search for new energy sources, and attempt to manage the impacts of global climate disruption. Some of these shared resources have finite limits, which are already stretched. Other resources can be stretched with new technology and shared for greater benefits. Ecosystems present many dilemmas, in many different forms. These eco-dilemmas can lead to insight regarding specific innovation opportunities and engagement.

Oceans are shared; no country, region, or person really owns them, yet all of us depend on them. The tidal zones, where land meets ocean, will be the focus point for dilemmas that are likely to become even worse in twenty to forty years. Compass (the Communication Partnership for Science and the Sea), for example, is a collaborative effort by scientists to bridge the fields of marine conservation, public interest, and marine policy. Their mission is to accelerate cooperation within the context of the challenges that they face. They start with a deep empathy for oceans and the value they provide.

BIO-EMPATHY AND FOOD

Created in 2000 as part of a merger, Syngenta is an agribusiness that has reframed its vision and its business as sustainable agriculture. Their focus is on plants, both seeds and crop protection. Growers of all kinds are their customers.

Syngenta has a very clear vision statement that is infused with bio-empathy: "We bring plant potential to life." This is a natural statement of future intent with bio-empathy and an aspiration built in. Notice how they frame their Winning Proposition in the context of external future forces:

> Over the next twenty years, the world's population will rise by about another two billion. Calorie demand will grow even faster, as diets in countries such as China increasingly shift to meat.
>
> In much of the world, agricultural land is limited and water scarce. So tomorrow's growers will have to produce much more food and animal feed with today's natural resources. At the same time, they will continue growing fibers like cotton and add crops for fuels such as bioethanol. And agriculture also has to protect the environment, for example, by reducing greenhouse gases and preserving natural habitats from the plow.
>
> This all means that growers must increase their yields—the amount of crop per field. Our products play a key role in making that possible.
>
> Bringing plant potential to life.[10]

Syngenta is using its own version of bio-empathy to address the challenges of food production, using science focused on plants. It is creating a business in the midst of the food web. So far, this seems to be working very well for the company and for its customers.

Food dilemmas will proliferate over the next decade and will reflect the rich–poor gap most dramatically. Even as many are hungry, some will be extremely and exotically well fed. Nobody knows how to solve this dilemma, but many leaders will figure out creative ways to flip this situation and make it better. In just the last few years, concepts like the "100-mile diet" and "locavores" (a word that designates those who eat only local foods) have become popular and—in at least some locations in some seasons—practical. Although some of the current focus on locally grown food could be a fad, the interest is indicative of deeper concerns about food sourcing. People want to know that their food is safe, and it seems safer if it is local or if they know where it comes from. People also want to consume less energy, and local food does not need to be transported.

In the world of the future, food chains are giving way to webs. Linear and mechanical procedures for distributing food are being replaced by cyclical, organic, flexible food webs. Food webs are the complex, interlocking, and interdependent feeding relationships among plant and animal species. Food companies traditionally used supply chains to distribute food for sale. In most corporations these chains are now referred to as "supply networks" or "supply webs." These webs will be challenged by global climate change, overdevelopment, and industrial waste, but they are also more robust than ever.

BIO-EMPATHY AT THE BALLPARK

Scott Jenkins is another example of a business leader with strong bio-empathy. Jenkins is the Seattle Mariners VP of ballpark operations for Safeco Field—where the Mariners play major league baseball. He was trained in construction management at the University of Wisconsin, with courses in environmental studies as well. Basically he is an outdoors person who spent a lot of time running along the shore of Lake Michigan when he was a kid in Kenosha. Jenkins has gained a reputation as a kind of "Mr. Green Stadium" for his work on the greening of stadiums for the Milwaukee Brewers, the Philadelphia Eagles, and now the Seattle Mariners. He has only limited formal training in environmental sustainability, but lots of passion for it. He was not taught bio-empathy in his formal course work, but he lives it.

Safeco Field is the stadium that I find most like Walt Disney World in terms of its family friendliness. If you use a four-letter word there, you will get warned once and then escorted quietly out of the park. The rule of thumb is that behavior must be appropriate in the company of a seven-year-old. The Safeco Field Code of Conduct is displayed around the park, and if you violate it, you get a red card that includes the following warning: "The Safeco Field Code of Conduct asks all of our guests to respect others around them by avoiding foul or abusive language, obscene gestures, and other abusive behavior. *If you receive this card, we believe that your behavior has crossed this line.* Please take this as a friendly reminder. Enjoy the game, but allow others to do so as well. Continued abusive behavior will require us to eject you from the ballpark without refund—something we don't want to do."

Part of being family friendly, according to Scott Jenkins, is being friendly to the environment. Bio-empathy relates to people as much as it does to plants and animals. When he came to Safeco Field, Jenkins asked his staff (it takes about 2,000 people to put on a single event at this stadium) how much energy it took to run the entire stadium for one day. Nobody actually knew at the time (including Scott), but they know now. Jenkins has put in feedback systems that let people know how much energy they are using and gives them rewards for saving energy. Safeco Field is looking for ways to give real-time feedback to its own employees (called team members) and to its fans.

Jenkins has great focus on the direction he is going as he greens Safeco Field while also improving the family experience, but he realizes that there are lots of steps along the way and many behaviors that must be changed. Jenkins himself bikes to and from the ballpark. His first car was the Honda CRX HF, one of the first hybrids, which averaged fifty to sixty miles per gallon, and he drove a Prius for a while, using hyper-mileage driving principles. (He told me that when he drives his car, he goes "as slow as [he] can without annoying people.") Now, he drives a Nissan Leaf where he is proud to get 200 miles on $4 of homegrown electricity. "The future is already here, folks just haven't figured it out yet," Jenkins declares.[11]

When I walked with Scott Jenkins around the stadium just before a game, he always stopped to pick up paper on the ground or clean any spills. He teaches everyone to take responsibility for the cleanliness of the park, which is a discipline that people at Disney follow as well.

One kind of feedback that Safeco team members get is from secret shoppers. The Mariners hire shoppers (disguised as normal fans, some with kids) to attend every game and give specific feedback about how they were treated and what they experienced. The feedback is not used in an evaluative way, but rather as a way to encourage staff to behave in a manner that is family friendly and green. The Mariners G.A.M.E. Plan is this clear statement of intent:

• Guests come first.
• Attitude is everything.
• Make memories.
• Everyone is empowered.

Staff members are rewarded around these principles and given encouragement about ways to improve. The secret shoppers are looking for behavior that I would call bio-empathy, especially empathy for the biological units called baseball fans.

The Mariners use the secret shoppers in a way that is reminiscent of the army and other public service agencies using After Action Reviews. The Mariners' "make memories" principle is similar to the way in which Walt Disney World park workers are encouraged to create magical experiences for the guests. They are not looking for someone to blame; they are looking for ways to give quick feedback on positive behavior that supports the overall fan experience they are trying to create. This is very motivational for the employees, since they get both the fulfillment of creating memories for the fans and also the quick feedback on their level of friendliness at the ballpark.

Bio-empathy gets played out within the context of the family-friendly vision and strategy for Safeco Field. Energy-saving behavior increased dramatically when employees were taught how they could save energy and given immediate feedback when they did. Much of the savings has come through behavior changes and creating a different set of disciplines at work. Team members are encouraged to treat the ballpark as they would their own home, as if they were paying the utility bills.

FIGURES 15 & 16 (left and above).
Captain Plastic is a family-friendly
voice of sustainability at Safeco
Field. He teaches kids to recycle as
part of the family experience at the
park. *Source:* Used with permission of
Ben VanHouten, photographer.

Changes in products and processes have helped as well. Safeco
Field now uses bottle-shaped recycling containers that are message-
branded with their own "Captain Plastic" logo and positioned all
around the park with requests for people to "Join the Green Team."
Captain Plastic recently got a new sidekick named Kid Compost, to
teach kids about the virtues of composting. (See Figures 15 and 16.)
The drinking cups for beer and soft drinks are not petroleum based
and can be recycled, for example.

The systemic changes, however, were all done in the context of behavior, and the behavior changes were done in the context of the family-friendly spirit of Safeco Field. This version of bio-empathy begins with the family—especially the kids. In Seattle's ballpark, family friendly is bio-friendly. These concepts are now being expanded to a wide range of other professional sports stadiums through the new Green Sports Alliance, which Scott Jenkins helped to create.[12]

DOGS AND BIO-EMPATHY

Cesar Milan is the star of the very successful National Geographic TV series called *The Dog Whisperer.* His mantra is "I rehabilitate dogs, I train humans." Certainly, Milan is a showman who has created a great story around himself and his presence with dogs. Behind the drama and the considerable hype, Milan is facilitating cross-species communication and is a maker of new relationships between dogs and humans.

Milan has great bio-empathy with dogs. He's lived with them all of his life, beginning on a farm in Mexico where he was born. His experience led him to a basic insight about what dogs want and need: exercise, discipline, and affection, in that order. This statement is a wonderful example of expressing intent with great clarity, but still with flexibility regarding how the exercise, discipline, and affection are delivered. All of us need exercise, discipline, and affection— though not necessarily in that order. Dogs, however, are different from humans in important ways that humans often forget in their efforts to cuddle and care for them. Dogs live in the moment and appear to be completely focused on their own immediate experience.

With a commander's intent and a strong presence with dogs, Milan's calm assertive energy, indeed his entire body positioning, shows strong clarity. He allows dogs to be themselves, but only within prescribed parameters. He doesn't train dogs; he rehabilitates them. He trains humans to have the same kind of bio-empathy with dogs that he has. People working with dogs should ask: what energy am I communicating? Certainly, every leader should also ask this question. Milan argues that a leader's energy must be calm and assertive—not nervous energy.

Just in time for the second edition of *Leaders Make the Future*, Adam Gopnik wrote a wonderful personal history for the *New Yorker* called "Dog Story." His is an elegantly written bio-empathy story inspired by the dog he brought home for his ten-year-old daughter. Gopnik shows us that we can have bio-empathy for dogs, but they can also have bio-empathy for us as they try to figure out what we want. Some dogs are very good at figuring out what humans want. Dogs, Gopnik reminds us, are descended from wolves some 30,000 years ago. Dogs can teach us to reach out beyond our immediate circle of life to the larger circles of natural life all around us. Dogs can teach us bio-empathy:

> And so the dog belongs to the world of wolves she comes from and to the circle of people she has joined. Another circle of existence, toward which we are capable of being compassionate, lies just beyond her, and her paw points toward it, even as her eyes scan ours for dinner.[13]

If you have a biology degree, it will be easy for you to grasp the importance of bio-empathy. If you don't have a biology degree and you want to learn bio-empathy, live with a dog as a mentor.

Bio-empathy Summary

There are many ways to develop bio-empathy, but the first step is to listen, observe, and appreciate the natural processes that are always going on around us. Bio-empathy contributes to person-to-person communication. Every organization's guiding principles should reflect bio-empathy and express it in organic—not mechanical—language. Bio-empathy takes big-picture thinking that respects all the multiple interrelated parts and nonlinear relationships, as well as cycles of change.

Bio-empathy is grounded in an ability to empathize with nature and understand its ways, its connectivity, and its resilience. One interesting strategy, for example, is to learn about nature through children's books, such as those published by Dorling Kindersley.[14] It is never too late to nurture your own bio-empathy.

6

Constructive Depolarizing

Ability to calm tense situations where
differences dominate and communication has broken down—
and bring people from divergent cultures
toward positive engagement.

Very little good has ever been done by the absolute shall.

ANONYMOUS CLERGYMAN IN
THE ERA OF PROHIBITION[1]

NEUROLOGIST ROBERT BURTON is studying the neuroscience of certainty. He writes: "Despite how certainty feels, it is neither a conscious choice nor even a thought process. Certainty and similar states of 'knowing we know' arise out of involuntary brain mechanisms that, like love and anger, function independently of reason."[2]

Burton's conclusions show how neuroscience will shake our understanding of leadership over the next decade. The title of his book on certainty is both revealing and provocative: *On Being Certain: Believing You Are Right Even When You're Not.* How many leaders have you seen who know they are right, even if they are wrong?

Clarity is critical for leaders, as I discussed in Chapter 2, but certainty is downright dangerous. In a VUCA World, many will be attracted to "absolute shalls" and leaders will have to engage with these polarized and polarizing advocates who drive wedges between others.

The quest for certainty will increase over the next decade because people will have an urgent need for certainty in the frightening face of uncertain times. I believe that the number of leaders who are clear, certain, and wrong will increase. I expect more zealous and self-righteous leaders who stridently advocate an absolute shall. Many of these prideful leaders will be well meaning and sincere, but dangerous nonetheless. The VUCA World will come with few absolutes, even fewer absolute shalls.

Nobody has created a VUCA index to measure just how volatile, uncertain, complex, and ambiguous our time is as compared to previous times in history. That would be interesting, but you don't need an index to tell you that the next decade will be tough and tense. I believe that the future will be more VUCA than what most of the world is experiencing today, and I think it's safest for leaders to assume this also. Whether the world is more VUCA or not, however, is less important than the fact that VUCA will abound. Leaders need to learn how to lead in an extremely uncertain age, perhaps the most uncertain that any generation has ever faced.

The more uncertainty there is in the external world, the more people will need to *feel* certain—or at least feel assured. Religious, political, social, and psychological fundamentalisms are likely to increase in an attempt to reel in the chaos of the external world. The neuroscience of certainty is likely to become an important field of study, along with other attempts to make sense out of certainty and extremism.

The tension between clarity and certainty will become a key dilemma for leaders to manage within themselves. According to Robert Burton and a growing number of neuroscientists, our brains will play a big role in our understanding of certainty—and our understanding of leadership. Leaders in the VUCA World will need clarity, but they must also be tempered about their own certainties. Knowing you know can be dangerous. Leaders must remind themselves of what they don't know, even while they maintain their own clarity about what they do. Again, clarity includes knowing what you don't know. Certainty does not.

In VUCA times, many different groups will believe that they are right; the most extreme of those *also* will believe that everyone else is wrong. I call this the *threshold of righteousness*. Extreme fundamentalist groups will *know* what's right with no sense of ambiguity, humility, or empathy. Dangerously, they also will "know" with great certainty that everyone else is wrong. Absolute shalls will abound.

Leaders will need to engage with extreme groups who may not even agree with other similar extreme groups. Extreme positions and polarization will be even more commonplace in the next decade. Engaging with those who are obsessed with certainty—whatever the source—will be difficult for leaders in particular.

In polarized situations, differences are sharply drawn and communication has disintegrated. In a chaotic world, there are often more than two points of view and there are usually many stakeholders. Leaders will need the skill of constructive depolarization in order to redirect the energy of conflict and bring the stakeholders toward constructive engagement and dialogue.

In times of change, simplified certainty will lure those who are most confused. When people go over their own personal threshold capacity for disruption, they will seek immediate solutions. If the uncertainty is too great for a particular individual, certainty is a logical psychological reaction. It may be a neurological demand. Certainty is a response not only to uncertainty in the external world, but also to inner needs. Leaders will need to show appropriate confidence while still having caution about too much, or false, certainty.

Constructive Depolarization Defined

Constructive depolarization is the maker instinct applied to conflict, an attempt to make polarization into dialogue. Constructive depolarizing begins with making calm. Often, polarized conflicts are dilemmas rather than problems than can be solved.

When leaders encounter conflict, the temptation is to pick sides. However, this is rarely a good strategy. The story of constructive depolarization is usually a drama, with many twists in the plot. Polarized conflict is rarely an either/or choice, even though it may look that way at first.

A background in cultural anthropology (the methodologies of ethnography), qualitative sociology (the methodologies of participant observation, which are quite similar to ethnography), or comparative religions will be very helpful for future leaders. International travel and living in a variety of places can be very instructive, as can language skills. Thomas Friedman's argument that the "world is flat" is true in one sense, but the world is also extremely jagged—with many varying cultural characteristics, religious beliefs, and economic pressures. The more comfortable a leader is with cultural diversity, the more likely he or she is to be able to lead in diverse and polarized situations.

Future leaders will need cross-cultural grace in order to constructively depolarize a situation: an ability to listen and learn from people who are very different from them, and perhaps different in a disturbing way. Grace in this sense means being nimble, poised, and engaging—like a good dancer. It is the ability to offer consideration and respect whether or not a person deserves it. Leaders with grace will be able to make the reconciliation process look easy. In exploring this critical future leadership skill, I turned back to the iconic anthropologist E. T. Hall, author of *The Silent Language: An Anthropologist Reveals How We Communicate by Our Manners and Behavior.* Hall argues that culture is communication and communication is culture. The "silent language" of culture will always be hidden, but Hall gives leaders some useful advice: "We must learn to understand the 'out of awareness' aspects of communication. We must never assume that we are fully aware of what we communicate to someone else."[3]

Hall worked for the State Department helping diplomatic leaders understand and learn from other cultures. Cross-cultural leadership is now much more complex than it was when Hall published *The Silent Language.* "Cross-cultural" does not just refer to ethnic, national, and regional beliefs. Leaders must take into account age, gender, disabilities, and other dimensions of difference. There are many cultures and subcultures, and the cloud will allow dispersed cultures to connect and influence each other—for better or worse. Polarization is most likely to occur between different cultures. Constructive depolarization is about grace across barriers of any kind, including those of culture, nationality, and ethnicity.

Dilemmas in the Future

The next decade will be characterized by diversity and polarization, much of which will trace to the growing and increasingly visible gap between the rich and the poor. One aspect of the gap is narrowing: even poor people are gaining access to cheap digital meeting tools that can be used for organizing. In general, extreme groups tend to be better at web organizing, which means that even very small extreme groups could have major impacts far beyond their numbers. Cheap ubiquitous cell phones, for example, can bring cohorts of people together and give voice to their concerns.

In ten years it is clear that pretty much everything will have a global and cross-cultural aspect—our differences will be visible to everyone. It will be rare to find situations that are exclusively local, simple, and homogeneous. For example, Wayne Sensor, former CEO of Alegent Health in Omaha, Nebraska, came to IFTF to talk about

Alegent's work on global health. When I asked why a local health-care provider that only serves the inland state of Nebraska would be so interested in global health issues, he responded, "Because planes fly into Omaha." Indeed, air travel increases the very real possibility of pandemics. Local organizations often have global suppliers, even if all employees are not aware of how globally connected they really are. Global issues will profoundly affect people who have previously seen themselves as operating on a local level. Food safety in China may seem like a far-away issue until you realize that some of the ingredients in your "local" food products may have come from China and may be tainted.

POLARITIES IN FAITH

The Consortium of Endowed Episcopal Parishes (CEEP) is made up of U.S.-based Episcopal churches, which are part of the global Anglican Communion, one of the largest social networks in the world. The Anglican Communion is a diaspora, with strong links based on values in spite of the great diversity of its members. Ironically, polarization has descended upon the Episcopal Church, in spite of its inclusive philosophy and globally networked connections.

Polarization in the U.S. Episcopal Church was sparked by the ordination of gay bishops, but there are deeper issues of authority within this diffuse global network. The debate over whether gay people should be ordained as bishops raises basic theological, psychological, and sexual questions that are difficult to discuss without emotion—sometimes extreme emotion. The situation is so polarized that dialogue among some people is often impossible. Key voices on each side know that they know, with self-righteous certainty. The absolute shall—or the absolute shall not—has fractured the community.

The Consortium asked IFTF to do an independent forecast of external future forces that will be important for Episcopal congregations to consider in the next ten years. Figure 17 shows the modified Foresight to Insight to Action Cycle that we created as part of this forecast, which we called *The Book of Provocation,* a conscious play on the Bible's Book of Revelation. Our forecast was designed to stimulate

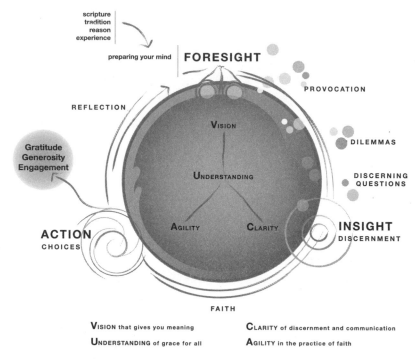

FIGURE 17. Modified Foresight to Insight to Action cycle for *The Book of Provocation. Source:* IFTF, *The Book of Provocation: Faith in the Future Conversations,* 2008. SR# 1123.

conversations among church members not only about present conflicts, but also about what they have in common as they think about the future. The case is still out as to whether or not we have contributed positively, but there are parishes around the United States using *The Book of Provocation* to spark conversations among people of faith. (See Figure 17.)

I believe that forecasting has the power to bring people together for dialogue across polarities, if they can step back as they look ahead. It is necessary, however, to find an internal logic for this dialogue.

In the Anglican Communion, there is a great history of openness and engagement. If participants start from their own scripture, reason, and tradition, a Ten-Year Forecast of external future forces can provide a context to provoke constructive conversations. A forecast, however, is not a prediction of the future. That future, we hope, will be shaped by people in the local congregations who become inspired by "Faith in the Future Conversations," as we are calling them.

Every ten years, the global Anglican Communion holds a nineteen-day summit for bishops. In the summer of 2008 the Lambeth Conference was held at the University of Kent in Canterbury. The polarizing issue on everyone's mind was the ordination of gay bishops. The one openly gay bishop, Bishop Gene Robinson from New Hampshire, was not invited to attend, but he was given space to meet with bishops from around the world as part of what was known as the "fringe" event. One hundred and fifty bishops decided not to attend the conference out of protest against the ordination of gay bishops.

This conference focused on person-to-person engagement and constructive depolarization. While the threat of a split church loomed, the goal of the conference was to honor the participants and their varied approaches to faith, so that the bishops from around the world could get to know each other as people—not polarities. They were trying to lay the groundwork for engagement with diversity, following principles that were not only Anglican, but also good for anyone trying to constructively depolarize a conflict.

The conference employed an African Zulu method called *Indaba,* used to allow villagers to meet and discuss problems in the community. In hopes that the Bible could provide a common starting ground, the conference began with Bible study groups of eight randomly assigned people reading the "I am" statements in the Gospel of John, as chosen by the Archbishop of Canterbury. Then groups of eight joined together to create assemblages of forty bishops, with an "animateur" to get things started and facilitate, a "rapporteur" to take notes, and a listener, who summarized.

These evolving groups put an emphasis on personal contact among the participants, rather than pushing through ideas or positions. While the *Indaba* methods seem similar to Western approaches, I expect that its African origin contributed to the sense of constructive engagement between developed and emerging economies. The African bishops were the apparent outsiders going in, but the use of a process that was familiar to them perhaps gave them a sense of trust that they would not have had otherwise. Canon Gregory Cameron, one of the chief mediators, summarized the challenges:

> No organization exists without internal conflict—not even the church. What is important is that organizations achieve enough unity to continue to fulfill their purposes. Our challenge is harnessing that which is best in the life of the church so that we have something to say not just to ourselves but also to the world.[4]

The goal of the conference was to hold the Anglican Communion together as a network, while allowing space for individual self-expression and differences in belief. Could they achieve clarity as a church while some of the members disagreed with such certainty?

The group process encouraged the participants not to judge too soon. Of course, many of the participants had pre-judged before they arrived, but this conference opening created a time to reflect and reconsider as the participants got to know each other as people.

The Lambeth Conference illustrates the polarized engagement we are all likely to experience in the next decade. The quality of the outcome from Lambeth is debatable, but at least the bishops engaged in thoughtful conversation to get beyond the polarities of certainty.

CIVIC ENGAGEMENT ACROSS POLARITIES

The technologies of cooperation are getting much better, and they will be able to help us bridge polarities and deal with controversial issues. One of the pioneers of computer support for large-scale meetings is Lenny Lind, who founded CoVision in 1985. The company mantra is "Building collective intelligence through high-engagement meetings." CoVision facilitates large in-person meetings by distributing laptops around the room to allow for instant polling and participation from more individuals than would be possible using conventional means. Trained facilitators solicit wide input and help the participants sort out common concerns, as well as create an action agenda. They use interactive panels through the electronic media to allow more voices to be heard.

For example, in 2005 CoVision worked with AmericaSpeaks to gather one thousand people in a large room for the Clinton Global

Initiative in New York. The focus was on four parallel tracks: energy and climate, global health, poverty alleviation, and mitigating religious and ethnic conflict. Former president Bill Clinton was the chair. World leaders were joined by senior government officials, public and private infrastructure experts, celebrities, business leaders, billionaires, philanthropists, and other notables—all sitting at round tables discussing the most important problems facing the world community. It was a marketplace of ideas and initiatives. The meeting was originally conceived of as a "world economic forum with an action plan." Indeed, hundreds of specific commitments to action were made and millions of dollars were raised. The process is continuing beyond this single event.

The electronic tools for civic engagement are getting much better, as are the processes for using the technology effectively. Over the next ten years, I expect that electronically assisted group processes like this will become more common in civic engagement. These media allow conversations that bridge polarities, using anonymity and simultaneous exchange in ways that are not possible in traditional face-to-face meetings. In this way, diverse groups can be brought together for constructive depolarization and engagement.

POLARITIES OF WAR

At one of our civilian/military workshops at the Army War College, I asked two strategy professors, one from Columbia Business School and one from the Army War College, to prepare an introductory lecture on strategy. About an hour before they went on, I asked them to exchange PowerPoint presentations and use each other's slides for their introductory lectures. Then I facilitated a panel discussion that compared strategy in business to the way it is practiced in the military.

There were many similarities in the basic concepts and principles. For example, Commander's Intent is basic to military strategy and it is quite similar to a Winning Proposition or strategic intent in the corporate world. What's different is that military strategy is *much* more complicated than business strategy. There are so many variables and so many stakeholders. In addition to the complexity of military strategy, war has life-and-death consequences.

If a military conflict involves religious beliefs, things get even messier. I've been very impressed in recent years with the approach coming to be called "faith-based diplomacy."[5] In traditional mediation, religion was considered out of bounds and the effort was toward a secular resolution. In faith-based diplomacy, religious representatives on both sides of the polarization get involved and share the precepts from each faith that speak to forgiveness and reconciliation. They look for common ground on which both sides can build. Of course, the introduction of faith adds even further to the complexity of the strategy discussion, but it is also closer to areas where lasting agreements might be achieved.

Thus, constructive depolarization is much more difficult in a military setting—especially if life-and-death decisions are involved. Leaders need a strategy for engagement and exploration, but they also need diplomatic skills that go far beyond the fighting and well into peacekeeping and even nation building. In one of our exchanges at the Army War College, I met a young man who had just returned from Iraq, where one of his tasks had been walking door to door to introduce the concept of democracy. Think of that. Certainly, his military training did not prepare him for going door to door talking about democracy, but that is what he had to do. This very human door-to-door process was critical to American attempts (some would say failed attempts) to depolarize a very bad situation and try to make it better. This young man was trying to be an agent of constructive depolarization. When I met him, he was reading the Koran in an attempt to understand the people he was meeting. The human contact may not have outweighed the negatives of the military tactics, but it certainly put forward a different approach to engagement that attempted to diffuse a very tense situation.

NEW POLARITIES OF NORMALCY

One of the big polarities in our society today is between people who are classified as "normal" and those who are not. People with disabilities have been marginalized by our society and by our policies toward them. Products, services, and technologies designed for people with disabilities have been treated as a do-good activity, if there has been any market activity at all. Public policy toward people with disabilities has been more or less stalled for the last decade, without much effort to constructively depolarize and build new definitions of normality. People with disabilities are likely to feel this polarization deeply.

The next decade will see some big changes in notions of normality. One of the few positive results of the Iraq War is the incredible effort in medical technology to rebuild broken bodies. Indeed, technology has evolved to the point where "normal" may just be a temporary zone on the way to becoming better than normal—depending on your definition of *better.* New drugs, for example, are likely to amplify leadership abilities by allowing people to stay awake and alert longer. People who can afford it will be able to understand their own genomic profiles so they can take better care of their bodies.

People with disabilities may be the earlier explorers of this future world, and since they already experience their own challenges of volatility, uncertainty, complexity, and ambiguity, they may in fact be more ready for the VUCA World than those who are "not yet disabled," as people with disabilities sometimes refer to the rest of the world. The true innovations are likely to come from the margins that are stretched, rather than from the mainstream.

CONSTRUCTIVE DEPOLARIZATION VIA YOUTUBE

In a BBC World News interview, Queen Rania of Jordan said,

> Violence has overtaken dialogue, and compassion has lost out to anger. I'm hoping this will become a channel of communication between East and West because I very much think our world is in dire need of that. . . . As Muslims we need to stand up and speak out about who we are. If we want to defy stereotypes we have to start defining ourselves, and we're not going to do that just by sitting quietly at home expecting people to just get it.[6]

Constructive depolarization involves both deep self-knowledge and the ability to communicate effectively across differences, using media appropriate to the task.

As Queen Rania pointed out, the Islamic faith is made up of many different diasporas with many different beliefs and practices. From the outside, Islam can look much more monolithic than it really is.

FIGURE 18. Jordan's Queen Rania has a video log on YouTube clarifying Islamic beliefs and Muslim traditions. *Source:* Used with permission of Ghada Al-Shami.

What looks like one diaspora is actually many, all loosely connected in the traditions of Islam. Stereotypes—false clarity, often stated with certainty—are dangerous because they oversimplify, and sometimes provoke extreme reactions.

In 2008, Queen Rania began using YouTube to present her own video log with a goal of clarifying Islamic beliefs and Muslim traditions for the rest of the world.[7] She created this site and invited questions and comments. (See Figure 18.)

Nobody yet knows the full impacts of Queen Rania's efforts, but they are certainly inspirational in their use of new media to constructively depolarize tensions between the people of Islam and the rest of the world.

Putting Something in the Middle

Chuck Palus and Wilfred Drath of CCL have studied constructive depolarization and explored the importance of "putting something in the middle" as a way of both calming a tense situation and moving toward a better path. CCL has created card decks and visual libraries of images that can become that something in the middle to help establish constructive dialogue:

Dialogue can be valuable in addressing complex challenges. In practice, dialogue is often difficult to initiate if not already present. Putting something in the middle—mediation of the conversation with various kinds of objects—has always been a way to achieve dialogue. The notion of mediated dialogue points the way to doing this deliberately and with skill.[8]

The CCL card decks and the process around them provide vivid points of engagement for people who are stuck in polarized conflict. If they are able to give up the moment, for a few moments anyway, the process of putting something in the middle allows them to relook at where they are and where they might go. Constructive depolarizing involves rethinking and reimagining what is possible. What is perceived as possible, of course, often depends on your point of view.

Constructive Depolarization Summary

Mentoring is great, but reverse mentoring is even better. Reverse mentoring is a simple but powerful strategy for bridging polarities.

Many innovative organizations already have reverse-mentoring programs, and they offer great benefit. For example, young scientists mentor senior executives with no science background; young Facebook users mentor their Boomer managers in social networking skills. Mentors have traditionally been experienced, often older, people who coach those who are less experienced and younger. In situations where young people are actually more skilled than older people—as is often the case with the new social media—why not reverse this process? Leaders and soon-to-be leaders should look for these opportunities.

Role reversal has always been a basic technique for conflict resolution across polarities. The idea is to try to see the world from the other side of an issue. Constructive depolarization starts with an ability to listen deeply and engage with people on all sides of a conflict. We need to seek out our common humanity and empathize with others who come from very different points of view.

Calming tense situations, however, is just a beginning. Creating constructive ways forward is much more difficult to sustain, particularly when key players know that they know with rigid certainty. Leaders will need to calm tensions and move through the conflict.

Extreme polarization will be a driving force for the foreseeable future, so leaders will need a personal strategy and style for constructive depolarization that goes way beyond picking sides.

7

Quiet Transparency

Ability to be open and authentic about what matters—

without being overly self-promoting.

THE *MAKE: MAGAZINE* MOTTO, "If you can't open it, you don't own it,"[1] is a call—really a demand—for transparency. Transparency is rooted in the maker instinct. People's curiosity and knowledge about how things are made has always been there but will increase dramatically. Where did those ingredients come from? What standards of safety were used? How green were the factories? Who were the workers and how were they treated? Quiet transparency is also necessary for constructive depolarization. Quiet transparency starts from being quiet and listening. Creating calm. Listening for the future.

New technology, such as cheap sensors everywhere and wireless connectivity, will fuel the growth of transparency—whether leaders like it or not. Transparency often won't be as easy or even as desirable as it sounds in the abstract. Although increasing transparency is inevitable, definitions of transparency will vary.

Companies and their leaders are being called upon to be transparent at every step of a product's life cycle. If leaders aren't transparent, others are likely to force it and the "transparency" they force may be neither accurate nor pretty. Transparency is in the eye of the beholder, or in the metrics of the people doing the measuring. If you don't measure yourself, you are likely to be measured by others. "Measure or be measured" is a current motto, but "measure *and* be measured" may be more accurate.

For example, many retailers now require a carbon footprint assessment for products they sell. This is one way to calculate a product's environmental impact. The idea is that carbon footprints can give potential buyers a measure that they can use to make choices. Carbon footprints, however, are not measurable in an absolute sense; they are only calculable.

The calculation of a carbon footprint depends on how far back and how far forward you go in the life cycle of the product you are footprinting. Detergents, for example, have a different carbon footprint in France than they do in the UK or the United States because power is generated differently in each country and the key variable is the water temperature at which the detergent is used.

A single carbon footprint number is based upon several assumptions—most of which are never even known by the person reading the label. It is debatable whether carbon footprint calculations are all that useful. It is just one example of how the demand for transparency will grow—even if the metrics for calculating it come into question.

Consumers will want a simple measure of environmental impact and retailers are anxious to give it to them. Manufacturers will often just have to do the best they can in difficult situations to provide the varying numbers that varying stakeholders want. In many cases, companies are likely to provide a simple number for something that is not simple. The good news is that we will have improved transparency. The bad news is that we may not know what the transparency reveals.

Transparency is more a dilemma than a problem, since few things are absolutely transparent in a way that everyone will agree upon.

Quiet Transparency Defined

Quiet transparency in leadership begins with humility. Leaders should be self-effacing and not self-promoting. Leaders must listen carefully. They should also be open. Why are you doing what you are doing? Why does it matter to you? More people will be interested in why leaders do what they do.

Quiet transparency goes beyond traditional command-and-control leadership styles, which operate on the need-to-know principle. (Unless you need to know something, you are not told.) In a transparent world, we all have access to more information—even if we don't have the need. In the future, leaders are more likely to be open about almost everything, unless there is a need to conceal, and concealment may not be easy.

Whether they are more or less transparent, leaders will definitely have to give up some control. They need to decide what they themselves can and want to manage, since they cannot directly supervise everything. Leadership control is often illusory. Most top executives are surprised when they reach the top and learn that they have less power than they'd imagined. In the world of the future, control will rarely be possible.

Some degree of transparency will be required of all leaders, certainly more than in the past. It will still be possible to keep some things private, but they will be limited. Business leaders, for example, may be able to protect their private lives more than politicians or celebrities will.

The evaluator of transparency, not the person or organization being assessed, usually gets to define what transparency means. Often, leaders will not get to decide how their own transparency is measured. If the customer, consumer, or public thinks it is important to be transparent about certain issues, then leaders will need to respond appropriately, using measures that others will trust. Quiet transparency requires trust from both the leader and from those who choose to follow. Leaders cannot be transparent if people don't trust them. Transparency implies the measurement is true.

Transparency is also about authenticity, as Joe Pine and Jim Gilmore state in their book, *Authenticity*.[2] Pine and Gilmore coined the term "experience economy," which refers to the overall direction of economic evolution: from commodity products to services to experiences to personal transformations. The further you get from products and the closer you get to transformations, the more important authenticity becomes. Leadership authenticity inspires credibility and trust. It also allows followers to see in their leaders not only a bit of themselves but also that which makes them aspire to be more.

Kerry Bunker from CCL talks about the importance of authenticity in leadership: "More than ever before, successful leadership hinges on learning agility and the experience necessary to navigate and lead others through complex situations. It's not the perfect pedigree or knowing all the answers anymore. It's about resiliency and openness."[3]

To further underline CCL's commitment to fostering authentic leadership, the center developed the Authentic Leadership Paradox Wheel (Figure 19). The wheel displays how, in times of transition, leaders must balance the "dynamic tension between six pairs of seemingly paradoxical leadership attributes related to managing change."

Authenticity, openness, and resiliency must go together. CCL's programs include 360-degree feedback to help leaders learn how to navigate this complex territory and try our varied approaches in order to find their own unique leadership voices.

Quiet transparency does not mix well with fame, celebrity, or acclaim. A leader doesn't need to be a celebrity to be successful, and in some cases, success and celebrity may be inversely correlated. Often, the best leaders get little credit for the changes that they bring about.

At Institute for the Future, we have found that many famous experts with wide public acclaim are not very good at forecasting the future. For our expert panels in the early days of IFTF, we would seek the most well-known experts in a particular field. We quickly found, however, that expertise at forecasting often does not correlate

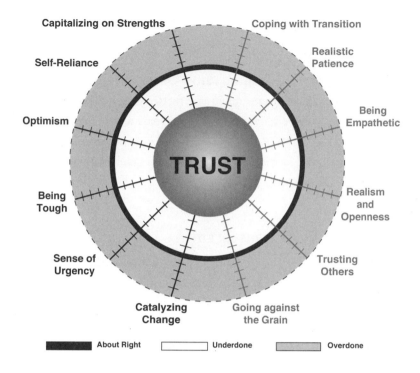

FIGURE 19. Authentic Leadership Paradox Wheel. *Source:* CCL.

with celebrity. There are just too many pressures on those who get the most publicity, such as audience demand for the same talk over and over again for large amounts of money. For our expert panels now, we seek out experts who either are not yet celebrities or do not want to be famous.

People who are used to the spotlight can get caught in their own bubbles, often losing not only their ability to forecast, but sometimes their ability to make the future. There are certainly exceptions where celebrities are great leaders, but it is a very tricky balance to sustain. Perhaps the most difficult challenge of quiet transparency is to become a great leader without becoming too much of a celebrity. This is certainly a dilemma, since successful leaders will always have to deal with some elements of fame, but they should resist the urge to be stars.

I realize that quiet transparency is not something that some aspiring leaders will find attractive. Many leaders or potential leaders will still want to be rock stars. They do not see self-promotion as bad, but rather as important in order to get to the top and achieve the success they desire—which they may measure in fame. I believe that humble strength, however, will win out in the future. I believe that the age of the rock star leader is over—with good reason. There still will be some rock star leaders, but I believe they will be less common and that most of them won't last long. Leadership and celebrity will not mix well in the VUCA World of the future.

Dilemmas of Quiet Transparency

Outside scrutiny of leaders is likely to grow in the world of the future as the tools of transparency—sensing, measuring, and monitoring—become cheap and ubiquitous. Also, it seems that there is more to be transparent about and more people who want to know what leaders are doing. In the future, they will have the tools to do it. Measuring devices will be everywhere, connected to people all around the world. In the world of social media, any record of bad behavior will be preserved and bad behavior is more likely to be discovered sometime—even if there is a long delay before discovery.

NEW TECHNOLOGY FOR TRANSPARENCY

The term *ubiquitous computing* has been around for many years (I believe Mark Weiser coined it years ago at what was then Xerox PARC), but over the next decade computing will become even more practical and truly ubiquitous. It is reasonable to expect a world instrumented with sensors, actuators, and information processors integrated with objects, activities, and many aspects of life.

A society that employs pervasive computing will be very different. Many things that are currently invisible will become visible through a vast array of measurement devices that make transparency so much more possible and accessible. Ubiquitous computing means that transparency will be mandatory in many environments, whether that transparency is "quiet" or not. The leaders of the civic structure and the grassroots actions of the community will set the specific measures of the transparency. Unfortunately, transparency does not necessarily mean accuracy. When everything can be measured, it will sometimes be more difficult to make sense out of the measures. It will also be easier to manipulate them to support your own point of view.

Citizens will be able to monitor their own bodies and the air quality around them, for example, as well as many other variables they think are important. The underlying architecture of pervasive computing networks has no center, grows from the edges, and cannot be controlled.

When the tools of measurement become pervasive, almost everything will be measured. It will be difficult to tell, however, when the transparency will be truthful and when it will be self-promoting (or both). Pervasive computing will provide the tools for transparency, but others will shape how those measurement tools get used—including regulators, advocacy groups, and those being measured.

Michael Conroy has explored this territory in great depth in his book *Branded!*[4] NGOs are creating new ways of monitoring and evaluating corporations. Global corporate branding and the global reach of brands make it impossible for single countries to regulate. NGOs are introducing their own certification systems: Fair Trade Certified monitors coffee and chocolate; Marine Stewardship Council encourages sustainable fishing practices; Health Care Without Harm and the Green Guide for Health Care promote environmentally friendly health care. This certification revolution will apply pervasive computing tools to reshape the kind of transparency that is possible. And what a given NGO looks for when measuring will be based on the values that they are advocating—which could narrow or broaden the public agenda.

Corporations and their leaders will be under much more scrutiny in this world. But there will also be new opportunities to work across companies, perhaps across industries, to establish new commons for trading that fit within the constraints of certification. Industry associations, for example, will have new opportunities to use pervasive computing to provide shared measures around important topics like safety. While corporations and NGOs will always be adversaries to some extent, it will also be possible to establish shared assets that benefit all concerned.

The big wave of change is from more closed to more open, although it will be a messy process of change along the way. Not everything will be completely open. Open-source thinking will be a fundamental driver of change in the future and it will add to and complicate the move toward transparency. Quiet transparency implies openness. It is based on a premise of trust that, if you give ideas away, you will get even better ideas back in return. Open-source logic teaches that leaders will need to release exclusive ownership and have the faith to be transparent. In addition, they must contribute to a greater good which is emerging but not yet apparent. Leaders need to be able to use open-source thinking to raise the bar for competition, and I will discuss this in more detail in Chapter 10 on Commons Creating.

Combine open-source thinking with pervasive computing—a world with wireless connectivity and sensors everywhere—and you get many new opportunities to interact, exchange, and collaborate. New possibilities will emerge as market demand and fear come together. For example, concerns about global climate change will result in the need to monitor progress or decline in a way that is trustworthy. New groups will arise to take on this responsibility. Will they be able to work together? Nobody knows yet, but the potential is very encouraging.

ECOSYSTEMS TRANSPARENCY

Energy and environment are ripe for measurement. Imagine that every house as you walk down the street had an indicator on the outside showing how much energy that household is using on a yearly, monthly, daily, or even minute-by-minute basis. The questions with such a system will be: who is doing the measuring? Will it be voluntary? Will everyone use the same standards? Will transparency for ecosystems be quiet or self-promoting or both?

Large-scale environmental sensing projects are already under way.

For example, the National Ecological Observatory Network (NEON) is laying the groundwork for distributing monitors of ecological systems continent-wide. MIT's Media Lab is pursuing what they call "wikicity" projects that combine data feeds from local utilities and services to show how much energy is used in major metropolitan areas. Australia's Commonwealth Scientific and Industrial Research Organization (CSIRO) has a Catchment Modeling Toolkit, which provides open-source modules for modeling water consumption. These are just a few signals from a recent IFTF Ten-Year Forecast, but we expect many more over the next decade.

More and more personal cell phones, for example, will be equipped with sensors to gather data in the field. Intel Research did an experiment recently with cell phone sensing devices to monitor pollution down to the level of a city block, a particular building, and potentially even individual rooms. The vast mobile network of cell phone users could be repurposed for pollution monitoring, with much more specific focus. Now, pollution levels tend to be measured by central sensors at the level of a city or region by corporate, government, or news organizations. In the near future, anyone could measure air quality and distribute the results—which may not be pleasant for those being measured. With sensors everywhere, environmental activists, community organizations, or health care agencies could organize citizen sensor networks around a variety of concerns. The degree to which the science is accurate, however, may vary.

You would be able to evaluate external air quality and track the amount of pollutants that your body can handle. Jason Tester at IFTF created an artifact from the future that models a handheld device that could advise an individual user "You should go inside within ten minutes" when pollution levels get too high for that particular person. Such services could be offered and supported by local health-care providers or even local community or religious groups. Our forecasts suggest that there will be an increasing number of bio-citizens, consumers whose concerns blend both personal health and environmental sustainability. Many will take it upon themselves to be watchdogs, using inexpensive sensors to measure what they think is important or dangerous.

A major challenge of these new ecological monitoring systems is how we will analyze and interpret the massive amount of data. Transparency suggests that we will see through the actions of leaders and organizations. Pervasive computing will help us measure, but who will make sense out of what we have measured? Certainly, a large array of governmental, advocacy, and corporate groups will interpret what the data is saying. Organizations will have varied degrees of control over what gets measured and how the results are perceived. Being informed so frequently, citizens are likely to be overwhelmed by the data.

Leaders Who Demonstrate Quiet Transparency

Leaders who are quietly transparent don't advertise themselves. This is a dilemma: leaders need to be known in order to lead; yet they need not be self-promotional. A strong résumé is wonderful for a leader, but it is much more powerful if someone else discovers the details about a leader's life. In fact, the most productive and happiest leaders may be those who are undiscovered and able to quietly practice their own forms of leadership.

Quiet leaders do not face the pressures of their more publicity-hungry counterparts. Quiet leaders are content to lead while others get the attention. The drawback to a lack of recognition is that they may not be having as much impact as they could. The core dilemma is this: how do you reach your full leadership potential and become well known without advertising yourself?

One leader I know who demonstrates quiet transparency is Ellen Galinsky, president and co-creator of the Families and Work Institute (FWI), a nonprofit in New York City. Ellen has explored the interactions between work and private life. She has reframed this work/life balance as work/life "navigation," since balance is really impossible to achieve. The interactions between work and private life are not a problem that can be solved, but rather an ongoing ever-changing dilemma that must be managed. Navigation implies that there are some fixed obstacles that must be avoided, but that there are also currents that are fluid and lots of choices regarding what to do. Work/life navigation is a clear and useful term, since it frames the life choices of a career very clearly but gives lots of room for individual variation. Navigation involves both fixed hazards and fluid currents, with lots of options for personal choice. In her own quiet way, Ellen Galinsky has seeded and cultivated a field of study around work/life navigation.

Ellen Galinsky is very energetic and outgoing, but she is not self-promoting. She writes, speaks, and organizes to spread her message. FWI has contributed to the human resource strategies of many major organizations and is transparent in the sense that it shares all of its research and methodologies. Both Ellen and FWI have a quietly transparent style. They are engaged and open, but they don't oversell.

I met Ellen on a panel at a conference on the implications of working from home. The next morning, I saw her on the *Today Show* talking about a new government policy for those who work at home. Ellen is one of the key people to be interviewed whenever issues arise around work and private life. People come to her. She is a person of renown, but she is also a humble public figure who doesn't take herself too seriously. Her style is understated by design. Her career is an example of how one can become an authority on a single substantive issue without developing an inflated ego.[5]

Timberland is a corporation that demonstrates transparency in its own low-key way. They don't hype their greenness, but anyone who is interested can see that they are environmentally responsible. Their mission statement gives a clear sense of their orientation and style, which is understated:

> Our mission is to equip people to make a difference in their world. . . . Our place in this world is bigger than the things we put in it. . . . Making new products goes hand in hand with making things better. That means reducing our carbon footprint and being

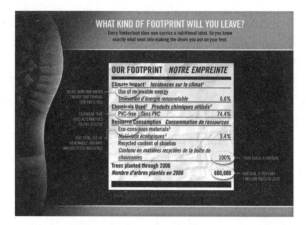

FIGURE 20. Timberland's measurement of the company's carbon footprint. *Source:* Used with permission of Timberland.

as environmentally responsible as we can. We love every minute we spend outdoors, and we work hard to create things that make that experience better in every way.[6]

The people of Timberland like hiking, which means that their interest in making boots is authentic. They also like the outdoors, which is why they were one of the first companies to calculate their own carbon footprint. Timberland is a large company with a quietly transparent style. When you walk in the woods, you walk quietly if you want to see the wildlife all around you. If you advertise your environmental values too loudly, you will become less credible. The Timberland carbon footprint label has become a model for transparency. (See Figure 20.)

Quiet Transparency Summary

There is one big lesson from quiet transparency: if leaders advertise themselves and take credit for their own performances, they will become targets. British Petroleum learned this when the company changed its name to BP, for "Beyond Petroleum." BP did a lot to live up to its new name, with many creative efforts around sustainability. Taking that bold position with regard to environmental policies, however, did little to advance relations with advocacy groups or regulators. In fact, this self-promotion seemed to make people even harder on BP, which was perceived in those days as a soft target. When the BP oil rig explosion hit the Gulf of Mexico in 2010, everyone was ready to attack BP. Their environmental credibility was low when the explosion occurred and it got much worse.

This example teaches us this: do the right thing and be transparent, but don't be self-promotional. Be willing to tell others what you are doing and why, but only when they ask. Anyone who is interested is more likely to see what you are doing and believe what you say. As a leader, you will need to make it easy for third-party organizations to notice your transparency as well as spread the word to others. In the increasingly media-rich world, someone will notice good behavior.

CCL's work also suggests that there is an "amazing power in vulnerability":

> Personal vulnerability opens the door to being genuine, human, and authentic with others, but the truth is that most leaders wear protective masks that they do not remove easily or lightly. It is as if they have been taught to hide or disguise any signs of fear, frustration, or personal pain lest it leak out and somehow undermine their credibility as a leader of others. However, our experience and research suggest that such masking actually tends to have precisely the opposite impact: those who deny valid concerns or pretend to fly above it all run the risk of being labeled as out of touch, clueless, cold and heartless, and disingenuous.[7]

Quiet transparency includes vulnerability. Quiet leaders are human and humble—but they have great strength. Quiet leaders have the ability to listen. Quiet leaders are vulnerable yet self-confident.

I believe that quiet transparency will make it more likely that leaders will succeed. Humble strength will be the best leadership profile for the future. Sometimes leaders will not get credit for the futures they make. The world of the future will not always be fair. Still, quiet transparency will be the best way to lead.

8

Rapid Prototyping

Ability to create quick early versions of innovations,
with the expectation that later success will require early failures.

———

When we change the way we communicate,
we change society.
CLAY SHIRKY

———

IN ORDER TO MAKE THE FUTURE, you have to prototype it first.
The resources for rapid prototyping will be magnified and amplified incredibly over the next decade, as Clay Shirky's work points out
convincingly:

> This linking together in turn lets us tap our cognitive surplus, the
> trillion hours a year of free time the educated population of the

planet has to spend doing things they care about. In the 20th century, the bulk of that time was spent watching television, but our cognitive surplus is so enormous that diverting even a tiny fraction of time from consumption to participation can create enormous positive effects.[1]

Prototyping is not new, but the art of rapid prototyping will be changed in profound ways by cloud-served supercomputing.

When I took my first computer programming class in 1970 at Northwestern, the professor noted that the two best programmers he had ever seen had extremely different strategies. One great programmer would carefully write out and mentally test his program before submitting it. (These were the days of batch processing where you brought your card deck to a large central computer.) The other great programmer would do a quick and dirty version and submit it right away to get the diagnosis of what did not work. The latter approach, I have now come to appreciate, was an early version of what we now call rapid prototyping.

Rapid prototyping enables us to learn from failure quickly, again and again. It is the trial-and-error method that has always been important for innovators, but on a faster cycle. The motto of rapid prototyping is to fail early, fail often, and fail cheaply as you make a better future.

Rapid prototyping is a perfect leadership strategy for the VUCA World—where truth emerges from engagement, trial, and error—because it allows leaders to try out their own ideas quickly, as well as tap into the maker instincts of a wide array of potential collaborators.

Few leaders get it right the first time, and it will get even harder in the future. Early failure will be key to later success. The failures of "computer conferencing" in the 1970s contributed to the eventual success of social media, for example. This lesson from failure took a very long time, however. In the future, leaders need to speed up the process. They should expect to go through multiple iterations of everything. As Alan Kay was known for saying when he was at Xerox PARC, "The purpose of research is to fail, but to fail in an interesting way." Rapid prototyping is all about failing cheaply, in interesting ways.

Rapid Prototyping Defined

Rapid prototyping is quick cycles of try, learn, and try again—in an ongoing sequence. Making sense in the VUCA World requires immersion in that world with a learn-as-you-go style. Prototypes typically have lifetimes measured in hours or days, not months. They are different from pilot or demonstration projects, which often take much longer to conduct.

Rapid prototyping is the Maker Instinct applied to innovation. While the concept of do-it-yourself will still be important, the next generation of innovation will be driven by "do-it-ourselves" leaders who don't get stuck on the idea of ownership since in this process people's ideas get mixed quickly and it is often impossible to sort out who thought of what.

Leaders can learn from people's pains, and innovation can help to relieve those pains. In rapid prototyping, the emphasis is not on abstract thought about possibilities or plans; it begins with real people, with the end users out in the field, and as early as possible in the innovation cycle. It begins with listening.

Companies can learn a lot from watching what people do with their products. Users are a remarkable source of new ideas for improving upon and reinventing products and services. The people who actually use a product can be a source of insight if companies are willing to learn along with them. Manufacturers create products, but no longer own them once they are purchased. The users may change them or use products in new ways. The innovation cycle is not necessarily over when the product is sold. The innovation cycle can keep going if the users continue to improve and the manufacturers learn along with them.

Leadership through rapid prototyping

- Is characterized by a trial-and-error mentality with an interest in starting quickly and learning continuously

- Emphasizes experience in the field, rather than advance planning

- Puts priority on extreme speed in learning

Traditional leadership has put a premium on thinking things through before acting. With rapid prototyping, leaders must expect to fail early in the process so they can succeed later.

In military conflicts, as I understand it, the rule of thumb is typically "one third, two thirds," where one third of the time is spent planning a mission, and the other two thirds is used for preparation in the field. It is tempting, even in battle, to spend more time planning and less time preparing. Rapid prototyping goes the other way: leaders should minimize planning, but maximize preparing in low-risk settings and learning in the field. The rule of thumb for rapid prototyping is less planning, more learn-as-you-go action. Of course, going into battle when your life depends on it may require more advance thought.

At IFTF, our former president Roy Amara often employed what he called the "jump to the end" strategy as we began a new project. For a six-month project, for example, Roy would say something like: "Let's do the entire project in a day. Then, we'll come back and fill in the holes and decide what to do next." It was an outrageous suggestion: do a six-month project in a day. But when we tried, we learned things about the project that we never could have imagined until we dove in. Rapid prototyping is learning by doing, but it is also doing by learning. It is a messy process, but it is also invigorating. The holes in logic become immediately apparent when you try to jump to the end.

Often the best way to do rapid prototyping is through the use of simulation or gaming to create realistic but low-risk learning environments. Rapid prototyping fits very well with the future leadership skill called immersive learning ability, which was described in Chapter 4. Leaders with immersive learning ability will find it much easier to do rapid prototyping. When faced with a new challenge, they could game out their possible responses before deciding what to do.

When I played basketball at the University of Illinois, we prepared for the next week's game by creating a "scout team" in practice. The scout team's job would be to simulate our opponents and run their plays. Scout team members would model their play on specific players from the other team. Our team would scrimmage against the scout team as a way of preparing our strategies and tactics of attack for the game—true rapid prototyping in action. Great practice teams usually do well during games because they have already prototyped and practiced in a realistic situation. Teams that spend too much time in the locker room planning and not enough time out on the court are at a disadvantage. The real learning happens on the court as the starting five prototypes ways of succeeding against the scout team. If the scout team does a great job, the starting five is more ready for the real game. You could also view this as a form of immersive learning, which links closely to rapid prototpying.

Dilemmas in the Future

Rapid prototyping is the first step in making the future. When I began my career in the early 1970s, much of the leading-edge innovation conducted at universities was funded by ARPA (Advanced Research Projects Agency, the research arm of the Department of Defense). The best ideas started with the military and gradually spread to consumer goods. Innovation tended to be top-down, driven and guided by central government policy. Leadership tended to be centralized and hierarchical. Now, just forty or so years later, it's become much more decentralized. Innovation tends to happen bottom-up, fueled by consumer electronics, gaming, and the maker instincts of many. Now, the best ideas start in gaming and gradually spread back to the military and government.

Leaders have to learn how to fail, and then try again—all with an expectation of much iteration. Of course, simulations and immersive environments can help leaders try and fail in low-risk ways, but try and fail we must—in order to ultimately succeed in the VUCA World.

Rapid prototyping allows us to scale up and find solutions to international dilemmas. Scholars, designers, and decision makers around the world grapple daily with the dilemma of providing clean and safe drinking water to one of every six people on this planet. A research team led by Ernest "Chip" R. Blatchley III at Purdue University has been designing and prototyping solutions for twenty years.[2] The team's most recent breakthrough is an inexpensive system that renders waterborne pathogens inactive through the creative use of the sun's ultraviolet rays. Blatchley's team successfully tested the product as part of Purdue's Global Engineering Program, with about two thousand systems currently in use in Kenya. The only way to succeed is to prototype your way to success.

PROTOTYPING IN DIASPORAS

Rapid prototyping works well within a diaspora because ideas spread more rapidly across a community of shared values and trusted relationships. News of the performance of a new beauty product, for example, will spread much more quickly among diaspora members who find the product beneficial. Testing a new idea is easier within a diaspora because it will circulate at a faster rate and reach a greater number of people—all in the same circle of trust. Diasporas are innovation breeding grounds if the innovations are a good fit with their values, priorities, financial resources, and availability of time.

Within a diaspora, rapid prototyping can begin with a small number of people but swiftly spread to many more. A diaspora is an army of potential prototypers—if the match is right. Active diasporas often make aggressive use of networked media. Offshore Chinese or Indian people, for example, are separated geographically from their homeland, but once they are joined electronically, word spreads in a flash.

PROTOTYPING CAN BE DANGEROUS

Innovation in the world of finance can be dangerous to everyone's health. The mortgage crisis of 2008, for example, was fueled by financial innovation gone amok. Personal home mortgages were intended as long-term financial agreements between a homebuyer and a bank giving the loan. As financial "innovation" accelerated, however, these long-term two-party agreements were packaged and sold to others, creating a growing chain of debt instruments that could be traded on a short-term basis. When the system started to break down, it was hard to know where to turn, since the original long-term instruments had been packaged and repackaged for market trading that benefitted only the traders along the way until things fell apart. To fuel the system, people were encouraged to buy homes they could not afford. The home mortgage market started to look a lot like gambling. The Wall Street culture has gotten very good at attracting people who are very good at creating and playing zero sum games where in order to win, someone has to lose. These complex mortgage instruments were certainly creative and innovative attempts to game the system, but they created many more losers than winners.

In public settings, it is tempting to borrow ahead rather than pay taxes today—even though the costs to future generations will be high. The current taboo on tax increases makes it more likely that financial "innovation" will grow to help improve infrastructure without revenue generation that is perceived as increasing taxes. The danger is that such innovation will hide new risk, just as it did with the mortgage crisis.

Rapid prototyping could help financial institutions, but caution is appropriate because the risks are so high. Often, prototyping in the world of finance happens in the market, where the definition of what works is who makes money. I am not a financial expert, but my instinct is that rapid prototyping logic may not apply to the financial sector in the way it does in other parts of the economy. I also have my doubts about its value in public policy making.

In the United States, compelling anecdotes often drive policy making. When a bridge collapses, there is a great public outcry and an immediate discussion of who is to blame and what can be done to prevent further collapses in the future. Unfortunately, however, it is very difficult to sustain the sense of urgency long enough to pass legislation to support the rebuilding and upkeep for infrastructure—until the next disaster happens. When demands increase but taxes don't, something else must be done to finance new infrastructure, and that something is not likely to play out well in the long run. The idea of rapid prototyping will often work better in business or research than in public policy. Public scrutiny and fear of failure sometimes discourage the practice of rapid prototyping.

Pilot and demonstration projects are often very useful to explore new policy ideas; rapid prototyping, however, moves much more quickly. New policies will be worked out in the field and rapid prototyping will be an important way to test out new ideas.

OPEN-SOURCE WARFARE

Terrorist groups, unfortunately, really get the concept of rapid prototyping. Insurgent warfare is focused on surprise and soft targets. Insurgent warriors try lots of tactics, and if one works, the new tactic spreads rapidly. If the terrorist group is a diaspora, the prototype results circulate even faster.

In the world of open-source asymmetrical warfare, the tactics will come from everywhere. Weapons will not just be traditional military-designed tools of war. Consumer electronics, games, and cell phones are the current weapon platforms of choice for many insurgent groups. In future warfare, rapid prototyping will be common terrorist strategy—which means that citizens and peacekeeping forces will need readiness training to prepare for surprise from many different directions.

Branches of the U.S. military and many other public service agencies, including police and fire departments, use a formal method called "After Action Reviews" (AARs) as a discipline for learning from everyday experiences.[3] AARs fit very well with rapid prototyping, since they focus on learning from failures. Unlike performance reviews, AARs are focused only on what can be learned and what can be improved. AARs explicitly avoid the subject of blame. The army does keep a central database of lessons from AARs over the years, but the real value of AARs is not the database but the discipline.

As best I can tell, many army personnel participate in several AARs every day, one for every significant experience, it seems; or there is at least informal learning that takes place. AARs can be used very effectively as the feedback loop in the rapid prototyping process. Indeed, this discipline fits in well with learning from the early failures and applying those lessons to achieve later success. In the world of warfare, AARs mean that the lessons from insurgent attacks can be quickly learned and reapplied in the field.

AAR discipline works well in the military, police, and fire services, but I've never seen a private corporation practice it broadly—other than a few successful pockets. Why? Most corporations are not able to separate learning from evaluation. They may have policies stating that it is important to learn from failures, but in reality employees know that if they fall short they will be punished. Failure is accepted in theory, but in practice it is almost universally unrecognized. The only exceptions I've seen are Silicon Valley companies, where failure is often seen as a badge of courage. If you haven't failed in Silicon Valley, it means you haven't taken enough risks. The AAR approach, however, would be too structured for many Silicon Valley companies.

ORGANIZATIONS DESIGNED FOR PROTOTYPING

Some organizations within large corporations are now designed to do rapid prototyping. P&G FutureWorks (futureworks.pg.com), for example, is a corporate group focused on potential new products and service innovations that P&G might consider beyond its current categories. The leader of this group, Nathan Estruth, comes from a background in political science and political campaigns. By nature, Nathan is an organizer with a keen interest in new ideas, working in the context of a very large corporation. FutureWorks makes the future.

Rapid prototyping is basic to FutureWorks. I remember in the early days of their work (when P&G was still active in food), they were deciding whether or not to go into the energy bar market. At that point, they wanted to learn as much as they could about energy bars. The idea was to try out lots of options, and they fully expected to fail "early, often, and cheaply," as was a motto in those days. They set up a room in their very flexible space that was dedicated to energy bars. Since I use them myself when I travel, I was very interested. When I went into the room, I saw more energy bars than I knew were in existence. Everyone on the FutureWorks team was using energy bars as part of their lifestyle, just to try out the concept. In parallel, they created a series of prototype energy bars that they tried out themselves, while also testing them with a variety of their target end users.

The first step in rapid prototyping is immersion in the world of end users with the aim of understanding their pains and their hopes. The second step is to begin prototyping. P&G FutureWorks decided not to pursue energy bars because it was impossible to isolate the benefits of the bar from the behavior of the person. The best of the bars contributed to weight loss, but only if the consumer developed an exercise program as well. Getting people to exercise is a lot harder than getting them to eat a tasty healthy bar.

Rapid prototyping should begin and stay as close as possible to the end consumers. For example (and this is an extreme example), when Nathan Estruth and his team created a new gravy dog food for the Iams brand, they literally ate dog food themselves as they developed the prototypes—as well as feeding the new food to dogs. In this case, prototypers really did eat their own dog food.

Rapid prototyping requires leaders to amplify their teams as much as possible—to immerse themselves in the future worlds they are trying to create. The best way to learn about these potential innovations is to try them out among the potential end users.

VISUAL PROTOTYPING

Rapid prototyping will benefit greatly from the tremendous improvements in our tools for visualization that will happen over the next decade. Visualization is a form of rapid prototyping in your mind and in virtual space. Pioneering work in this field is being done by The Grove Consultants International, founded by organization consultant and information designer David Sibbet.[4] This organization teaches people to use visualization to imagine future possibilities and bring them to life. The Grove provides leaders with a method to rapidly prototype their own thinking and evolve their own stories about how things work in their world—similar to the way a design firm would prototype a new product. Conceptual prototyping can be just as effective as product prototyping, for many of the same reasons. Along the way, The Grove has developed graphic templates that help people imagine new strategies and make them practical.

Stimulated by new visual tools, leaders will be able to improve

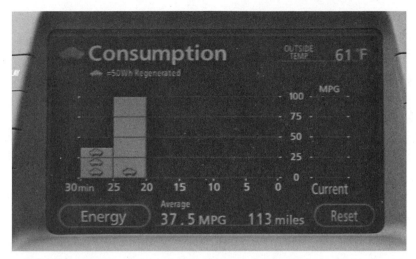

FIGURE 21. Dashboard of a Toyota Prius showing gasoline consumption. *Source:* Used with permission of Toyota.

their visual literacy—the ability to understand and communicate in pictures, drawings, and other forms of imagery. Visualization, like other pervasive computing tools, will be available in much more decentralized ways and at far less cost. The new visual tools will allow much more realistic forms of rapid prototyping in virtual and enhanced worlds. Visual computing will also allow many things to be visible that were invisible before.

An example is the dashboard of the Toyota Prius, Figure 21, which shows a real-time display of gasoline consumption while you drive. Behavior change happens best when it is influenced by immediate feedback, which is exactly what the Prius dashboard gives to a driver. In fact, it is sometimes difficult to concentrate while driving a Prius because it is so tempting to look over at the display and try to influence it with your driving. My guess is that that dashboard has saved a lot of fuel, but has caused a few accidents because the display is so engaging to watch. The Ford Focus hybrid uses the same principle, but the display—instead of a histogram—shows a leaf that wilts when a person is wasting gas, but looks healthy when the person is driving well.

Imagine a Prius-like or Focus-like dashboard that visualizes the measures that are most important for the organization you lead. Leaders could use this tool to test changes that you might make. In a virtual visual world, you could reap the benefits of rapid prototyping without the risk of actually making those changes out in the real world. Of course, there is the challenge of designing virtual world measures that accurately reflect the real world. It will not be as easy as measuring gasoline consumption.

A Rapid Prototyping Leader

Institute for the Future is located about two blocks from IDEO—arguably the world's leading design firm—in downtown Palo Alto, California. IDEO is a model for rapid prototyping. "IDEO University" teaches rapid prototyping as a way of engaging people in the design and innovation process.

IDEO's workspaces are unique. Founder David Kelley believes that design groups should be no bigger than about thirty people and that each studio should be designed in a way that adds to the creativity of the group. One design group used their office furnishings budget to purchase the tailpiece from an old DC-3 aircraft. Another purchased heavy curtains from a theater that was going out of business. My favorite studio at IDEO is a gutted Volkswagen bus rebuilt as a work environment, created as a joke on a designer while he was on vacation. This combination of good design and playfulness is stimulating and very helpful for rapid prototyping.

Rapid prototyping shows up in all the products that IDEO has designed. About a hundred versions of the Palm Pilot are on display at the Palo Alto office, from a crude foam cutout to a machine shop prototype to a commercial product. Seeing all of them together, one gets a sense of the evolution from first idea to final product. The failures along the way reveal lessons that get built into the next generation of the prototype.

IFTF has worked together with IDEO on several different projects. Thinking ten years ahead, we provide the foresight, which

IDEO incorporates into their prototyping process. Essentially, we are looking for waves of social change that can be ridden by the product. David Kelley once commented to me that he likes working with futurists because, in the past, IDEO was sometimes called in so late in an industrial design process that they built great products that never should have been built in the first place. Now, IDEO is reaching upstream from industrial design to innovation. A ten-year futures perspective provides context for ethnographic studies of real people in their native habitat—the environment in which the new product will be used.

One project we worked on involved the creation of healthy, portable, and inexpensive food. First IDEO looked at current products. Cheerios with nonfat milk scored pretty well on the nutrition and price scales, for example—but they are not very portable. IDEO then combined consumer insight with foresight to help generate new ideas. From the first day of the project, they were roughing out prototypes, using any material that could be easily formed and reformed. Each studio has a tech box that contains materials that their designers have collected from all over the world to use in creating new prototypes.

IDEO has institutionalized rapid prototyping, though their designers have avoided over-standardizing it. This learn-as-you-go spirit lets the process of creativity happen without trying to control it.

Rapid Prototyping Summary

Rapid prototyping is a practical way to tap into the maker instinct. Leaders with maker instinct will get the idea of rapid prototyping easily and use it to succeed. The big challenge will be for them to accept failures as important ingredients of success and learn from them. Many leaders do not like failure of any kind, but in the future, they will have to change their expectations and learn to play through them.

Leadership in the future will be about high-speed, perpetual prototyping. The best leaders will be those who embrace the process and develop the ability to discern the patterns across the prototypes, the ideas that really do work. As Winston Churchill said, "Success is the ability to go from failure to failure with no loss of enthusiasm."[5]

Rapid prototyping accepts failure as critical to success. Rapid prototyping requires enthusiasm to fuel the energy of innovation. Enthusiasm breeds innovation. Winston Churchill's struggles with depression may have prepared him to survive failures with enthusiasm.

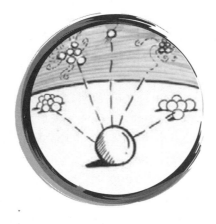

9

Smart-Mob Organizing

Ability to create, engage with, and nurture
purposeful business or social change networks
through intelligent use of electronic and other media.

A SMART MOB SPARKED DISRUPTIVE CHANGE in Cairo,
Egypt, in January of 2011. Fueled by educated young people who
could not find jobs and were frustrated by the policies of Egyptian
President Hosni Mubarak, this smart mob (actually, a loosely orches-
trated collection of smart mobs) was amplified by social media in
2011. The "Arab Spring" that followed only hints at what will be possible ten years from now, when the digital natives are in their twenties
and social media are much more sophisticated than they are today.

I was surprised that these creative young people were able to
organize themselves with today's relatively crude social media. It is
obvious to me that ten years from now, however, the smart mobs will

be so much smarter since social media will be so much better and digital natives will be coming of age. The Arab Spring is just an early signal of what is likely to happen if serious economic rebalancing is not undertaken soon.

When I was in graduate school, Saul Alinsky was an iconic community organizer working on the south side of Chicago. He was the model for social activism. It may be that the Saul Alinsky of cyberspace turns out to be a network, rather than a single person. Tomorrow's version of community organizing will be smart-mob organizing— sometimes mixed with in-person gatherings such as those in Tahrir Square in Cairo in 2011. We are beginning to see this today, but the smart mobs of the future will be much smarter and much more amplified by social media.

Leaders are what they can organize. Leaders make connections and draw links. Everyone is part of a network and electronic media will amplify networks for business and social change. Future leaders will be expert users of the next generation of online social media that will be foreign to many of today's leaders.

Some social networks will have intense values linkages, and leaders will need to mesh with those values. Indeed, a leader's own networks and connections will be their most powerful assets. This has always been true to some extent, but the connections in the future will be amplified.

Smart-mob organizers must choose the best medium for each situation. Most of today's leaders communicate well in person, but have limited skills using electronic media. Leaders of the future will need to have a strong online identity, as well as a compelling in-person presence. Younger people are more likely to have strong online identities, since they grew up with the web.

Knowing how to use electronic media is not what makes a smart mob smart. The people must provide the intelligence, but the media could make smart people smarter. (On the other hand, the media could also make dysfunctional leaders even more dysfunctional. The media are amplifiers.) Powerful collaboration technologies are now practical, after more than thirty years of testing.

Smart-mob organizing is the maker instinct applied to social connectivity, or vice versa. Solo makers are coming together into smart mobs of makers. All that maker energy has the potential to be channeled in new and highly creative ways, if leaders are able to engage with it.

Smart-Mob Organizing Defined

Smart-mob organizing brings together large groups for a common business or social change purpose, making savvy use of available media. Smart mobs are smart because the media amplify their collective intelligence for greater impact. They are mobs because their behavior is emergent, unpredictable, and sometimes unruly. Of course, how smart a smart mob is depends on the resources of the members, the talent of the leaders, and the effectiveness of their media.

The father of smart mobs is Bay Area visionary Howard Rheingold, who in 2003 coined the term in his very important book, *Smart Mobs.*[1] With remarkable speed, "smart mobs" entered the vocabulary to the point where I saw it used in major publications within one year of the book's release, without quotation marks and without attribution.

Howard Rheingold's Web site (www.smartmobs.com) continues to explore the evolution of smart mobs. Rheingold calls smart mobs "the power of the mobile many." Now, almost ten years after it was introduced, some experts in the field say that the term has become dated. I disagree. It can be transformative when a leadership team, an NGO, or an industry association reimagines itself as a smart mob. Terms like "smart mobs" are also provocative; they get people to think about the future and to realize that not all mobs are smart, nor are they necessarily well intentioned. Unfortunately, hostile mobs often seem more sophisticated in their use of new media than do positive smart mobs.

As forecasters, we seek out terms that provoke people constructively without turning them off. I like to call this process of futures provocation "forecaster's haiku." If you get a forecast headline right, it draws people toward the future. If you get it wrong, it repels people or doesn't stretch them enough to be provocative. Referring to "smart networks" or "smart connectivity" would describe the same space, but would not be as provocative as "smart mobs." Merely saying "smart mobs" can start a very interesting conversation about leadership in the future. What if you thought about your own leadership team as a smart mob?

Face-to-face meetings are still useful at some stages in smart-mob organizing, especially for orientation and trust building, but often they are not possible. Luckily, the range of media options is getting much wider and the new media work much better than they used to. Organizing smart mobs is already practical, and it will become required for effective leadership in the future. Consider the following example from today, but presaging tomorrow.

Lyn Jeffery, the cultural anthropologist at IFTF I mentioned earlier, is studying the Chinese language Internet. One of the disruptions that she observed is the growing popularity of "tuangous," which are smart mobs organized to buy things. One of the earliest cases was a group of about thirty people who all wanted to buy new BMWs. The tuangou went to a BMW dealer and asked "What is the price if we buy thirty all at once?" This was not a pleasant question for the BMW dealer, since it was not the model of retail that he had in mind.

Tuangous are now starting to organize to purchase much less expensive products and services. They come together, often through the Internet, around a particular purchasing need. Leadership emerges on an ad hoc basis, and there is clear benefit for all of the buyers. Tuangous preceded the very popular Groupon on the English language Internet.

These kinds of smart mobs are changing the rules of the marketplace.

Dilemmas in the Future

Smart mobs and not-so-smart mobs will become much more common over the next decade. Leaders will need to learn the skills of smart-mob organizing and develop their own online presence and leadership styles. In-person leadership will not be enough.

SMART MOBS IN CIVIL SOCIETY

As best I can tell, Howard Dean's early presidential campaign in 2004 was the first to make serious use of the Internet for political organizing, and it established models that spread quickly. The 2008 election, however, was the first to make heavy use of media for smart-mob organizing; the techniques were more creative and the platforms more stable. This, however, was just the beginning of smart-mob politics in civil society. Expect much more in future elections.

Barack Obama's 2008 campaign proved the value of online smart mobs for fund-raising, making very sophisticated use of social media to organize for their candidate. Neither Obama nor his opponent, John McCain, was a natural in these media, and neither grew up with them. Obama, however, invested much more time and effort, and his followers skewed young, which helped accelerate the campaign's use of the Internet. Obama's use of online smart-mob organizing was much more sophisticated in getting him elected than it was in governing once he came into office. Partly, this is because leading a complex government is much harder than leading a campaign, but smart-mob organizing skills in government are only beginning to be understood.

At this early stage, YouTube has been used most visibly for "gotcha" videos that caught candidates or endorsers saying the wrong thing at the wrong time. In the 2008 presidential campaign, we all learned about the downside risk of a candidate receiving endorsements from anyone who had ever said something stupid on video. By this criterion, it will be difficult to get any endorsements at all in the future, and it will be increasingly difficult to find anyone who has *not* said something stupid on video. Now, the "gotchas" have moved over to social media of varied forms, including Facebook and Twitter.

Smart mobs can amplify misinformation just as rapidly as they can spread the truth. The take-home lesson: smart mobs can boost a candidate rapidly, but other smart mobs can bring that same leader down just as fast. Smart mobs are not necessarily fair, nor are they necessarily right. Sometimes, smart mobs will be dumb.

The new civil society will have platforms that allow much greater participation across the population, for better or for worse. The founders of the United States were skeptical about direct democracy—but there was no way to provide direct democracy using the technology of the time. The founders were very leery about mobs. Pervasive social media, however, create new potential for direct democracy. Smart mobs (or dumb mobs) could soon become the carriers of the people's message. Electronic media will soon make direct democracy possible and perhaps even practical. The new media may, in effect, challenge the founders' logic and give us a structure that could allow full participation and direct democracy. Do we really want a more direct democracy, even if we can do it? Smart mobs are already forming and creating new modes of civil engagement. Using rapid prototyping to create a new form of civil media-enhanced society, smart mobs will have their say—like it or not.

I hope that the United States will never adopt a governmental structure run by smart mobs—even if it does become possible. Still, the direction of change over the next ten years is likely to be from representative to direct democracy—but the process of change will be messy. The good news is that the new networks make it possible to collaborate and cooperate in ways that were never before available. The bad news is that destructive mobs will be active as well, and they are likely to have highly developed media skills.

SMART MOBS FOR HEALTH

Most households are very concerned about health, and the person most often at the center of the household is, according to most research, Mom. Indeed, some of the groups we work with that develop new health products now refer to the "HMM," or "Health Management Mom" (a play on the old Health Management Organization, or HMO). The mom-led health smart mob for a particular family includes not only the family physician but also specialists (when they are needed), family, friends, retailers who give advice, online medical sources, and online communities. Our forecasts suggest that health insecurity will grow in all parts of the world, which will create more need for health-oriented smart mobs.

The challenge on a larger scale is to create a health-and-wellness platform that allows smart mobs to form, re-form, and multiply. At this time in the United States, the closest thing we have to this is the Centers for Disease Control and Prevention (CDC), which is indeed focusing on creating a new culture of health—as well as responding to disease threats. There are also a number of virtual smart mobs for health arising—most of them targeting people suffering from particular medical conditions. Web sites like MyDaughtersDNA.org and PatientsLikeMe.com are efforts to organize smart mobs to manage sickness. Indeed, sharing information with others who have similar health issues has been, still is, and will continue to be a very important use for the Internet.

Kelly Traver is a physician focused on health and wellness who could not find a way to sustain a wellness-oriented practice within the traditional financial structure of the health-care system in the United States—which is actually more of a sick care system.[2]

Dr. Traver organized a kind of smart mob around healthy living. She created her own start-up as the first prototype of a new kind of health commons, called Healthiest You, where the principles of healthy living can become a shared asset for much larger groups of people. She began by providing health coaching to Google's employees. Now she is working with a range of companies and broadening her approach to spreading the twelve principles of healthy living that she has developed.

I participated in the prototype for Healthiest You and was very impressed. I already had some pretty good healthy living practices, but her twelve principles are the best summary I have ever seen. More importantly, the principles are packaged with a process and delivered in a practical way that I found easy to apply. The principles provide the content, but a smart mob of healthy living practitioners will be necessary to spread the word and the behaviors.

I don't believe that there is any single path to health and fitness, but I found this program both solid and flexible enough to help me change a number of my behaviors in a more healthy direction. In effect, I've formed my own little smart mob (with coaching from a handful of others) that is focused on my health. I am also part of a smart mob that Dr. Traver is organizing to make sure these principles reach a much larger portion of society.

Over the next ten years, a global health economy will emerge as a major economic driver. Within this economy, smart mobs will organize and spread health practices in unusual ways that are likely to have major social benefits.

THE DIRECTION IS TOWARD OPENNESS

The term "open source" comes from open-source software, which refers to source code under a license that permits others to study, change, and improve the software—under the condition that they share improvements with the creator and others. The everyday understanding of open source is not an either/or choice; it is a sliding scale from completely open to completely closed. Leaders will decide where they want to position their organizations on that scale.

The forecast map inside the book jacket reflects the direction of change from more closed to more open. Smart mobs will accelerate the trend toward increasing openness. You cannot control a mob. Smart mobs will skew toward open, even though some of them will be extremely closed.

Open-source practices still need to have a structure of some kind, and intellectual property will not go away. For example, in the world of R&D, a very interesting range of open-source networks has emerged, such as InnoCentive. InnoCentive is a kind of highly structured smart mob of scientists interested in ad hoc assignments for pay. They are prequalified for participation in a network of scientific problem solvers. Companies offer bounties for solutions to chemistry problems, or other specific scientific tasks. Scientists in the network bid on the work and InnoCentive manages the transactions.

YourEncore is similar, but includes only retired scientists from R&D organizations in top companies. YourEncore is particularly fascinating, since it also provides meaningful work opportunities for scientists who are officially retired but still want to work in the field of science, although under new terms of engagement. Thus, it is a bridge between individual scientists and corporations with specific

R&D needs. YourEncore makes it easier to form smart mobs that match retired scientists with tasks they could do for hire. It represents individual scientists looking for meaningful work, as well as the corporations looking for support in their scientific endeavors. YourEncore also feeds the corporate and scientific diasporas of which the individual scientists are a part.

These open-source efforts are highly structured and focused, yet they are also smart mobs with the purpose of delivering high quality ad hoc R&D services in a decentralized pay-for-the-task structure. One could argue that these mobs are very smart since they are mostly scientists with graduate degrees. Appropriateness of structure will play a key role in how smart a mob can become.

SMART MOBS AT WAR

Terrorist groups can be smart mobs too. In fact, from a purely sociological point of view, many of the terrorist groups are very sophisticated indeed in their use of new media—even if they have religious beliefs that call for return to a simpler time. Many of these smart-but-threatening mobs are far more sophisticated in their use of social media than more moderate groups. Network-based warfare is now a mainstream practice, and there are few rules of engagement that can be trusted. The new forms of war that are likely to emerge over the next decade are frightening.

Meme warfare, for example, will be very attractive for smart mobs. Memes are self-propagating ideas that spread like a virus. Vannevar Bush wrote a classic article right after World War II envisioning the "Memex" to allow ideas to be shared across large communities.[3] In this groundbreaking article Bush imagined a network like the Internet long before 1968 when its precursor began. Richard Dawkins used the term in 1976, drawing from the fundamentals of natural selection. Meme warfare will add a nasty twist to mob organizing. The point of conventional warfare is, in the words of George Patton, "not to die for your country, but to make the other poor bastard die for his." The point of meme warfare could be, conversely, to make the "other poor bastard" unwilling to die for his.[4]

Smart mobs can also use countercultural means to effect social change and corporate social responsibility. Anti-corporate "subvertising" (as compared to advertising) is one such approach, where corporate brands are spoofed and appropriated in ways that subversively lead to social change and question the basic integrity of the brand.

Another approach to meme warfare is "shop-dropping," which is the opposite of shoplifting. Instead of stealing from a store, urban street artists are now bringing in cans and boxes to display on the shelves. Imagine armies of smart-mob organizers who shop-drop local stores with a particular message to disrupt normal practices. Meme warfare in the future will attempt to undermine ideas and social practices in ways that challenge the underlying beliefs of a society.

A Smart-Mob Leader

One of the most successful smart-mob organizers is Jimmy Wales, creator of Wikipedia. Wales started with a clear, compelling, and outrageous vision: to reach everyone in the world with a free encyclopedia for all human knowledge. As with any good intent statement, he had great clarity about where he wanted to go, but great flexibility with regard to how to get there. Wales is a leader with great clarity, who also has a gift for smart-mob organizing.

Wales clearly envisioned Wikipedia as a social experiment built upon an existing technology platform that would be extended. Wikipedia is much more of a social innovation than a technological one. He clearly saw himself as a community organizer like Saul Alinsky, but with a different goal in a different medium. Volunteer editors enter and maintain the encyclopedia entries, but anyone can revise and update them. The editors watch the pages closely, however, and mistakes are usually corrected within minutes. Wikipedia has become a great place to start a research project, even though it would be a mistake to end there.

The Wikipedia vision took a smart mob to implement, and it takes many smart mobs to maintain it now that it has grown to such a massive scale. It is evolving into a permanent smart mob, a community others can build upon, or what we call in the next chapter a commons.

Smart-Mob Organizing Summary

Smart-mob organizing is an important ability for leaders of the future. I began using group communication through computers (similar to what we now call social media) with small groups of scientists and engineers on the ARPAnet in 1972. After I facilitated those early online conversations, I realized that I did not have the ability or the patience to be a smart-mob organizer myself. Still, I saw its value and I have always worked with people who have these skills. Leaders do not have to do everything themselves.

As a ten-year forecaster and a book writer, I choose to try out new media as they appear, but I focus on the two media I love—writing books and doing workshops around my books. I have tried a wide range of social media, but—for my particular role in life as a ten-year forecaster (and an introvert in an extrovert's role)—today's social media are not a good fit for what I'm trying to accomplish. For many leaders, however, today's social media are critical to their work and their role. The key here is to assess the media options and make intelligent choices. Also, as the media evolve, rethink your choices of which medium is good for what, and which are a good fit for you as a leader.

My point is not that all leaders need to be smart-mob organizers personally—although it is better if they use the media themselves and do at least some of their own organizing. Rather, it is that all leaders must be respectful and understanding of the importance of smart mobs. I suspect that all leaders will at least need to have smart-mob organizers working for them closely. A. G. Lafley, the former CEO at P&G, for example, made frequent use of the Internet to share his message, but he did not always make the entries personally. Leadership should not only be expressed face to face or through broadcast media—it must be expressed through the Web. Leaders must be smart about which medium works best to deliver the message at hand. Smart-mob organizing is a skill that all leaders must utilize in order to make the future—and each one must use that skill both directly and indirectly, with his or her own personal style.

10

Commons Creating

Ability to seed, nurture, and grow shared assets

that can benefit all players—

and allow competition at a higher level.

COMMONS CREATING IS THE ABILITY to make common cause
with others for greater benefit.

Digital connectivity will radically improve our ability to grow new
commons and new forms of value exchanges. I believe that the more
connected you are, the freer and safer you will be—in spite of the
new dangers that connectivity will introduce. Connectivity can only
make you free and safe, however, if you nurture it and keep the social
network alive. As a planet, we are searching for new common ground.
What is it that we have in common that could make the world a better
place for more people?

New commons are shared resources that create platforms for generating wealth and value. Commons grow out of connectivity. New commons employ win-win logic, rather than win-lose logic. New commons allow multiple parties to win.

Commons creating is the most advanced and the most important of the ten future leadership skills. As we move into the next decade, expect a wide range of new commons structures. Consider these diverse examples from today's world as prototypes for where we will be going.

• Svalbard International Seed Vault: a storage facility built into a mountain near the North Pole, the vault was created and is supported by the Global Crop Diversity Trust and the Norwegian government. It opened in early 2008 and is a commons dedicated to the preservation of crop diversity for future generations. (See Figure 22.)

• Ponoko: an online site that builds products one at a time from user designs. Users can buy, sell, create, and customize their designs. Thus, Ponoko has become a commons for open-source design.

• Unified Grocers: a California-based cooperative that distributes food for retailers up and down the West Coast of the United States. Unified is owned by its members and is structured to benefit them all. It is a traditional food cooperative that is transforming itself to a new model of commons creating—to allow more advanced forms of competition that build upon shared resources.

• Global Lives Project: an international "collaborative online video library of human life experience." Founded by IFTF Research Director David Evan Harris, the project engages filmmakers to document the everyday lives of demographically representative individuals from across the globe. With over 400 volunteer collaborators, the Global Lives Project offers a firsthand view of the lives and worldviews of its participants, broadening understanding and creating an innovative multimedia platform for exchange.

FIGURE 22. The Svalbard International Seed Vault: a storage facility built into a mountain near the North Pole. *Source:* Used with permission, Svalbard Global Seed Vault. Mari Tefre, photographer.

• CCL Senior Fellow and innovation expert Stan Gryskiewicz created one of the earliest commons for managers of innovation in 1981, calling it the Association for Managers of Innovation (AMI).[1] AMI is a meeting of the minds where innovation leaders from various organizations and companies come together. AMI members participate in a "Beg, Borrow, or Brag" session at every meeting. A "beg" is an ask, a "borrow" is a request to share, and a "brag" is an exclamation of something that a leader is proud of and members should know about. This commons is limited to leaders who are responsible for at least two aspects of creativity and innovation at their organizations, and membership is limited to 200 members.

Future leaders will be called to create new commons, to grow new places within which collaboration and mutual success can occur. There will be many opportunities to create new commons between public and private, social and economic, digital and physical. Cloud-served supercomputing will create a powerful new infrastructure for commons creating.

Essentially, the search for new commons is a search for goodness that benefits multiple parties simultaneously. In a world constrained by problem-solving mentalities, having a winner usually implies that there is a loser as well. However, in the VUCA World of dilemmas, the potential for win-win solutions is increasing, if leaders can figure out ways to flip the dilemmas into opportunities.

Peter Barnes describes this space between public and private as the "third economic sector" in his book *Capitalism 3.0*.[2] This title is an example of dilemma flipping itself. Capitalism as currently defined has an inherent tension between the public and private sectors. This is not a problem that can be solved, but a dilemma to be flipped. The balance could be better or worse—depending on your point of view. *Capitalism 3.0* brings new Web networking language to a very old concept—to reframe how we view capitalism.

Traditional capitalism assumes that self-interest is the driver. Barnes understands the pressures of profit in capitalism, but he challenges unexamined assumptions and creates a space for exploring beyond the traditional balance of power between public and private sectors. It is in this space that interesting new approaches to leadership will occur over the next decade, opportunities to create new commons.

InnoCentive, NineSigma, and YourEncore provide a commons exchange for scientific consulting. Each of these efforts started as a smart mob, but evolved into an ongoing commons aimed at sharing R&D resources organized in a network similar to eBay. Where smart mobs are ad hoc, commons are sustainable over a long period of time.

Maker Faire has evolved into a commons for makers, a place for them to convene and share what they do. More importantly, it is a place where makers learn from each other. Every maker is part of a network and the Maker Faire celebrates and amplifies those networks. Leaders can use commons events like the Maker Faire to prototype their own ideas and learn from how others adapt their products. I expect that is why Microsoft sponsored an entire pavilion for makers who hack Microsoft products in creative ways.

Before hacking became synonymous with digital criminals, the term was used to describe ingenious individuals who pushed the technology to its extreme and came up with imaginative new uses or ways of using. Hackers pushed the edges, building better systems by breaking the old ones and rebuilding them. Hackers blaze trails for the rest of us through new territory. Increasingly, instead of litigating against them and policing their customers who "misuse" their products, companies are rewarding hackers who come up with new ideas. Hackers could be prototypers in disguise for the next generation of products and services. They also help explore the possibilities for creating new commons, including shared resources for the hackers themselves. Obviously, there is a criminal side to hacking as well, but the positive energy cannot be ignored.

When I was in graduate school, I read the classic article by Garrett Hardin called "Tragedy of the Commons," in which individual self-interest in grazing one's sheep led to collective disaster, since there was not enough grass for everyone if all the sheep took their fill.[3] This was a world of clearly limited resources and a self-contained system that was very difficult to grow. Commons logic in the world of cloud-served supercomputing, however, does not necessarily lead to tragedy. Indeed, the potential for new commons will become greater than at any time in history.

In the future, we will be able to shift resources from one area to another to form new commons. New network-amplified commons will allow new opportunities for win-win solutions and new potentials to synchronize individual self-interest with larger common interests. New commons can create new clarity with regard to sharing resources and rules for engagement. Traditional notions of individual self-interest can expand. Competition will still be important, but it will be in a new context that can make it even more profitable.

It will take genuinely creative thinking for leaders to identify potential new commons opportunities both within and outside of their own organizations.

Commons Creating Defined

A commons is a shared asset that benefits multiple players. If a team improves its playing field, all the teams that play there will benefit. Commons creating is about growing markets, not just market share.

There are many different kinds of commons, including parks, town squares, beaches, and markets. While many commons are clearly organized for the public good, market-oriented commons are focused on providing a platform of shared assets that allows competition to take place at a higher level.

The term "commons" may not work for some people. A more business-like term such as "shared assets" might communicate better to some people, but I am drawn to the aspirational notion of a commons.

What is it that organizations and people could share in order to make all of their lives better? What do you have in surplus that could be given away to grow a shared asset? A commons is a platform on which individuals and groups can build for some greater good. The dilemma for leaders is to perform for their own organization while also growing a commons around them to benefit the surrounding community. For example, if a company does something that's good for itself and the industry, the entire industry grows—not just one company.

There is a fuzzy line between a smart mob and a commons. Commons, however, tend to have a long-term view toward sharing assets and continuing value for the participants over an extended period of time. Smart mobs can evolve into commons, but many of them are ad hoc. Smart mobs come and go. Commons have continuity.

eBay is a market commons for people to buy and sell through the Web. It also provides structures for evaluating buyers and sellers, so that fair exchanges can occur. It has become a very large commons platform that allows people to operate businesses and make purchases through the eBay protocols of exchange.

Leaders with strong commons-creating abilities will be able to mobilize shared resources. This vision of leadership is, in some ways, timeless and has always been a part of public and corporate life. In the world of cloud-served supercomputing, however, leaders will need to move beyond their own interests and beyond smart-mob organizing to create new terms of engagement, new environments in which they can make the future they want to make.

Leaders will use smart mobs to build new collaborative structures, not just for the common good but to allow competition at a higher level—typically competition with profit margins higher than they were before the commons was created. The creation of a new commons can create new clarity within which both cooperation and competition can thrive. The commons game is not a zero-sum game, where some people must lose in order for others to win. In a commons game, win-win solutions are the goal. By expanding the playing field and upping the level of play, everyone could benefit.

Even though leaders are facing challenges of unprecedented scale, the tools and media for creating new platforms for cooperation—particularly cloud-served supercomputing—will get better than ever before. The currency of the cloud will be reciprocity.

The tragedy of the commons will still apply in some cases, such as fishing in oceans, but the use of networks allow commons to extend win-win opportunities in new and exciting ways.

Commons creating is the culmination of the other nine future leadership skills. Because it is complicated and there are many stakeholders, creating commons is often frustrating but also very satisfying for leaders who can do it. As the most important future leadership skill, it benefits from all of the other future leadership skills explored in this book.

Commons Creation in the Future

Leaders will have an opportunity in this next decade to reframe and broaden the purpose of their organizations. In the world of global interactive media, companies will have new potential to create both market value and more commons. Companies will be able to become stronger protectors of the commons that are already here and advocates for new commons that need to be created. Target, for example, already gives 5 percent of its profits to the communities where its stores are located. This is an example of contributing to commons that are already established locally, but what if that notion was extended to create new commons in areas like community economics or clean and affordable water? Business profits are important, of course, but long-term social profit is necessary for business to be sustainable. Inherent in creating commons is a leader's motivation to promote not only business profit but social profit as well.

DIASPORAS AS COMMONS

Diasporas are commons by definition: they have strong shared values and common points of view on the world. Since sharing is already practiced regularly within their communities, diasporas can create new commons structures for themselves more quickly.

The challenge for diasporas is to grow new commons that extend beyond their own constituencies. While growing commons is typically easier within a diaspora, it is likely to be harder when it involves outsiders: diasporas may not play well with outsiders or with other diasporas. They may develop commons for their own benefit, but they could exclude those on the outside.

One fascinating example of a commons geared toward diasporas is the Genographic Project by *National Geographic*. The project maps humanity's historical migrations, so that current diasporas can understand their histories better and new ones can be created based on ancestral DNA. As a planet, we have only just shifted from being a primarily rural to a primarily urban place. Over the next decade, migrations will continue at an alarming pace, including climate-induced migrations due to storms, earthquakes, and other shifts. The Genographic Project is one attempt to track the flow of DNA. The lesson: most diasporas can be sustainable if they come up with a commons that preserves their basic values.

Indian Institute of Management professor Dr. Anil Gupta launched the Honey Bee Network in India, a commons for documenting traditional knowledge and grassroots innovations. Honey Bee Network was born out of a partnership between India's National Innovation Foundation, the Council for Scientific and Industrial Research, and the Society for Research and Initiatives for Sustainable Technologies and Institutions.

The "honey bee philosophy," as Anil Gupta calls it, is one based on the cross-pollination of ideas, collaboration, and bringing innovations to the public domain. Today, the network boasts 100,000 ideas, innovations, and traditional knowledge practices from India, Mongolia, Kenya, Vietnam, Uganda, Colombia, Ecuador, and North America. Its newsletter is received in seventy-five countries.

GOVERNMENT-SUPPORTED COMMONS

In recent years, Brazil has become a fascinating case study of government support for seeding the open source movement. This shift to increased transparency is writ large with the move from Microsoft software to Linux software in many quarters. Microsoft's source code is not open, meaning that it remains the property of its developers, and cannot be studied or changed. There is a cost for purchasing the software, and usually charges associated with upgrades.

In contrast, Linux's open-source software is free; it is also much more transparent and accessible. Some see this as a much-needed balm that would help to close the rich–poor divide between areas that are technologically enabled and technologically deprived.

Sérgio Amadeu, author of *Digital Exclusion: Misery in the Information Era,* argues that governments should phase out closed-source software in government work and invest in developing open-source software, which can be fueled by Brazilian ingenuity, thus creating a kind of commons around open-source software that benefits the entire economy of Brazil.[4]

There are other leaders in the open source movement in Brazil. For example, Ronaldo Lemos is known for his work with the national body of Creative Commons, which envisions a continuum of copyright options beyond closed ownership of intellectual property. With Creative Commons licensing, information may be designated as "some rights reserved" or completely in the public domain. Depending on the kind of Creative Commons license, information can be built upon, altered, or redefined by other users of that information. Lemos is also a pioneer of Overmundo, a Web 2.0 tool for collaborative community reporting of local cultural news. Articles undergo a peer review process by contributors and are voted on before they are published.[5] Overmundo gives voice to cultural perspectives that would otherwise have gone unheard and does so in a way characterized by active engagement and participation in shaping the stories.

Brazil has now become a leader in open-source thinking and applying that logic to the creation of innovation spaces (virtual and physical) that seed science and technology innovation.

OPEN LEADERSHIP COMMONS

Amy Schulman is a leader in the practice of law. Formerly a partner at DLA Piper and currently working for Pfizer, Schulman is a commons creator.[6] Known for her ability to build the right team for a project, Schulman is strong at cultivating mutual benefit and allowing competition at a higher level. Her colleagues say, "Amy is a very good listener and understands what her own strengths are, and in turn where she might have weaknesses that will not help with a particular problem. She is good at finding others to fill in for those weaknesses."[7]

Schulman created a commons for female attorneys to focus on career advancement. Heidi Levine, a younger associate, describes how Amy coached her on the mechanics of the law, but also on business strategy: "Learning directly from her helped me to grow in a way that I would not have otherwise experienced that early in my career. I have tried to pass that along to the women I work with. People, especially one's supervising partner, are usually hesitant to share that type of information as it could make them vulnerable. But Amy did, and in my eyes, it made her much stronger."[8] Through her efforts to stimulate advancement for others, she created a commons, a shared space in which both mutual benefit and greater responsibility occur.

Commons creating is the work of leaders, but these leaders are not necessarily always found at the top of an organization. Sometimes commons creating can come from the lower ranks. What is really crucial here is that the leader step back to create a space and to hold that space for the common good in an act of open leadership. This will allow others to enter and fill that space.

This kind of commons being created from below is evident at the beginning of Schulman's career when she was at the law firm of Cleary Gottlieb Steen & Hamilton based in New York. She went from a summer associate position to a full-time assignment where she soon bore responsibility for individual state cases for a large international client. Her role involved coaching local lawyers, many of whom were older and more experienced than she was, so the job required interpersonal skills and sensitivity to their situation. Consensus building appeared more and more crucial to her as she learned how to build teams and get them to perform at their best. She was not focused solely on her own performance, but on stimulating and growing the team.

Digital Natives and Commons Creating

As part of the Leadership Beyond Boundaries initiative (discussed in the chapter on Immersive Learning), CCL has leveraged its expertise in leadership development and has tailored the youth-specific program called Early Leadership Toolkit. CCL President John Ryan says, "Leadership is like a muscle: the earlier you start flexing it the stronger it will become." The program allows young people to develop basic self-development skills, learn facilitation skills, and understand the CCL philosophy. In 2011, IFTF partnered with CCL and hosted a "Train the Trainers" module on futures thinking in Palo Alto. This module was divided into two parts: *Knowing the Future* and *Leading the Future*. The training introduced participants to the range of opportunities and challenges youth will face over the next decade as well as how futures thinking capabilities can lead youth to make better decisions today. IFTF led an immersive scenario workshop with artifacts from the future specifically designed to provoke participants to think about the future. This is an effort to grow a commons around youth leadership development.

FINANCIAL COMMONS

Some financial institutions are examples of commons, such as credit unions or those banks focused on particular communities or purposes. Indeed, financial markets are, in some sense, commons—although most of these commons are geared more heavily toward individual greed than social profit.

Home mortgages began as commons when communities started banks to share risk and make loans to local people so they could build houses and businesses. Now, however, home mortgages have been packaged and resold as instruments for short-term trading. It is more challenging to find financial commons that support local communities.

The money commons idea is not dead, however. The Lending Club, for example, is one of several new social lending networks where members can borrow and lend money among themselves at better-than-market interest rates. These networks are creating new models for entrepreneurs who are interested in doing well while doing good, through commons-based services.

Another approach has been developed by Kiva.org, which combines the practices of micro lending and commons creating. Muhammad Yunus, whom I referred to earlier in reference to his clarity, created new commons to enable very small loans to people (mostly women) who were part of communities where paying back the loan became a social responsibility. Yunus and his micro lending philosophy have had major impacts on local communities through a very large number of very small loans. Kiva has now created an online structure that allows anyone online to be a Yunus-like social investor. Kiva provides arm's-length structures through the Web where specific individuals can request specific loans. Contributors decide whom they want to lend to, agree upon terms for repayment, and follow the progress of the loan through Kiva. Kiva gives contributors a way to lend to a specific entrepreneur in the developing world, to help empower that person to work him- or herself out of poverty. These are one-on-one personal loans, through the Kiva commons structure.

OTHER COMMONS EXAMPLES

Since commons creating is the most difficult future leadership skill, I want to provide a range of examples that are consistent with it. Of course, there are traditional commons that should be considered, such as the European Union, the United Nations, and NATO. But the next generation of commons will be different. Consider these examples, some of which may not use the word "commons" to describe their activities:

- MDVIP: a for-profit network of physicians, who have restructured their practices to limit the number of patients per doctor (to allow for more personal consultation) and provide services geared toward healthy living for a monthly fee. MDVIP is a business based on the foundation of shared health resources across a dispersed network.

- OScar: a project that functions like a commons to develop different cars from the same base of open-source standards and materials. The goal is to break away from the constraints of the current automobile industry and reinvent mobility, using open-source principles.

- COMPASS: Communication Partnership for Science and the Sea is a collaborative effort of scientists to bridge the fields of marine conservation science, public interest, and marine policy. Their focus is on marine ecosystem services and ecosystem-based management. The oceans border many different countries, and COMPASS is one attempt to bridge the different interests.

- The Wild Farm Alliance (WFA): This is an agricultural commons effort to protect and restore wild nature, envisioning "a world in which community-based, ecologically managed farms and ranches seamlessly integrate into landscapes that accommodate the full range of native species and ecological processes."[9] This is what I think of as a restorative commons, with an eye to the future.

This short list of future-oriented commons efforts is only intended to be illustrative. The very concept of a commons will evolve over the next decade, with lessons from past efforts being transformed into very new kinds of commons organizations and networks. Leaders will have a chance to connect and build common platforms in ways that have never been possible before.

Reciprocity-Based Innovation

Commons creating is a special kind of innovation that begins with reciprocity. Reciprocity is all about exchange and the interpersonal terms of engagement that include many imbedded transactions. Self-interest is still an important part of reciprocity, but the focus is on more than self-interest. In many transactions, the individual players each focus exclusively on getting the greatest value for themselves. With reciprocity, the frame is larger: what is the potential value for a wider range of players—including yourself? How can shared interests or commons be created that would benefit more players? Reciprocity is different from altruism or philanthropy. There must be value for all the players, not just a gift from one to another. In order to get value over the long run, however, all the players must contribute to the commons even as they benefit from it.

Reciprocity-Based Innovation (RBI) is giving things away in intelligent ways, in the trust that you will get back even more in return over a designated period of time. By giving things away in "intelligent ways," I mean careful consideration of what you have in surplus that may have value to others. Reciprocity-Based Innovation is not a simple transaction. It is giving things away, but it is giving away with careful thought about the commons that could be seeded by each gift.

There is a leap of faith involved in RBI. There are no guarantees. The trust that is required is a kind of faith that the gift will lead to great value for you and for others.

Reciprocity-Based Innovation requires some return over time if it is to be sustainable. A commons must be created that has an ongoing life. Again, RBI is not philanthropy. The period of time for reasonable return, however, will be longer than with a traditional transaction. The period of return for RBI is typically measured in years, not months, and certainly not days or hours.

When I began my career in the 1970s, IBM sold large machines for small margins. Now, IBM is pretty much out of that business. It tends to give away or undercharge for software, while it sells services for high margins. Its initiative, "A Smarter Planet," now frames both the

IBM brand and its reciprocity: it is giving things away in the trust that it will get back even more in return. While the company does not call it that, IBM is practicing Reciprocity-Based Innovation and making money from it—while also creating new commons that are shared assets for others far beyond IBM. IBM is seeding a smarter planet, and its services support the growth.

As I have discussed earlier in this book, the future forces are clearly moving from more closed to more open—even though it will be a messy process along the way. This larger direction of change will mean that Reciprocity-Based Innovation will become more common and, in some cases, difficult to avoid. Not surprisingly, IBM is now a leader in the shift toward more openness. Even if a company is not open, however, there are strong external forces that will urge it in that direction.

In the early winter of 2010, for example, Microsoft introduced its Kinect platform for the Xbox 360 video gaming platform. The code name for Kinect as it was being developed was Natal and excitement mounted as it moved toward the marketplace. It is the first gestural interface for computers, so it is a threshold product that will seed many types of innovations. Kinect allows users to interact with computers by moving their bodies or speaking. While it was introduced as a gaming interface, it has much broader application potential.

Days after the Kinect was introduced, it was hacked. Microsoft quickly announced that it would sue anyone who hacked the Kinect platform. As a counter effort, a prize was offered for the best Kinect hack. A few months later, Microsoft opened the Kinect platform.

The Kinect story is a vivid example of what I'm starting to call Involuntary Reciprocity-Based Innovation. Microsoft tried to protect its intellectual property, but decided that it could not. Now, they have opened their strategy in some very creative ways.

In the future, it will be increasingly difficult to protect new ideas. In many cases, it will be much easier to give away new ideas and stay ahead of the innovation cycle than it will be to defend them—providing you can find a way to monetize the value of the new idea. Over the next decade, Reciprocity-Based Innovation will become practical on a very large scale. New commons will be created based on seed gifts that grow into new markets and new value creation opportunities.

Reciprocity-Based Innovation won't be easy—commons creating is the most difficult of the ten future leadership skills—but the potential for innovation is unprecedented. Innovation can come from anywhere.

As I introduced in Chapter 3, I first started working with P&G's global R&D organization in the early days of the ARPAnet in the 1970s. The notion of the invisible college of P&G scientists was powerful, and the network was a great amplifier of this power for creativity *within* P&G. When A.G. Lafley said with great clarity that half of the new ideas for P&G products had to come from *outside* P&G, it opened the invisible college. In the near future, with cloud-served supercomputing, innovation can start anywhere in the world—with anybody. And it will not be just very large innovative companies like P&G. These innovation resources will be available to anyone with access to the cloud—which will mean *anyone*.

Reciprocity-Based Innovation will be, I think, the biggest innovation opportunity in history. In an increasingly open world connected by cloud-served supercomputing, the opportunity to create new commons will be everywhere—and available to everyone.

Commons Creating Summary

As I said earlier, this is the most frightening ten-year forecast I've ever done, but it is also the most hopeful. The reason I am so hopeful is because of our new commons creating potential.

We will be facing unprecedented challenges of global climate disruption, pandemics, bioterrorism, and other stark realities. Of course, every generation seems to think that it has it worse than any previous generation, but arguably, the future appears more threatening now than at any other time in history.

Our connectivity, however, can be our strength. Leaders will have new opportunities to create commons that address even the most frightening challenges. The more connected we are, the safer and the more powerful we are—if we realize our interconnections. Through the growing global electronic webs of cloud-served supercomputing, we will be able to communicate and cooperate better than ever before.

The ten new leadership skills described in this book all build on each other, from the Maker Instinct on through Clarity, Dilemma Flipping, Immersive Learning, Bio-empathy, Constructive Depolarization, Quiet Transparency, Rapid Prototyping, Smart-Mob Organizing, and finally Commons Creating.

The ten future leadership skills build from individual instinct to collective action. Making comes from an inner urge. Commons Creating is extremely complex and very social. The Maker Instinct is where the commons are rooted: the urge to grow a sustainable, shared wealth. Commons Creating requires Dilemma Flipping and engagement with polarized conflict, but the best leaders will see through the mess with a clarity that articulates the essence of the commons they are trying to create. Nature provides insight regarding commons. Leaders will have to rapid-prototype their way to their new commons, using smart-mob organizing techniques that have the promise to become sustainable.

These ten skills will give leaders a great chance to make the world a better place—in spite of the many challenges.

As we think about and plan for the future, children are what we all have in common. Children keep us humble, especially those of us who are parents. The next generation of kids—the digital natives—will create new commons that we can only begin to imagine. Thinking about the world we want to leave for our children and grandchildren gets everyone in a good space to create new commons and make a better future.

In a world of volatility, uncertainty, complexity, and ambiguity, these ten future skills will be basic to successful leadership. The broken-planet issues will be daunting, *and* networked connectivity will create incredible opportunity.

11

Future Immersion for Leadership Development

SINCE THE FIRST EDITION of *Leaders Make the Future* came out three years ago, I have contributed to more than 150 leadership development programs for a wide range of corporate, nonprofit, and government organizations. I'm typically scheduled on the first day, to set a futures context for leadership development by providing an outside-in view.

I'm convinced that the best way to learn about the future is to immerse yourself in it. Since the future is "already here," your challenge will be to listen for that unevenly distributed future and figure out a way to navigate through it.

Leadership development programs, when designed as immersive learning experiences, can prepare leaders for the future. Traditional lecture or classroom-based training programs will not be enough.

This book is not meant to replace current talent and leadership models but rather to provide a futures lens for you to reconsider the models you are using and the programs that you employ to develop leaders.

Figure 23 shows CCL's model for developing individual leaders: Direction, Alignment, and Commitment (what many in the leader-

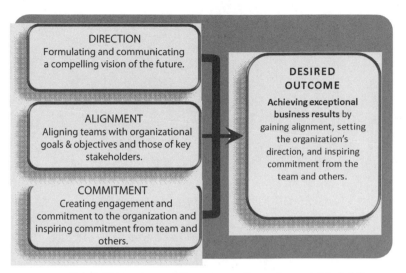

FIGURE 23. DAC (Direction—Alignment—Commitment) Model for Leadership Development. *Source:* CCL.

ship development world call the DAC Model). Leadership development programs, at their best, provide vivid experiences at direction setting, alignment nurturing, and commitment building. Leadership Direction is particularly important in a VUCA World where confusion is everywhere. Alignment is also extremely difficult in a world that is increasingly polarized. Leaders need the ability to see beyond the polarities of the present. Dilemma Flipping and Constructive Depolarizing will be critical leadership skills to achieve alignment in a VUCA World. Alignment requires openness to others. Exclusionary thinking can make alignment impossible, particularly if leaders get caught in a bubble of their own rigid beliefs. Commitment is necessary to move from insight to action, to make things happen. Creating engagement and commitment will be increasingly difficult in the jagged world of the future. Commitment comes through reciprocity, giving to get larger value over the long run.

Direction, Alignment, and Commitment involve a creative mix of Foresight, Insight, and Action, as summarized in Figure 24. This blended model provides grounding for future-oriented leadership development programs.

FIGURE 24. "Leading from the Future": A blending of IFTF's
Foresight to Insight to Action Cycle with CCL's Direction,
Alignment, and Commitment Model. This is leading from
the future—but with practical links to the present. *Source:*
IFTF and CCL.

Direction lives between Foresight and Insight. A ten-year perspective on external future forces gives a futures context
within which the direction of an organization can be envisioned. What external waves of change could an organization
ride? Which waves should be avoided?

Alignment happens between Insight and Action. Foresight can provoke Insight, even if you don't agree with the forecast. After the
insight leads to a direction, it is possible to align—but not before.

In the United States, many business teams with which I
have worked tend to rush for alignment before it is possible to
truly align. Alignment takes time. If you force alignment too
early, it is more likely to fall apart later.

Commitment happens both before and after Action. Building
commitment happens before you act. Maintaining commitment happens afterwards. Commitment must be nurtured
constantly by leaders in order for it to be sustainable.

Where CCL works with today's leaders to help them prepare for
the future, IFTF practices a foresight-based approach. I'm convinced

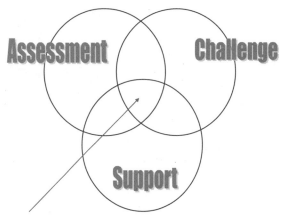

Powerful Development Experience

FIGURE 25. Assessment Challenge Support Model for Powerful Development Experience. *Source:* CCL.

that with new skills, leaders can make better organizations, better communities, and a better world. The last three years since the first edition was published have revealed both hopes and fears for leaders.

Leadership development programs must create opportunities for personal growth—not just organizational engagement. Figure 25 shows the basic Center for Creative Leadership model for personal leadership development: Assessment, Challenge, and Support.

Assessment is really self-assessment, in which you take stock of where you are in your leadership development journey and where you need to go.

Challenge represents the variety of learning experiences that you choose to immerse yourself in as you improve.

Support focuses on what people, money, and other resources you will need in order to succeed in your own leadership development program.

In the IFTF world of Foresight to Insight to Action, Assessment lives between Foresight and Insight, as suggested in Figure 26. Foresight sets a futures context within which you can assess your own leaders and ask where they are in their own development. Foresight

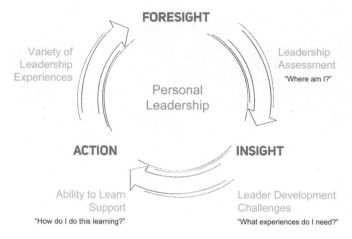

FORESIGHT

Variety of
Leadership
Experiences

Leadership
Assessment
"Where am I?"

Personal
Leadership

ACTION

INSIGHT

Ability to Learn
Support
"How do I do this learning?"

Leader Development
Challenges
"What experiences do I need?"

FIGURE 26. Future Immersion for Leadership Development Process. *Source:* IFTF and CCL.

precedes self-assessment by describing the future world within which you need your leaders to lead.

With this perspective—the current skills of your leaders in a futures context—you are ready to design a leadership development program. What immersive experiences do your leaders need? The challenges you provide will live between Insight and Action, leaning toward Insight. Insight is the aha moment that is provoked by Foresight. As you read this book, what are your aha moments with regard to your own organization and your leaders? Where does your organization need more readiness in order to be prepared for this VUCA World?

Finally, you will need personal support for your leaders in order to advance your development programs. This is the Action stage, where you decide what you need in order to take the next step in learning. Everyone has some ability to learn, but everyone needs support from others in order to extend that inner ability. The exact kind of support, however, varies dramatically from person to person.

CCL provides a variety of leadership experiences that bring the cycle of Assessment, Challenge, and Support to life. *Leaders Make the Future* gives you the futures perspective you need to put leadership development in the context of the future forces of the next decade.

Immersive Experiences

The best leadership development programs have lots of opportunities for first-person learning, not just reading about leadership, or listening to lectures. The ten future leadership skills are designed so that they can be used in leadership development programs and workshops as part of immersive learning experiences. For example, I often use the ten future leadership skills in workshops as a way of linking the ten-year forecasts I am presenting to the individual leaders in the room—and to the leaders as a team. What are the most important leadership skills for your particular organization to consider? This is a discerning question for leaders to consider thoughtfully.

Reading this book in advance of the leadership development program, or as a follow-up, can also help get people oriented to the future leadership skills so that they can engage with them and apply them. This book is designed to be a practical takeaway for leadership development programs.

I have tried to create titles for the ten future leadership skills that will provoke people without turning them off. Certainly, however, the names of the future leadership skills will be different from your current talent profiles or leadership models. View this as an opportunity. Create a matrix that compares your current model with the ten future leadership skills and look for matches and holes. What do the ten future leadership skills suggest about your current model? What could be improved? Use language that starts good conversations in your culture.

Several of our clients have done detailed matrices of their skills models and compared them to the ten future leadership skills. Some of them have changed their talent profile after considering the kinds of future skills that are emerging. One company, for example, was focusing on problem-solving and analytic skills—rather than the ability to win in a world of dilemmas, where the problems cannot be solved but leaders have to figure out a way to win anyway. This company changed both their recruitment criteria and their leadership development strategies to emphasize what I call dilemma flipping—although they called it something slightly different.

People and cultures vary and some terms communicate better than others for particular groups. It is a good idea, after working with the skills for a while, to ask the group what skills are missing. The ten future leadership skills are meant to be provocative but not exhaustive. Sometimes, letting groups identify and name their own future leadership skills could work better than staying with my list. Perhaps my list will inspire a group to come up with others that are better suited to them.

It is important to remind workshop participants that they do not have to agree with these ten leadership skills to find them useful. Looking at the list may prompt leaders to articulate leadership skills that are unique to their own environments but not fully expressed in the ten skills described in this book.

I have now used the ten skills with many groups, and I'm convinced that they are constructively provocative for a wide range of leaders. My goal in presenting the ten future leadership skills is to spark conversations about future leadership in a very personal and practical way.

Often, I ask groups of leaders to do their self-assessments (see Chapter 12) before I present the Ten-Year Forecast. Sometimes I ask them to assess their leadership team. When I'm working with a graphic artist, I ask questions and have participants answer by simply raising their hands, after which the artist creates a quick histogram of the leadership team's skills.

For the second edition, Berrett-Koehler is offering an online self-assessment that I recommend using before or after leadership development experiences. This online tool is available at www.bkconnection .com/leaders-sa and volume discounts are available for workshop or classroom use. You can also have people do their own self-assessments in their book and take notes as they do it. The online took is a bit better because it automatically does a nice display of results, but making notes in your own book is useful as well—either in a physical book or an e-book.

I sometimes ask leaders to choose the top four leadership skills (out of the ten) that they believe they already have as strengths. If they feel they are strong in more than four skills, I ask them to choose the top four that best describe their current leadership skills. If they say there are fewer than four skills at which they feel strong, I ask them to just select those they are already good at. Every leadership team has some areas where it already feels strong. It is very interesting to see which skills are most attractive to a particular leadership team and which are most foreign. Each time I've done this exercise with a leadership team, we have gotten an interesting distribution of skills, and a great conversation has ensued.

Figure 27 shows a wall chart that was created for one of my workshops at the McDonald's Leadership Institute. For groups of up to twenty-five or so participants, I use a wall chart like this and small sticky dots. I ask participants to do a self-rating and then come and put dots on the chart that show their self-rating. If they line up the dots carefully (I coach them on that), you get an instant histogram that is a great conversation starter. I start by asking the group: "What do these results suggest to you?" It is always interesting to see where they rate themselves as most advanced and where they feel they need the most work.

If you do this exercise with a leadership team, you can ask what's missing on the team. Do the results suggest the need for new members of the team who would add different future leadership skills? Do the results suggest some areas where the leadership team needs to do some development?

Many of the leadership teams I work with are not very strong on bio-empathy, for example. That is an area where many decide they need to improve. Many of the teams with whom I work come from engineering backgrounds, so bio-empathy is not comfortable for them—unless they have also had experiences in nature as they grew up.

Also, most leaders today consider dilemma flipping very tough, since they were trained to be problem solvers and that's how they got to where they are today. Many still believe they can problem-solve their way to success in the VUCA World. They don't want to hear

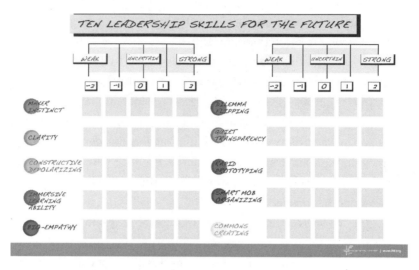

FIGURE 27. Wall chart version of future skills self-assessment. *Source:* IFTF and McDonald's Leadership Institute.

about problems that they cannot solve or that won't go away. Problem solvers are likely to be very frustrated in the future if they are in top leadership positions. Many problem solvers refuse to believe they have anything to learn.

Finally, smart-mob organizing and commons creating are skills that seem most unusual for today's leaders, but will be mandatory for leaders of tomorrow.

The best workshops involve some form of immersive learning experience. IFTF has designed a variety of gameful experiences that immerse leaders in the VUCA World to give them a firsthand taste of each of the future leadership skills. In this context, participants self-organize based on their top leadership skill scores and complete missions that draw on certain combinations of skills. This gives them a chance to practice the skills in a low-stakes way and to determine what areas of transfer there may be to their high-stakes business environments.

I have also found it useful to present the ten future leadership skills at the beginning of a workshop, before I dive right into the Ten-Year Forecast. The discussion about the forecast often links back to the leadership skills. Toward the end of the workshop, I ask participants to review their self-ratings, since they will then have a much better understanding of the skills after having a while to think about them and apply them in the context of the Ten-Year Forecast. Their final ratings are usually much more useful than the ones they did at the start. It takes a while for people to get comfortable with the ten future leadership skills and to draw similarities and differences to their own leadership styles.

As I am introducing the ten future leadership skills, I like to bring in an example of a leader who embodies the skills. One of my favorite examples is Jay Rogers, the CEO of a very interesting startup called Local Motors (http://www.local-motors.com/). Local Motors is a signal in that it exemplifies many of the external future forces that I discuss in *Leaders Make the Future.* Jay Rogers personally embodies all ten of the future leadership skills. In workshops, I often show a video clip from the Local Motors Web site and then ask participants to tell me how this CEO demonstrates all ten of the future leadership skills.

For example, Local Motors crowdsources the design of their cars—all of which are targeted to local markets. This is smart-mob organizing and, if Local Motors succeeds, it will become commons creating. Instead of making designs internally and convincing people to buy a new car, Local Motors goes out and solicits designs. They only build those that get the most enthusiastic responses. (See Figure 28.)

Local Motors taps into the Maker Instinct by bringing people to their factories so that they can feel as if they are part of the car-building process. You don't have to actually make a car in order to feel that you were involved in the process. These factory visits are also examples of Immersive Learning, since the customers are immersed in the factory where the cars are made—rather than a sterile showroom.

Jay Rogers and Local Motors embody the Clarity leadership skill, since they are very clear about what they are doing and what they are not doing. They don't, for example, manufacturer taillights or even engines. For clarity in the VUCA World, it is important to be clear about what you are doing and what you are *not* doing. Picking a rich example like this helps to bring the ten future leadership skills to life.

FIGURE 28. Local Motors "Future Car." *Source:* Flickr user cocoate.com.

It is important to bring the pressures of leadership to life with specific examples and experiences that allow people to immerse themselves in the pressures of the emerging future world.

While I was writing this book, I taught a workshop on senior leadership development for Chevron. Also on the program was Robert Rosen, author of *Just Enough Anxiety.*[1] Even the title is a gift for leaders. Expectations are so important and so fragile. Leaders should expect anxiety and seek out situations that have "just enough" of it to fuel their own leadership. The Local Motors case provides a vivid example that provokes great conversations about leadership.

Volatility, uncertainty, complexity, and ambiguity are not new. Everyone experiences moments in life that have all of these characteristics. To better understand the future leadership skills at the core of this book, it helps to look at a ten-year futures perspective. Leadership development programs should be designed to immerse people in the future so that they can learn how to flip the VUCA World from threat alone to threat laced with opportunity. The following directional shifts can be built into leadership development experiences:

VOLATILITY YIELDS TO VISION

In a VUCA World, leaders need a compelling sense of the future they want to create. Do your leadership programs encourage participants to develop their own vision and personal legacy—given the external future forces with which they are going to need to cope? Leadership development programs can help leaders develop their own vision and align it with the organization's vision. They can help leaders make their way through the external future forces in order to make the future.

Vision gets rewarded because most people are so overwhelmed by the present. In a world of dilemmas, future intent is needed to provide a sense of focus and grounding. Leaders must be very clear where they are going, but very flexible how they get there. Each of the ten future leadership skills has lessons about vision. Bio-empathy, for example, provides natural principles that are important clues about where to go and what to avoid. Commons Creating is a vision of shared assets that a wider community can use in constructive ways. Vision, however, should be carried out with a leader's own sense of Quiet Transparency and strength.

UNCERTAINTY YIELDS TO UNDERSTANDING

Leadership development programs can help leaders understand the cross-cultural worlds they will be serving. Immersive Learning ability will be critical to understand worlds that are unfamiliar and threatening. In some situations, Constructive Depolarization will be needed before any progress can be made. Bio-empathy can help, since natural principles often yield new insights about what's really going on. The Maker Instinct provides curiosity to spur leaders on to a better understanding of the situation and how things can be improved. Leaders must avoid exclusionary thinking. Understanding is impossible if you don't listen to others who are different from you.

COMPLEXITY YIELDS TO CLARITY

Since Clarity will be rewarded even if it is wrong, leaders need to be not only clear, but also trustworthy, accurate, and transparent. Leadership development programs can give leaders a chance to practice these skills in a low-risk setting. The urge for clarity will seduce people toward polarities and extremes because absolute statements are comforting. Clarity must be both compelling and simple—but not simplistic. Bio-empathy can help leaders make sense out of complexity and find a deeper clarity in the principles of nature. The best leaders will express Clarity with Quiet Transparency, yet with power that people find meaningful. Leaders will need to be very clear about the commitments they are making and the commitments they seek. There is a big difference between leadership clarity, which asks for commitment, and blind faith, which demands obedience. Clarity is mandatory, but certainty is dangerous. Leadership development programs should help leaders develop their own clarity, but moderate their certainty.

AMBIGUITY YIELDS TO AGILITY

Leaders need great flexibility within the frame of their own vision. Indeed, all ten of the future leadership skills require agility in order to bring them to life. Leadership development programs should find ways to immerse leaders in all ten of the future skills in ways that allow them to practice dealing with ambiguity and developing their own agility.

The Maker Instinct encourages an ongoing cycle of new projects, but an agile mind is needed to orchestrate them all and work with others in the making. Clarity is like the martial arts principle of being centered in the pit of your stomach, so you can respond with agility to attack. Dilemma Flipping depends upon the agility of absorbing and reacting with creativity—even while stumbling. Immersive Learning often leads to disorientation, and you will need agility to recover your balance in the new setting from which you are learning. Bio-empathy teaches agility in the form of resilience, a basic principle of successful natural systems. Constructive Depolarization, which often necessitates agile communications with people who disagree, will be mandatory to cope with the extreme polarities of the future. Quiet Transparency, an agile balance of strength and humility, is the best leadership self-presentation style for the future. Rapid Prototyping is all about agility and learning on the fly. The best leaders will be perpetual prototypers. Smart Mobs require agility to grow organically in the midst of fluid times, using a variety of media. Commons Creating will demand agility to create new territory with multiple winners and shared assets.

Learning the Ten Future Leadership Skills Yourself

———

It is often the statement made with an eye to
the future that is most suspect.

JULIAN BARNES
IN *THE SENSE OF AN ENDING*

———

I WANT TO END this second edition with a focus on what you can do to prepare yourself for the VUCA World of the future—even if you don't have a progressive leadership development program to attend. Many people asked me after the first edition: "What can I do to develop my own future leadership skills?" This chapter is my response to that question. Leaders can make the future if they have the right skills. Leaders can even win over skeptics who view these statements about the future as suspect. Making the future is much better—and often easier—than talking about it.

Given the future forces of the next decade, where do you stack up? Are you ready to lead in a future that will be volatile, uncertain, complex, and ambiguous? How could you improve your own readiness? Your own resilience? How could you develop and use the ten future leadership skills described in this book?

This chapter will help you rate your own readiness for the future—given the forces of the next decade—as well as draw some conclusions about leadership in the years to come. Berrett-Koehler is offering an online self-assessment that you can use before or after you read the book. The self-assessment will be particularly useful to use in conjunction with this chapter, which guides you on how to improve in each area. The online self-assessment is available at www .bkconnection.com/leaders-sa and volume discounts are available for workshop or classroom use.

Looking back at the ten core chapters, you now have an opportunity to assess yourself. Don't consider this assessment absolute, since nobody can predict the future. Rather, use it to spark your own thinking about leadership and how you might like to develop yourself as a leader in the future. This chapter is designed for individuals, but it can also be used as part of leadership development programs. I hope that this book will provide a futures lens through which you can evaluate yourself as a leader and develop ways to become an even better leader. You have to decide what kind of leader you want to become, but immersion in the future can help you bring out your own innate leadership gifts. I believe that there will be many new skills for future leaders to learn—in addition to the many enduring leadership resources from which you can draw.

Answer the questions below as candidly as you can. I have grouped the questions around the ten future leadership skills, each of which was described in an earlier chapter. Review the chapters if you need to as you answer these questions for yourself. They are intended to help you personalize the ten future leadership skills and point to how you might improve your own leadership skills.

I realize that these are personal questions, but leadership begins from the inside, from your own history, values, and point of view. Leaders can make a better world, but it will take an inner balance and personal discipline. It will also take physical, mental, and spiritual fitness to thrive in a VUCA World.

Ponder these questions as you reflect back to the ideas in each chapter. These are meant to be discerning questions that cannot be answered with a yes or no; you need to decide what they mean for you. These questions are designed to help you assess your own leadership skills and where you might need to improve.

Chapter 1: Are You Expressing Your Own *Maker Instinct*?

* When you were a child, think back to the ways in which you played in sand or dirt. What kinds of things did you make? What did you enjoy the most? How has your early maker experience contributed to your leadership style as you have matured? Do you still have child-like abilities to make and enjoy making?

* How would you describe your interests as an adult in *how* things work, beyond just what gets produced as output? How does this interest translate into your own leadership style and skills?

* How do you express your own do-it-yourself urges to cook, sew, knit, work with wood, design, write, or do other tasks where you are either making or remaking? How do these instincts contribute to your role as a leader?

Actions You Can Take to Bring Out Your Own Maker Instinct:

* Read *MAKE: Magazine* or other maker publication and go to a Maker Faire. Everyone gets enthused about making at a Maker Faire. Your Maker Instinct, even if it is suppressed, will be revived.

* Hang out with makers, either in person (the best way to learn) or virtually. A TechShop is a great place to do this, but there are many local hangouts where makers or craftspeople meet to make things together.

* Express your own inner maker. Tackle a task to make something you've never made before, or at least engage with the making. Get your hands dirty.

Chapter 2: How Can You Improve Your Ability to Communicate with *Clarity*?

- Think back to a recent meeting in which you had trouble getting your point across. What were the characteristics of that situation? How did you respond when you were not being understood?

- Have you ever been complimented about your clarity of expression? How often do you receive such compliments? Think of some specific examples. If you have never been complimented for your clarity, what do you think that means?

- How would you express your own personal leadership legacy in a single compelling sentence? Which of the ten future leadership skills will be most important in order for your legacy to be successful?

- How would you express your organization's strategic intent or winning proposition in a single compelling sentence? How do you contribute personally to that winning proposition?

Actions You Can Take to Improve Your Own Clarity:

- Ask your team, your boss, your friends, your family, or someone else close to you to assess your clarity in communicating with them. Ask them to give some specific examples where you were either clear or not clear with them.

- Read about military history and the importance of Commander's Intent in a variety of battle situations. What might these military leadership lessons have to teach you?

- Think about people you have known or whom you have seen in public life who were decidedly NOT clear. What lessons do you have to learn from them?

Chapter 3: How Could You Improve Your Ability to *Flip Dilemmas*?

- Think about a specific dilemma you have faced in your recent experience. When you could not solve it, how did that make you feel? How did you respond? How did you explore ways to flip the dilemma around so that it could become an opportunity?

- Do you get energized when you are in the midst of doing a puzzle, *before* you solve it, or even if you cannot solve it? How do you apply that energy (the space between knowing too soon and deciding too late) to explore ways to flip dilemmas into opportunities?

- Are you willing to decide and move ahead when a decision needs to be made, even when you don't have a solution? Think of a decision you've had to make when there was no apparent solution but you had to decide anyway.

Actions You Can Take to Improve Your Own Dilemma Flipping Ability:

- Watch the news for one week and record examples where politicians have described a dilemma in problem-solving language. Consider the risks they are taking when they promise to solve something that cannot be solved.

- Keep a dilemmas journal for at least one month. List each challenge you face in your work or your life and assess whether they are problems that can be solved or dilemmas.

- Find a video game that attracts you that involves dilemmas (rather than clear solvable problems). Ask a Digital Native for advice or, better yet, reverse mentoring. Once you find a game you like, practice your dilemma flipping skills in this low-risk environment.

Chapter 4: Are You Growing Your Own *Immersive Learning Ability*?

- How do you seek out new experiences from which you learn—especially situations that make you feel uncomfortable in the pit of your stomach? Think of a recent example and how that experience has contributed to your leadership. What did you learn? How did your learning get expressed in your leadership?

- How are you interested in the experience of and lessons from video gaming? Do you seek to understand how and why serious and casual gamers are playing?

- How have you participated in management games or simulations in your organization? Would you be willing to do so if someone else suggested it? Do you encourage the use of gaming and simulation as a learning medium for your organization?

- Study how the military is using gameful experiences to help people learn. Since the military is ahead of business in its use of gaming, how might you learn more from their experiences?

Actions You Can Take to Improve Your Own Immersive Learning Ability:

- Find a Digital Native (fifteen or younger) and figure out a way to engage with him or her as a reverse mentor in video gaming. (Clue: you will probably need to offer something in return. What might you offer? This will also test your commons creating abilities.) If you are lucky, you will have a child, relative, or young friend who is a Digital Native with whom you can immerse yourself and learn about gaming and why it is so engaging for so many people.

- Take an adventure or eco-vacation, one that makes you feel uncomfortable. If you have the option, take an international assignment—even if it is for a relatively short period of time. If you cannot travel, find a group in your local area that makes you uncomfortable and embed yourself with them to try and understand what they are all about.

- Go to a gamers conference and spend some time there. What motivates serious gamers? What can you learn from serious gamers?

Chapter 5: How Could You Seed and Cultivate Your Own *Bio-empathy*?

- As you were growing up, did you live in or frequently visit outdoor spaces like forests, oceans, farms, ponds, or parks? How did you play outside in nature? How does this experience contribute to your leadership today? Do you have a child-like ability to appreciate nature?

- Do you have an emotional need to be in natural settings and learn from the experiences you have in nature? How do you satisfy that need? How does this emotional connection to nature contribute to your leadership?

- When you were in school, were you attracted to biology, life sciences, zoology, geography, anthropology, or other similar courses? Do you think of yourself as an amateur or professional life scientist, biologist, geographer, or natural scientist?

- How do you look to nature for insight about challenges you have in your life? How do these life lessons get translated into your leadership style and skill set?

- What could you learn about leadership from your dog or cat? How do animals help us understand our choices as leaders?

Actions You Can Take to Improve Your Own Bio-empathy:

- Take an introductory biology course or read an elementary school biology textbook or video.

- Volunteer to be an assistant for a working biologist in the field.

- If you have dogs, cats, or any other pets, spend at least a week watching them very closely and trying to develop your own empathy toward them. Watching or reading Cesar Milan or another dog observer may help you develop your own bio-empathy.

Chapter 6: How Might You Improve Your Abilities to *Constructively Depolarize* Conflict Situations?

- How do you look at the world through the eyes of others, especially those with whom you do not agree or who make you feel uncomfortable? How do you express a curiosity about other cultural practices that are different from your own?

- How do you listen and learn from people who come from unfamiliar cultures where you have little experience? How are you judgmental—if at all—about cultural habits and practices that do not conform to your own beliefs and values? Do you ever exclude or write off some groups as not worth trying to understand?

- How have you traveled internationally or lived abroad as a way of learning about people who think differently from you? When you do travel, do you seek out opportunities to learn how people in other cultures live?

- Think about how you relate to other languages, including those you do not understand. Do you speak multiple languages? What have you learned about Constructive Depolarization by thinking across languages and how different languages express varied aspects of life?

- Think of an example where you have calmed a polarized situation and constructively engaged people toward some new path forward. How did you engage with the dissenting parties? What worked? What did not work?

Actions You Can Take to Improve Your Own Constructive Depolarizing Abilities:

- Seek out situations that are polarized, where neither side has empathy with the other. Try to figure out what is going on—without picking sides. How do people interact with each other? Are some people looking for ways to constructively depolarize? What strategies do they try?

- Tap into the current literature on conflict management and anger management. What themes come out that you might use in your leadership?

- Think back over your life to situations where you have been in polarized situations. For each case, what did you do and what might you have done to help constructively depolarize the situation? Don't forget, constructive depolarization does not imply that you solve the disagreement—just that you calm the situation and make it better. Unfortunately, some polarized situations may be dilemmas that cannot be solved.

Chapter 7: As a Leader, Do You Present Yourself with *Quiet Transparency?*

- How do you share your reasons for doing things with others, especially with those whom you are leading? Would the people you lead characterize you as quiet? As transparent?

- How do you embody trust and express it toward others—particularly people you are leading? Do the people you lead feel that you trust them? How do you embody this trust in your leadership style?

- Do you have a strong need for others to recognize your accomplishments? Would the people you lead say that you have a strong need for personal recognition and getting credit for accomplishments? Can you think of a recent experience where you demonstrated quiet transparency in your leadership, showing both strength and humility simultaneously?

- Has anyone ever referred to you as humble? What do those situations where you have shown humility have to say about your own leadership? If nobody has ever referred to you as humble, what do you think that means?

Actions You Can Take to Improve Your Own Quiet Transparency:

- Watch people in a public place (on a plane, in a train station, or in a park, for example) and decide which people are presenting themselves with Quiet Transparency—with both humility and with strength. How do they do it? How do their bodies communicate both strength and humility? How do their voice and word choices communicate strength and humility?

- Arrogance is very different from quiet transparency—perhaps even the opposite. Seek out a person who shows arrogance in his or her behavior and ways of dealing with people. How is arrogance communicated? What can be learned from these negative models?

- There is no such thing as absolute transparency. Pick an environment in which you work or play. How is transparency defined in that world? Who are examples of people you see acting with Quiet Transparency?

Chapter 8: How Might You Develop Your _Rapid Prototyping_ Abilities?

- Are you anxious to try out things as soon as possible in order to learn what works and what does not? Think of an example where you kept trying out different approaches to a new idea over and over again, in a rapid prototyping process. What did this experience reveal about your own leadership style? What additional skills could help you do this better?

• Early on in a new task, do you get frustrated or impatient if things don't work right away? If so, how do you express and work through that frustration?

• What is an example where you were able to learn from your own failures? How does your approach to failure fit in with your own leadership style? Do you encourage people you lead to learn from their own failures?

Actions You Can Take to Improve Your Own Rapid Prototyping:

• The next time you take on a project, do a prototype on the first day—literally the first day. Consciously try to fail early and fail often as you learn. Keep trying and see what you learn.

• Hang out with designers and read some of the current literature of design. See how they use rapid prototypes as part of the design process—which begins with design thinking.

• What is the opposite of rapid prototyping? Do you see any examples in your work world or private life? What are the tradeoffs of *not* doing rapid prototyping?

Chapter 9: How Might You Reimagine Your Leadership Role as *Smart-Mob Organizing?*

• Do you find it satisfying to bring together groups of people? What are recent examples where you have done this? What aspects of this process do you find most satisfying?

• Do you like to reach out and network with others, both in person and through online media?

• Do you have a personal rule of thumb with regard to which medium is best for a given situation? How do you decide when to meet in person, as compared to through some electronic medium?

- Are you able to use online social media in your role as leader? Have you practiced your leadership skills through a range of different media? How does your use of online media leadership compare to your in-person leadership?

Actions You Can Take to Improve Your Smart-Mob Organizing:

- Look for examples of smart mobs in your work, community, or public news world. Are these mobs really smart? What media choices do they make?

- Consider a committee or team with whom you work. What difference might it make if you viewed yourselves as a smart mob?

- Think through your own criteria for choosing which medium is good for what. When do you choose to travel to exert your leadership? How do you express your leadership through various electronic media?

Chapter 10: How Might Your Leadership Legacy Include *Commons Creating*?

- How do you seek out and try to create situations where multiple parties benefit (as opposed to a situation in which you alone win)? Can you give recent examples when you have tried to do this, whether or not your efforts were successful?

- Think of an example where you have given something away in order to get more in return. Think back and describe how this process worked. Was it a win-win situation in the end? Did you succeed? Did others succeed as a result of your actions?

- Read about historical efforts to create commons that rewarded both individuals and larger groups. What lessons do you take away from these historical experiences? What is different about the new commons that are becoming possible with cloud-served supercomputing?

- Read fantasy fiction or scenarios about how things could be or might be in the future. What commons are created in fictional works? What fiction writing do you find most provocative for your own leadership?

Actions You Can Take to Improve Your Own Commons Creating Abilities:

• What do you or your organization have in surplus that you could give away in the faith that you would get even more value in return over a period of time?

• Think back to examples when you have given gifts to others. How has it made you feel? Did you receive anything back in return? How might you and your organization develop a give-to-get philosophy?

• What commons (shared assets) do you see in your local community and business community? What value do those shared assets provide? What challenges do they present? How are new media likely to affect these commons?

Rate Your Own Leadership Skills for the Future

I developed the revised self-rating system below with Sylvester Taylor from the Center for Creative Leadership. I have used it with a wide range of organizations, with very provocative results. Completing this form will give you insight about your own future leadership skills. If you prefer, you can use the online self-assessment at: www .bkconnection.com/leaders-sa.

FUTURE LEADERSHIP SKILLS INDICATOR

For each statement, use the following scale to rate your own future-oriented leadership skills. Once you have finished rating yourself on the ten leadership skills for the future, please answer the questions again while considering the *most* future-oriented leader with whom you have personally worked. Finally, answer the questions having in mind the *least* future-oriented leader with whom you have personally worked. Both the most future-oriented leader and the least future-oriented leader should be real people, not someone you imagine. Please rate to what extent the following statements are true:

1 = To no extent
2 = To a very little extent
3 = To some extent
4 = To a great extent
5 = To a very great extent

LEADERSHIP SKILL	YOU	MOST FUTURE-ORIENTED LEADER	LEAST FUTURE-ORIENTED LEADER
1 Maker Instinct Sees his or her inner drive to build and grow things, as well as connect with others in the making.			
2 Clarity Sees through messes and contradictions to a future that others cannot yet see. Leaders must be clear about what they are making but flexible about how it gets made.			
3 Dilemma Flipping Can turn dilemmas—which, unlike problems, cannot be solved—into advantages and opportunities.			
4 Immersive Learning Ability Can immerse in unfamiliar environments to learn from them in a first-person way.			
5 Bio-empathy Sees things from nature's point of view, to understand, respect, and learn from its patterns.			

FIGURE 29. Future Leadership Skills Indicator

	YOU	MOST FUTURE-ORIENTED LEADER	LEAST FUTURE-ORIENTED LEADER
6 Constructive Depolarizing Calms tense situations where differences dominate and communication has broken down. Brings people from divergent cultures toward positive engagement.			
7 Quiet Transparency Is open and authentic about what matters—without being overly self-promoting.			
8 Rapid Prototyping Has the ability to create quick early versions of innovations with the expectation that later success will require early failures.			
9 Smart-Mob Organizing Can create, engage with, and nurture purposeful business or social change networks through intelligent use of electronic media and in-person communication.			
10 Commons Creating Seeds, nurtures, and grows shared assets that can benefit all players—and allows competition at a higher level.			
Total for Questions 1-10			

Take a Personal Look Back at Your Own Leadership

As you look forward, I also recommend that you look back at your life and the choices you have made that influence your leadership abilities and style. Our past shapes our future, but there are also opportunities to break out of your own pattern. Understanding where you have been is an important part of determining where you want to go and what you need to learn.

The ten future leadership skills are meant to be provocative, to cause you to consider your own leadership skills and think ahead to the next stage in your professional life. There may be parts of your own background that you want to revisit and perhaps resurrect as part of your leadership style. There may be things you tried to do earlier in your career that failed, but that would work now. On the other hand, there may be things you need to unlearn or change. As in any effort to think systematically about the future, it is important to look much further back than you are looking forward and to think personally about your own experiences as a leader and the choices you have made.

I got to meet the management visionary Peter Drucker twice late in his life, when he was in his nineties. When we asked him about leadership and how to create an organizational climate that can help leaders grow, he suggested that people try out many roles in life and work with many different types of people when they are young (essentially using rapid prototyping), since they don't yet know who they are. In the second half of life, he said that people should only work on things they are passionate about and with people they admire.

I found this very optimistic advice, since Drucker lived to be ninety-five and worked productively up to the end. What Drucker saw as the first half of life—almost fifty years—allows leaders plenty of time to take on different identities and seek their own styles of leadership. It also gives all of us time to learn new leadership skills like those introduced in this book.

Each of us has taken steps toward leadership from early in life, even if we don't realize it. As an undergraduate at the University of Illinois in Champaign-Urbana, for example, I led a relatively protected life as a college basketball player on scholarship. Since Illinois was a land grant college, I was required at that time to take part in the Reserve Officer Training Corps. When John F. Kennedy was killed in 1963, I found it very strange that we were called together and ordered to march around in a vacant field—with nobody watching. Thinking back, that experience was an important part of my leadership learning. It was a vivid experience of possible responses to the VUCA World, circa 1963.

As best I can tell, marching in a vacant field was an attempt by the ROTC leaders to put order around the disorder that had shaken us all. We were doing something familiar in a situation that was suddenly unfamiliar: our president had been killed. We were marching to bring back our sense of order. With this experience, I got an early taste of how leaders respond to volatility, uncertainty, complexity, and ambiguity. It seems like 1963 was a simpler time, at least from my perspective. My lesson: when something awful happens, put some order around it that at least allows you to engage with and experience the moment actively—not just sit back watching twenty-four-hour news in passive shock.

I had another leadership moment of truth in graduate school. It was a big identity shift for me to go from thinking of myself as a basketball player to thinking of myself as a serious student. I was a very good high school player, but only a marginal player in the Big Ten and certainly not good enough to be a pro. It was painful to realize that my early leadership identity as a basketball player was over.

I found myself very attracted to studying the future, but it was hard to know where to start and how to engage. I have a vivid memory of the exact moment I first learned about Institute for the Future. As a research assistant in divinity school, I was in my professor's office and looked down on his table and saw an article in a new publication called *The Futurist*.

I was frozen in place. "That's where I'd love to work," I thought with a clarity that I didn't even know that I had.

Seeing that article about the Institute for the Future was a major turning point in my life. I had an immediate attraction to thinking about the long-term future, but it took me some years to develop a leadership role in that space. In 1972, at the conference in Washington, DC, where the ARPAnet was publicly introduced, I presented a paper based on my dissertation at Northwestern. By good fortune, I was on a panel with Andy Lipinksi, a senior researcher from Institute for the Future, who invited me to apply for a job. I got the job and, remarkably, I am still working at IFTF thirty-five years later, immersed in my fifth different career there. Lesson: look back at the turning points in your life and consider how you could build on them even more as you create your own leadership legacy.

I am very fortunate that I have been able to work on things I am passionate about since I first came to Institute for the Future in 1973. My leadership roles at IFTF have varied, but it has become a home where I can thrive. By Drucker's criteria, I found my calling early—well before my life was half over.

My leadership lessons from early life helped me figure out what I could do and what I could not. I was a leader in sports up to playing at Illinois, but then I needed another identity in order to be a leader. I had topped out as a basketball and baseball player. There was no place else to go, unless I traded on my sports identity as an insurance agent or some other career in the small town where I was raised or where I went to college, where people might remember who I once was as a player. As I went on to graduate school and continued to try out different roles, I gradually figured out what I could do well—and how I wanted to continue to learn. I realized, painfully, that I had to move on. What worked for me early in my life was not going to work any longer.

Each leader has to figure out a path that works for him or her. My experience was a form of prototyping. I was practicing for the life I am now living. Lesson: if you are unhappy with your current work, how might you use rapid prototyping to find something more engaging and meaningful? Gaming and immersive learning are particularly good ways to do that kind of rapid prototyping.

Leaders are likely to do better in situations they have experienced before, in situations for which they have practiced. Once in a VUCA situation, leaders will be disoriented. The discipline of practice and preparation (immersive learning ability) really is useful *before* a crisis so that decisive action can happen rapidly—especially in situations where there is no time to consider all the options. The challenge, of course, is to simulate experiences that will be useful in the future world. Leaders don't want to be caught playing out-of-date games in new situations that demand new approaches.

Once you are in an uncertain world, you may not have much time to think—you will be immersed, like it or not. Clarity becomes extremely important in crisis situations. In my days as a basketball player, for example, I often found myself flipping back and forth mentally between playing and watching myself play, or thinking about what I needed to do next or the consequences of missing a shot at a critical time. I learned to my surprise that I could actually shoot better without my glasses. Seeing details (the basket, the crowd, the cheerleaders) often caused me to lose my focus. Without the detail, I could get into the flow of the game more much easily and my muscle memory allowed me to shoot well even when I could not see well. Leaders need muscle memory, and immersive learning can help develop those muscles in a low-risk environment.

It is great to try out lots of different leadership roles until you find one that really fits you. Rapid prototyping is wonderful—especially when you are young. Daniel Seddiqui is an extreme example: he was in his mid-twenties and had a hard time finding a full-time job. He came up with a clever alternative: finding lots of one-week jobs to grow his experience base, since most employers wanted people with experience. He found a series of fifty jobs in fifty states, working one week on each.[1] He wrote a blog to record his experiences, which are now incredibly broad for someone who has never had a full-time job. Finally, he wrote a book about his experiences. Now *that* is rapid prototyping. Along the way, he developed a good sense of what he would like to do on a more permanent basis. This kind of creative turnaround is exactly what leaders need to do in the VUCA World.

Conclusion

These ten skills are challenging to master, but each of them can be learned and there are many resources.

Maker Instinct is the most basic of the skills, and it is certainly necessary in order to make and remake organizations. Clarity is very personal (what is *your* clarity?), but others can help you shape your clarity. You can start Dilemma Flipping based on your own view of the world, but others can help you figure out how to do it. All the other leadership skills can be done jointly with others, as long as the leader understands and believes in the approach. Bio-empathy, for example, can spread across an organization, but it will not work if the leader tries to control things in mechanical and linear ways. Leaders do not need to do all the Smart-Mob Organizing themselves, but they must set the vision and encourage the organizers—who must take on the authority to act.

Again, what works in the VUCA World is not only great clarity about where you are going, but great flexibility about how you get there.

Foresight is the ability to look over the horizon and see the big picture. It requires a combination of the Maker Instinct, Clarity, and Dilemma Flipping—but the other leadership skills will contribute as well. All effective leaders must have the ability to think ahead, beyond the usual planning horizon. Thinking ten years ahead will give you a much more robust perspective from which to make decisions today.

Insight is discernment, an aha moment. A forecast, whether or not you agree with it, is a great way to provoke insight. In the next generation of the Internet age, everyone will know what's new. The challenge for leaders will be to derive insight from the messiness around them and sense what's important. Anger is the enemy of insight. These days, it is difficult not to be angry at something or somebody. An angry leader, however, is rarely effective.

Action depends upon the ability to decide on a strong path ahead. It requires Rapid Prototyping, Smart-Mob Organizing, and an aptitude for Commons Creating. All ten future leadership skills will contribute to a leader's ability to act. Leaders may be known by their vision, but their actions will be evaluated most vigorously. The best leaders will innovate through reciprocity, giving and getting.

The best future leaders will have their own styles of cycling continuously through foresight, insight, and action. This book gives you the skills to do that.

Flipping from the frightening VUCA (volatility, uncertainty, complexity, and ambiguity) to the hopeful VUCA (vision, understanding, clarity, and agility) will be the ultimate dilemma for leaders in the future. As a leader, you will need to have all ten of the future leadership skills in a blend that becomes you. Connectivity will bring the leadership skills to life and amplify your impact. The best leaders will develop the skills necessary to

- make sense out of volatility
- make concise what is uncertain
- make clear what is complex
- make common cause with ambiguity

Leaders will make the future, but they won't make it all at once, and they can't make it alone. This will be a make-it-ourselves future. Listen for the future. Develop your clarity. Moderate your certainty.

Leaders can learn by immersing themselves in the future, but we all must return to the present in order to make a better future. Leaders can make the future.

Notes

Preface

1. The Ten-Year Forecast is an ongoing research program led by Kathi Vian at Institute for the Future. See http://www.iftf.org for details.
2. The VUCA World terminology was developed at the Army War College in Carlisle, Pennsylvania. I learned about it when I was there the week before 9/11/2001.
3. Bob Johansen, *Get There Early: Sensing the Future to Compete in the Present* (San Francisco: Berrett-Koehler, 2007).
4. Institute for the Future published a map to the 2008 Maker Faire; it is published under a Creative Commons license available to everyone. David Pescovitz and Marina Gorbis were the lead authors, and this map was part of IFTF's Technology Horizons Program, which is now led by Lyn Jeffery. See www.iftf.org to access and download the map.
5. William Gibson, "Broadband Blues," *Economist* 359, no. 8227 (June 23, 2001), 62.

Introduction

Epigraph: Confucius as quoted by James Geary, *Geary's Guide to the World's Great Aphorists* (New York: Bloomsbury, 2007), 72.

1. Johansen, *Get There Early*, 45–68. The original definition of VUCA was volatility, uncertainty, complexity, and ambiguity. In *Get There Early*, I introduced the idea of a VUCA turnaround with an emphasis on vision, understanding, clarity, and agility.
2. You can access this data in IFTF's Ten-Year Forecast 2011. See www.iftf.org.

3. Map of Hurricane Katrina's Diaspora, October 2, 2005. See www
   .nytimes.com/imagepages/2005/10/02/national/nationalspecial/20051
   002diaspora_graphic.html.

4. Governor of Massachusetts Deval Patrick attributed this phrase to
   Barney Frank in a speech he gave on August 26, 2008. Full text available at http://www.demconvention.com/deval-patrick/.

5. This is a term from Linda Stone's work at Microsoft Research. See
   www.lindastone.net.

6. Liisa Välikangas, *The Resilient Organization: How Adaptive Cultures Strive
   When Strategy Fails* (New York: McGraw-Hill, 2010), 91.

Chapter 1: Maker Instinct

1. See www.instructables.com.

2. Selected from the TCHO Web site: www.tcho.com.

3. "Chicago Chef Invents Edible Menu," *Wikinews*, Sunday, February 13,
   2005. http://en.wikinews.org/wiki/Chicago_chef_invents_edible_menu.

4. "CBS News Sunday Morning," February 11, 2009. www.cbsnews.com/
   stories/2007/06/03/sunday/main2878788.shtml.

Chapter 2: Clarity

1. As I tell this story, I recall the early days of my career when business
   and government leaders were not allowed to make decisions in the first
   hours after international travel due to jet lag. International travel was
   longer and more difficult then, but some of the rigors of time shifting
   remain, and they certainly affect my mental state.

2. Apparently my experience was not unusual. I read this after I
   returned: "'BA lost one bag for every 36 passengers in April, May and
   June—nearly double the European industry average of one lost bag
   for every 63 passengers,' an Association of European Airlines (AEA)
   survey said." "British Airways Worst for Losing Luggage," *Money
   Times,* August 4, 2007. www.themoneytimes.com/news/2007084/
   British_Airways_worst_for_losing_luggage-id-107545.html.

3. Sylvester Taylor, "KEYS® to Creativity and Innovation Diamond
   Model for Creative Climates." CCL, 2010.

4. Gary Hamel and C. K. Prahalad, *Competing for the Future* (Boston: Harvard Business School Press, 1996), 141.

5. Willie Pietersen, *Reinventing Strategy: Using Strategic Learning to Create and Sustain Breakthrough Performance* (New York: J. Wiley and Sons, 2002), 42.

6. For more, see www.ogilvy.com.

7. For more, see www.southwest.com.

8. For more, see www.pg.com.

9. For more, see www.syngenta.com.

10. Nassir Ghaemi, *A First-Rate Madness: Uncovering the Links Between Leadership and Mental Illness* (London: Penguin Press HC, 2011).

11. Nassir Ghaemi, "Depression in Command: In Times of Crisis, Mentally Ill Leaders Can See What Others Don't," *Wall Street Journal*, Saturday/Sunday, July 30–31, 2011.

12. Kelly Hannum, *Social Identity: Knowing Yourself, Leading Others* (Greensboro, NC: Center for Creative Leadership, 2007).

13. CPT Joel C. Dotterer, "Commander's Intent: Less Is Better," *Field Manual* 100-15, 14 June 1993. www.GlobalSecurity.org.

14. See www.pbs.org/weta/carrier/ for a synopsis and video clips, as well as instructions for ordering the entire series.

15. Martin Luther King Jr., speech, the Mason Temple Church, Memphis, TN. April 3, 1968. To view a clip of this speech, see www.american rhetoric.com/speeches/mlkivebeentothemountaintop.htm.

16. Alan Jolis, "The Good Banker," *Independent*, May 5, 1996. www.gdrc .org/icm/grameen-goodbanker.html.

Chapter 3: Dilemma Flipping

Epigraph: F. Scott Fitzgerald as quoted by Edmund Wilson, ed. *The Crack-Up* (New York: New Directions, 1945), 69. I thank Nathan Estruth, leader of FutureWorks at Procter & Gamble, for pointing me to this quote early in my writing of this book.

1. See Johansen, *Get There Early*, 74, for a longer description and analysis of modern dilemmas.

2. Lt. Commander Charles Swift, *Esquire*, March 2007. www.esquire .com/features/ESQ0307swift?click=main_sr.

3. Barack Obama, speech, the White House, August 8, 2011. www.white house.gov/the-press-office/2011/08/08/remarks-president.

4. Roger Martin, *The Opposable Mind: How Successful Leaders Win Through Integrative Thinking* (Boston: Harvard Business School Press, 2007).

5. See www.selectminds.com.

6. Ingar S. Skaug, "Breaking Free in Turbulent Times." *Business Leadership Review IV: III.* July 2007. http://www.mbaworld.com/blr.

7. Porter B. Williamson, *Patton's Principles: A Handbook for Managers Who Mean It!* (New York: Simon & Schuster, 1982).

8. Larry Huston and Nabil Sakkab, "Connect and Develop: Inside Procter & Gamble's New Model for Innovation," *Harvard Business Review* 84, no. 3, March 20, 2006.

9. A.G. Lafley and Ram Charan, *The Game-Changer* (New York: Crown Business, 2008).

10. Winston Churchill quoted by James Geary, *Geary's Guide to the World's Great Aphorists*, 72.

11. Flip-flopping is usually a pejorative term to refer to changing one's position back and forth, often depending upon the audience. It allows politicians to be attractive to a wider range of people. Flip-flopping, or even the appearance of it, is something that politicians seek to avoid. There are cases, however, when what appears to be flip-flopping is actually an authentic dilemma flipping based on insight or a changing set of variables.

12. See Johansen, "What's Different About Dilemmas?" *Get There Early*, 69–84, for detailed discussion of distinguishing dilemmas from problems. See also "It Takes a Story to Understand a Dilemma," *Get There Early*, 87–100.

13. See Johansen, *Get There Early*, 78–81, for a fuller discussion of the threshold of righteousness.

Chapter 4: Immersive Learning Ability

1. Scott F. Dye, MD, "Conscious Neurosensory Mapping of the Internal Structures of the Human Knee Without Intraarticular Anesthesia," *The American Journal of Sports Medicine* 26, no. 6 (1998), 774.

2. Constance Steinkuehler and Sean Duncan, "Scientific Habits of Mind in Virtual Worlds," *Journal of Science Education and Technology* 17, no. 6 (2008). The authors downloaded the content of 1,984 posts in 85 threads from a discussion board for players of World of Warcraft. I thank Zach Mumbach from Electronic Arts for pointing out this research to me and for reviewing this chapter as I was writing it. http://website.education. wisc.edu/steinkuehler/papers/SteinkuehlerDuncan2008.pdf.

3. Sian Beilock, *Choke: What the Secrets of the Brain Reveal About Getting It Right When You Have To* (New York: The Free Press, 2010).

4. Ellen Van Velsor, Cynthia D. McCauley, and Marian N. Ruderman, *The Center for Creative Leadership Handbook of Leadership Development*, 3rd ed. (San Francisco: Jossey-Bass, 2010).

5. Just google "Jane" and "games" to glimpse the range of her gaming activities, as well as to see how a person with a great online identity presents herself without a business card. For more on this, see www .newyorker.com/online/video/conference/2008/mcgonigal and Jane's Web site, www.avantgame.com/.

6. Jane McGonigal, *Reality Is Broken: Why Games Make Us Better and How They Can Change the World.* (New York: Penguin, 2011).

7. See Johansen, "Immersion: The Best Way to Learn in the VUCA World," *Get There Early*, 101–21. This chapter provides more detail on the range of immersion experiences and explores how they can be used in the foresight to insight to action process.

8. Robert Johansen, Jacques Vallee, and Kathleen Spangler, *Electronic Meetings: Technical Alternatives and Social Choices* (Reading, MA: Addison-Wesley, 1979), Appendix. The boxed version of *Spinoff* is now out of print.

9. For details on the most recent online forecasting games, see the Ten-Year Forecast portion of IFTF's Web site (www.iftf.org) and particularly this article on the first Massively Multiplayer Forecasting Platform: www.iftf.org/node/2319.

10. Sue Halpern, "Virtual Iraq: Using Simulation to Treat a New Generation of Traumatized Veterans," *The New Yorker* (May 19, 2008), 32–37.

Chapter 5: Bio-empathy

Epigraph: Wendell Berry, "The Pleasures of Eating," *What Are People For?* (San Francisco: North Point Press, 1990). www.stjoan.com/ecosp/docs/pleasures_of_eating_by_wendell_b.htm.

1. Essentially they are grass farmers who just happen to produce other products from the grass, like meat.

2. Taken from Polyface Farm's Web site: www.polyfacefarms.com/principles.aspx.

3. Scott F. Dye, MD, "The Pathophysiology of Patellofemoral Pain: A Tissue Homeostasis Perspective," *Clinical Orthopaedics and Related Research* no. 436 (2005), 100–110.

4. Katherine Jefferts Schori, *A Wing and a Prayer: A Message of Faith and Hope* (New York: Morehouse Publishing, 2007), 8.

5. The forecast map and a video describing it are available on the GEMI Web site: www.gemi.org.

6. Operation Purple is run by the National Military Family Association and The Sierra Club. Please direct questions regarding Operation Purple to operationpurple@nmfa.org.

7. Ibid.

8. For an example of how this phrase is in use, see this article from the *Journal of Soil and Water Conservation*. Available online: www.jswconline .org/content/63/5/149A.short.

9. This course was taught by Professor Linda L. Golden, Marlene and Morton Meyerson Professor in Business, McCombs School of Business, University of Texas, Austin.

10. Taken from Syngenta's Web site: www.syngenta.com/en/about _syngenta/visionandbusiness.

11. Scott Jenkins, e-mail correspondence, October 10, 2011.

12. For more information on the Green Sports Alliance, go to their Web site: http://greensportsalliance.org.

13. Adam Gopnik, "Dog Story," the *New Yorker*, August 8, 2011.

14. See, for example, Dorling Kindersley's *Eyewitness Books* series. Some of these books are explicitly future-oriented, but all are solid introductions to science and nature. Reading children's books is a kind of do-it-yourself reverse mentoring. http://us.dk.com/nf/Search/AdvSearchProc/.

Chapter 6: Constructive Depolarizing

1. Quoted in the Ken Burns and Lynn Novick documentary film *Prohibition*, PBS, 2011.

2. Robert A. Burton, MD, *On Being Certain: Believing You Are Right Even When You're Not* (New York: St. Martin's Press, 2008).

3. Edward T. Hall, *The Silent Language* (Garden City, NY: Anchor Press/ Doubleday, 1959), 29.

4. Ian Wylie, "Meetings Resolve Almighty Issues," *Financial Times,* July 15, 2008. I was able to talk with a number of people about the Lambeth Conference, but I thought that this article about conflict management was a very good summary of the approach. It is fascinating that the *Financial Times* and Ian Wylie did this analysis, looking at Lambeth as a source of insight about conflict management in business. I thank Professor Ian Douglas for his review of this account of the Lambeth Conference.

5. Douglas Johnston, *Faith-Based Diplomacy: Trumping RealPolitik* (Oxford: Oxford University Press, 2003).
6. Beth Jones, "Queen Rania Takes on Stereotypes," *BBC News/Middle East,* July 25, 2008. http://news.bbc.co.uk/1/hi/world/middle_east/7524933.stm.
7. See www.youtube.com/user/queenrania?ob=4.
8. Charles J. Palus and Wilfred H. Drath, "Putting Something in the Middle: An Approach to Dialogue," *Reflections* 3, no. 2.

Chapter 7: Quiet Transparency

1. See http://makezine.com/04/ownyourown/.
2. James Gilmore and Joseph Pine, *Authenticity: What Consumers Really Want* (Boston: Harvard Business School Press, 2008).
3. Kerry A. Bunker, Douglas T. (Tim) Hall, and Kathy E. Kram, *Extraordinary Leadership: Addressing the Gaps in Senior Executive Development* (San Francisco: Jossey-Bass, 2010).
4. Michael E. Conroy, *Branded!: How the "Certification Revolution" Is Transforming Global Corporations* (Gabriola Island: New Society Publishers, 2007).
5. That said, her work takes root more broadly in the realm of changing workforce, changing family, and changing community.
6. Taken from Timberland's Web site: www.timberland.com.
7. Ellen Van Velsor, Cynthia D. McCauley, and Marian N. Ruderman, *The Center for Creative Leadership Handbook of Leadership Development*, 3rd ed. (San Francisco: Jossey-Bass, 2010), 219.

Chapter 8: Rapid Prototyping

1. Clay Shirky, *Here Comes Everybody: The Power of Organizing Without Organizations* (New York: Penguin, 2008).
2. For a description of Chip Earnest (Chip) R. Blatchley's work, see http://krannert.purdue.edu/centers/dcmme_gscmi/conferences/speakers_S11.html.
3. See www.au.af.mil/au/awc/awcgate/army/tc_25-20/table.htm.
4. For a description of the work done at Grove and for access to their designers' visual templates, see www.grove.com.
5. Winston Churchill as quoted by James Geary, *Geary's Guide to the World's Great Aphorists,* 72.

Chapter 9: Smart-Mob Organizing

1. Howard Rheingold, *Smart Mobs: The Next Social Revolution* (New York: Basic Books, 2003). Howard continues to be a thought leader in this field and a continuing source of inspiration.
2. See www.healthiestyou.com.
3. Vannevar Bush, "As We May Think," *Atlantic,* July 1945.
4. Richard Dawkins, *The Selfish Gene* (Oxford: Oxford University Press, 2006).

Chapter 10: Commons Creating

1. For more information, see AMI's Web site. http://aminnovation.org/.
2. Peter Barnes, *Capitalism 3.0* (San Francisco: Berrett-Koehler, 2007).
3. Garrett Hardin, "The Tragedy of the Commons," *Science* 162 (1968), 1243–1248.
4. For more information, see www.cio.com.au/index.php/id;1491647901; fp;4;fpid;21;pf;1 or www.wired.com/techbiz/it/news/2003/11/61257 or www.nytimes.com/2005/03/29/technology/29computer.html.
5. For more information, see http://icommons.org/articles/web-20-in-brazil-the-overmundo-case.
6. See http://blogs.wsj.com/law/2008/05/28/dlas-amy-schulman-lands-top-legal-job-at-pfizer/.
7. Boris Groysberg, Victoria W. Winston, and Shirley Spence, "Leadership in Law: Amy Schulman at DLA Piper," *Harvard Business Review* (Case 10.1225/407033), 5. Further, "the experience taught Schulman that . . . 'good leaders are actually consensus builders and work to elicit the best from their teams. It's not a solo star opportunity.'"
8. Ibid.
9. Taken from Wild Farm Alliance Web site: www.wildfarmalliance.org.

Chapter 11

1. Robert H. Rosen, *Just Enough Anxiety: The Hidden Driver of Business Success* (New York: Portfolio, 2008).

Chapter 12

Epigraph: Julian Barnes, *The Sense of an Ending* (New York: Alfred A. Knopf, 2011), 20.
1. Ian MacKenzie, "Daniel Seddiqui Works 50 Jobs in 50 States," *Food for Thought,* October 7, 2008.

Bibliography

Allen, Nate, Tony Burgess, Nancy M. Dixon, Pete Kilner, and Steve
    Schweizer. *Unleashing the Power of the Army Profession.* West Point, NY:
    Center for the Advancement of Leadership Development & Organiza-
    tional Learning, 2005.

Altman, David G., Jennifer J. Deal, and Steven G. Rogelberg. "Millenials
    at Work: What We Know and What We Need to Do (If Anything)."
    Journal of Business and Psychology 25.2 (2010):201–210. Print.

Ashby, Meredith D., and Stephen A. Miles, eds. *Leaders Talk Leadership.*
    New York: Oxford Press, 2002.

Austen, Hilary. *Artistry Unleashed: A Guide to Pursuing Great Performance in
    Work and Life.* Toronto: University of Toronto Press, 2010.

Barnes, Julian. *The Sense of an Ending.* New York: Alfred A. Knopf, 2011.

Barnett, Thomas P. M. *The Pentagon's New Map.* New York: G. P. Putnam's
    Sons, 2004.

Bell, Wendell, and James A. Mau, eds. *The Sociology of the Future.* New York:
    Russell Sage Foundation, 1971.

Bennis, Warren, and Patricia Ward Biederman. *Organizing Genius: The
    Secrets of Creative Collaboration.* Reading, MA: Addison-Wesley, 1997.

Betof, Edward. *Leaders as Teachers: Unlock the Teaching Potential of Your Com-
    pany's Best and Brightest.* San Francisco: Berrett-Koehler, 2009.

Botsman, Rachel, and Roo Rogers. *What's Mine Is Yours: The Rise of Collab-
    orative Consumption.* New York: HarperCollins, 2010.

Bunker, Kerry, and Michael Wakefield. *Leading Through Transitions: Facilita-
    tor's Guide Set.* San Francisco: Pfeiffer/A Wiley Imprint, 2010.

————. *Leading with Authenticity in Times of Transition.* Greensboro, NC: Center for Creative Leadership, 2005.

Burnside, Robert M. "Encouragement as the Elixir of Innovation." *Issues & Observations* 8-3 (1988): 1–6. Print.

Burton, Robert A., M.D. *On Being Certain.* New York: St. Martin's Press, 2008.

Chrobot-Mason, Donna, and Chris Ernst. *Boundary Spanning Leadership.* New York: McGraw-Hill, 2011.

Conroy, Michael E. *Branded!: How the "Certification Revolution" Is Transforming Global Corporations.* Gabriola Island: New Society Publishers, 2007.

Cramer, Aron, and Zachary Karabell. *Sustainable Excellence: The Future of Business in a Fast-Changing World.* New York: Rodale, 2010.

Crandall, Doug. *Leadership Lessons from West Point.* San Francisco: Jossey-Bass, 2007.

Davis, Stanley M. *Future Perfect.* New York: Addison-Wesley, 1987.

————, and Bill Davidson. *2020 Vision.* New York: Simon & Schuster, 1991.

Dawkins, Richard. *The Selfish Gene.* Oxford: Oxford University Press, 2006.

DeGeus, Arie. *The Living Company.* Boston: Harvard Business School Press, 1997.

Doctorow, Cory. *Makers.* London: HarperVoyager, 2009.

Drucker, Peter F. *The Future of Industrial Man.* New York: The New American Library of World Literature, Inc. 1965.

Finkel, Donald L. *Teaching with Your Mouth Shut.* Portsmouth, NH: Boynton/Cook, 2000.

Friedman, Stewart D. *Total Leadership.* Boston: Harvard Business Press, 2008.

Friedman, Thomas L. *The World Is Flat: A Brief History of the 21st Century.* New York: Farrar, Straus & Giroux, 2005.

Fromm, Erich. *The Forgotten Language.* New York: Grove Press, 1951.

Gansky, Lisa. *The Mesh: Why the Future of Business Is Sharing.* New York: Penguin, 2010.

Geary, James. *Geary's Guide to the World's Great Aphorists.* New York: Bloomsbury, 2007.

Ghaemi, Nassir. *A First-Rate Madness.* New York: Penguin, 2011.

Goffman, Erving. *Frame Analysis.* New York: Harper & Row, 1974.

Goldsmith, Marshall, Cathy L. Greenberg, Alastair Robertson, and Maya Hu-Chan. *Global Leadership.* Upper Saddle River: Prentice Hall, 2003.

Goleman, Daniel. *Emotional Intelligence.* New York: Bantam Books, 1995.

Greer, Scott. *The Logic of Social Inquiry.* Chicago: Aldine Publishing, 1969.

Gryskiewicz, Stan S., and Sylvester Taylor. *Making Creativity Practical: Innovation That Gets Results.* Greensboro, NC: Center for Creative Leadership Press, 2003.

Gupta, Anil J. *Honeybee Network.* SRISTI (Society for Research and Initiatives for Sustainable Technologies and Institutions). Web. 05 October 2011.

Hall, Edward T. *The Hidden Dimension.* New York: Anchor Press/Doubleday, 1966.

———. *The Silent Language.* New York: Anchor Press/Doubleday, 1959.

Halpern, Belle Linda, and Kathy Lubar. *Leadership Presence.* New York: Gotham Books, 2003.

Hannum, Kelly. *Social Identity: Knowing Yourself, Leading Others.* Greensboro, NC: Center for Creative Leadership, 2007.

Harman, Willis. *Global Mind Change.* New York: Warner Books, 1988.

Harter, Jim, and Tom Rath. *Well-Being: The Five Essential Elements.* New York: Gallup, 2009.

Heider, John. *The Tao of Leadership.* Atlanta: Humanics New Age, 1985.

Heifetz, Ronald A. *Leadership Without Easy Answers.* Boston: Harvard University Press, 2003.

Hock, Dee. *Birth of the Chaordic Age.* San Francisco: Berrett-Koehler, 1999.

Hoffer, Eric. *The True Believer.* New York: Harper & Row Publishers, 1951.

Jaworski, Joseph. *Synchronicity: The Inner Path of Leadership.* San Francisco: Berrett-Koehler, 1996.

Johansen, Robert. *Get There Early: Sensing the Future to Compete in the Present.* San Francisco: Berrett-Koehler, 2007.

Johansen, Robert, and Rob Swigart. *Upsizing the Individual in the Downsized Organization.* Reading, MA: Addison-Wesley, 1994.

Johansen, Robert, David Sibbet, Suzyn Benson, Alexia Martin, Robert Mittman, and Paul Saffo. *Leading Business Teams.* Reading, MA: Addison-Wesley, 1991.

Johnson, Steven. *Where Good Ideas Come From: The Natural History of Innovation.* New York: Riverhead, 2010.

Johnston, Douglas. *Faith-Based Diplomacy Trumping Realpolitik.* New York: Oxford Press, 2003.

Keen, Peter G. W. *The Process Edge.* Boston: Harvard Business School Press, 1997.

———. *Shaping the Future.* Boston: Harvard Business School Press, 1991.

Kelley, Tom, and Jonathan Littman. *The Ten Faces of Innovation*. New York: Doubleday, 2005.

Kelly, Matthew. *The Dream Manager*. New York: Hyperion, 2007.

Kidder, Tracy. *The Soul of a New Machine*. New York: Avon Books, 1981.

Kolditz, Thomas A. *In Extremis Leadership: Leading as If Your Life Depended on It*. San Francisco: Jossey-Bass, 2007.

Kuhn, Thomas S. *The Structure of Scientific Revolutions*. Chicago: The University of Chicago Press, 1962.

Lafley, A. G., and Ram Charan. *The Game-Changer*. New York: Crown Business, 2008.

LeGuin, Ursula K. *Lao Tzu: Tao Te Ching: A Book About the Way and the Power of the Way*. Boston: Shambhala Publications, 1997.

Lencioni, Patrick. *Silos, Politics and Turf Wars*. San Francisco: Jossey-Bass, 2006.

Martin, Roger. *The Opposable Mind: How Successful Leaders Win Through Integrative Thinking*. Boston: Harvard Business School Press, 2007.

Maslow, Abraham H. *Toward a Psychology of Being*. Princeton: D. Van Nostrand Company, 1962.

Mathews, Ryan, and Watts Wacker. *The Deviant's Advantage*. New York: Crown Business, 2002.

McCauley, Cynthia D., Marian N. Ruderman, and Ellen van Velsor. *The Center for Creative Leadership: Handbook of Leadership Development*. San Francisco: Jossey-Bass, 2010.

McGonigal, Jane. *Reality Is Broken: Why Games Make Us Better and How They Can Change the World*. New York: Penguin, 2011.

McGuire, John B., and Gary B. Rhodes. *Transforming Your Leadership Culture*. San Francisco: Jossey-Bass, 2009.

Mills, C. Wright. *The Sociological Imagination*. New York: Oxford University Press, 1959.

Muoio, Anna. "Beg, Borrow, Stimulate." *Fast Company*, 31 Jan. 2001. Web. 05 Oct. 2011.

O'Hara-Devereaux, Mary, and Robert Johansen. *Global Work Bridging Distance, Culture and Time*. San Francisco: Jossey-Bass, 1994.

Pfeffer, Jeffrey, and Robert I. Sutton. *Hard Facts, Dangerous Half-Truths & Total Nonsense: Profiting from Evidence-Based Management*. Boston: Harvard Business School Press, 2006.

Pietersen, Willie. *Reinventing Strategy*. New York: John Wiley & Sons, 2002.

Pinchot, Gifford, and Elizabeth Pinchot. *The Intelligent Organization*. San Francisco: Berrett-Koehler, 1994.

Platoon Leaders. *A Platoon Leader's Tour.* West Point, NY: Center for the Advancement of Leader Development & Organizational Learning, 2010.

Progoff, Ira. *Jung, Synchronicity, and Human Destiny.* New York: Dell Publishing, 1973.

Prothero, Stephen. *God Is Not One.* New York: HarperCollins, 2010.

Rheingold, Howard. *Smart Mobs: The Next Social Revolution.* New York: Perseus Publishing, 2002.

———. *The Virtual Community.* New York: Addison-Wesley, 1993.

———. *Virtual Reality.* New York: Summit Books, 1991.

Rose, Frank. *The Art of Immersion: How the Digital Generation Is Remaking Hollywood, Madison Avenue, and the Way We Tell Stories.* New York: W. W. Norton & Company, 2011.

Rosen, Robert H. *Just Enough Anxiety.* New York: Penguin Group, 2008.

Rosenfeld, Robert, with John Kolstoe. *Making the Invisible Visible: The Human Principles for Sustaining Innovation.* Bridgewater, NJ: Replica Books, 2006.

Schori, Katharine Jefferts. *A Wing and a Prayer.* Harrisburg, PA: Morehouse Publishing, 2007.

Shirky, Clay. *Cognitive Surplus: Creativity and Generosity in a Connected Age.* New York: Penguin, 2010.

———. *Here Comes Everybody: The Power of Organizing Without Organizations.* New York: Penguin, 2008.

Shostak, Arthur B., ed. *Putting Sociology to Work.* New York: David McKay Company, 1974.

Sibbet, David. *Best Practices for Facilitation.* San Francisco: The Grove Consultants International, 2003.

———. *Fundamentals of Graphic Language: Practice Book.* Graphic Guides, 1991.

———. *Principles of Facilitation: The Purpose and Potential of Leading Group Process.* San Francisco: The Grove Consultants International, 2002.

———. *Team Performance: Creating and Sustaining Results.* San Francisco: The Grove Consultants International, 1996.

———. *Visual Meetings: How Graphics, Sticky Notes and Idea Mapping Can Transform Group Productivity.* Hoboken: Wiley, 2010.

———. *Visual Teams: Graphic Tools for Commitment, Innovation, and High Performance.* Hoboken: Wiley, 2011.

Skaug, Ingar. "Breaking Free in Turbulent Times." *Business Leadership Review IV: III.* July 2007. http://www.mbaworld.com/blr.

Smith, W. Stanton. *Decoding Generational Differences*. New York: Deloitte Development LLP, 2008.

Sproull, Lee, and Sara Kiesler. *Connections: New Ways of Working in the Networked Organization*. Cambridge: MIT Press, 1991.

Steffen, Alex. *Worldchanging, Revised and Updated Edition: A User's Guide for the 21st Century*. New York: Abrams, 2011.

Sutton, Robert I. *The No Asshole Rule: Building a Civilized Workplace and Surviving One That Isn't*. New York: Warner Business Books, 2007.

Taleb, Nassim Nicholas. *The Black Swan*. New York: Random House, 2007.

Taylor, Sylvester. "KEYS® to Creativity and Innovation Diamond Model for Creative Climates." CCL, 2010.

Theobald, Robert. *Futures Conditional*. New York: The Bobbs-Merrill Company, 1972.

Tichy, Noel M., and Warren G. Bennis. *Judgment: How Winning Leaders Make Great Calls*. New York: Penguin Group, 2007.

Toffler, Alvin, ed. *Learning for Tomorrow: The Role of the Future in Education*. New York: Vintage Books, 1974.

Tohei, Koichi. *Aikido in Daily Life*. Tokyo: Rikugei Publishing House, 1973.

Traver, Kelly. *The Program: The Brain-Smart Approach to the Healthiest You: The Life-Changing 12-Week Method*. New York: Atria, 2009.

Välikangas, Liisa. *The Resilient Organization: How Adaptive Cultures Thrive Even When Strategy Fails*. New York: McGraw-Hill, 2010.

Vallee, Jacques. *Computer Message System*. New York: McGraw-Hill, 1984.

———. *The Network Revolution: Confessions of a Computer Scientist*. Berkeley: And/Or Press, 1982.

Watson, James D. *Avoid Boring People*. New York: Alfred A. Knopf, 2007.

———. *The Double Helix*. New York: New American Library, 1968.

Watts, Alan W. *The Wisdom of Insecurity*. New York: Vintage Books, 1951.

Wheatley, Margaret J. *Leadership and the New Science*. San Francisco: Berrett-Koehler, 2006.

Whitehead, Alfred North. *Science and the Modern World*. Toronto: The McMillan Company, 1925.

Williamson, Porter B. *Patton's Principles: A Handbook for Managers Who Mean It!* New York: Simon & Schuster, 1982.

Wilson, Edmund, ed. *The Crack-Up*. New York: New Directions, 1945.

Acknowledgments

A lot of what I know about leadership I learned from Roy Amara, who was president of the Institute for the Future in 1973 and brought me to Silicon Valley. Roy passed away on New Year's Eve, 2007. He had leadership qualities that I have come to think of as "Roy's gift" for future leaders. I started writing the first edition of this book right after Roy's death. I feel called to share Roy's gift of leadership with future leaders, as best I can.

Roy was a systematic thinker who focused on disorderly futures. He was a very strong leader in his own quiet and self-effacing way. Roy always treated people with respect, even if he disagreed with them. He encouraged spirited exchange of ideas at the Institute; there were—and are—many debates. But Roy wanted high conflict about ideas *and* high respect for people. The few times I saw him angry, he was still respectful to those who had upset him. Roy kept his commitments and had many long-term friendships. He was a leader that you could count on.

Roy Amara had an ability to be both strong and be humble—in the face of a complex future, an overwhelming present, and a wild mix of personalities at the Institute. The essence of Roy's gift is the wisdom to hold diverse thoughts together. Roy's combination of strength and humility allowed him to engage with others who were very different from him. But Roy's gift also presents a dilemma for leaders: how can you be both strong *and* humble? The leadership skill I call Quiet Transparency came to me based on my experience with Roy.

Roy Amara was both a leader and a maker. He was an engineer and, in a real sense, he made the Institute for the Future and he helped make or remake so many effective organizations with which he worked over his long career. *Leaders Make the Future* is dedicated to Roy Amara in the hope that I can share Roy's gift as we strive to make the future a better place.

I have many others to thank as well, beginning with my colleagues at the Institute for the Future. Marina Gorbis is the Institute's executive director, and she encouraged me to embark on this volunteer effort at a time when the Institute was extremely busy with paying projects. Marina's work on "socialstructed" organizations has been inspiring to me, particularly in Chapter 10 on Commons Creating. Kathi Vian is the leader of the annual Ten-Year Forecast, and this book builds directly on her base of wisdom and foresight. The ideas of both Jane McGonigal and Jason Tester were very constructive for me as I was writing. Thanks to Andrea Saveri and Howard Rheingold for their groundbreaking work on commons and cooperation.

Rachel Lyle Hatch joined IFTF as I was writing the book and added so much to the project in so many ways. Rachel somehow manages to be a great content contributor, an extremely well-organized person, and a positive life force all at once. My assistants Kathy Seddiqui and Laurel Funkhouser helped clear the way for this project and manage it to completion while still carrying a full-time project load. Natalie Matzinger Fernández, a global business student from Brazil, did an internship with us and added a unique perspective at an important time for the book. Deepa Mehta joined me at IFTF as I was completing the second edition and added greatly to the manuscript.

Berrett-Koehler is a very unusual publishing house. I have done books for large publishers and I have had several famous editors. Nothing in my experience, however, compares to the quality of BK. My editor Steve Piersanti is by far the best editor with whom I have ever worked. In fact, Steve is the best editor I can imagine. I come away from each session with Steve exhausted, but he inspired me to take the second edition to a new level. Rick Wilson was a great help with the cover and production. Indeed, I thank everyone at BK, since it seems as though every single person gets involved with every book. I certainly feel supported as an author. Jeevan Sivasubramaniam assembles a remarkable group of reviewers who give constructively critical feedback. My reviewers for this book were Valerie Andrews, Danielle Scott, Frank Basler, and Douglas Hammer. Each provided great insight, in four very different ways. BK has a unique approach to external review and I find it extremely useful. I'm sure that this process has made this a much better book, and I hope I have lived up to their aspirations for the final product. Jim Levine of Levine Greenberg Agency is my literary agent. Jim has the insight of an author and the constructive guidance of a great agent. I am very grateful for Jim's support. Tanya Grove and Dave Peattie at BookMatters did a wonderful—very dedicated and personal—job editing this manuscript.

While this book is about my point of view on leadership in the future, I have learned so much from my experiences at Institute for the Future. I am very grateful for this opportunity, which continues to be inspiring for me.

The current Board of Trustees at Institute for the Future is a wonderful mix of people that includes: Aaron Cramer, Kelly Traver, Karen Edwards, Deborah Engel, Marina Gorbis, Ellen Marram, Bob Sutton, Rod Falcon, Jean Hagan, and Lawrence Wilkinson. Thank you so much for your support.

The current Institute for the Future community is the most exciting mix of people I have worked with in my thirty-five-year history at IFTF. My sincere thanks to Richard Adler, Dawn Alva, Robin Bogott, Jamais Cascio, Mathias Crawford, Vivian Distler, Jake Dunagan, Rod Falcon, Marina Gorbis, Jean Hagan, David Evan Harris, Rachel Lyle Hatch, Lyn Jeffery, Andy Lam, Kim Lawrence, Harvey Lehtman, Mike Liebhold, Karin Lubeck, Miriam Avery Lueck, Rachel Maguire, Jane McGonigal, Lisa Mumbach, Sean Ness, Neela Nuristani, Alex Pang, David Pescovitz, Jody Radzik, Kathy Seddiqui, Chuck Sieloff, Rob Swigart, Jason Tester, Anthony Townsend, Kathi Vian, and Anthony Weeks.

Index

ABOUT THE AUTHOR

Bob Johansen has worked for more than thirty-five years as a ten-year forecaster. Focusing on the human side of new technologies, Bob was one of the first social scientists to study the human and organizational impacts of the Internet when it was called the ARPAnet. He also has a deep interest in the future of religion and values.

Bob served as the Institute for the Future's president from 1996 to 2004. He now invests his time with IFTF sponsors, writing, public speaking, and facilitating top-executive workshops across a wide range of organizations. Bob is the IFTF Distinguished Fellow.

Bob is the author or co-author of seven previous books, including *Upsizing the Individual in the Downsized Organization,* a guide for organizations undergoing technological change and reengineering; *GlobalWork,* a guide to managing global cross-cultural teams; and *Get There Early,* an introduction to the foresight to insight to action cycle that helps leaders engage with the future context in constructive ways.

A social scientist with an interdisciplinary background, Bob holds a BS degree from the University of Illinois, which he attended on a basketball scholarship, and a PhD from Northwestern University, where he focused on sociology of religion but was also introduced to the ARPAnet and interactive computing. Bob also has an MDiv degree from what is now called Colgate Rochester Crozer Divinity School, where he studied comparative religions.

ABOUT IFTF

The Institute for the Future (IFTF) is an independent nonprofit research group in Silicon Valley. It works with organizations of all kinds to help them make better, more informed decisions about the future. IFTF provides independent foresight to provoke insights that lead to action. The Institute is based in Palo Alto, California, a community at the crossroads of technological innovation, social experimentation, and global interchange. IFTF was founded in 1968 by a group of former RAND Corporation researchers with grants from Arthur Vining Davis Foundation and the Ford Foundation to take leading-edge futures research methodologies beyond the world of classified defense work.

For more information, visit http://www.iftf.org.

ABOUT CCL

The Center for Creative Leadership (CCL) is a top-ranked, global provider of executive education that unlocks individual and organizational potential through its exclusive focus on leadership education and research. The *Financial Times* has ranked CCL's public programs in the top ten internationally for ten consecutive years. Founded in 1970 as a nonprofit, educational institution, CCL helps clients worldwide cultivate creative leadership—the capacity to achieve more than imagined by thinking and acting beyond boundaries—through an array of programs, products, and other services. CCL is headquartered in Greensboro, North Carolina, with campuses in Colorado Springs, Colorado; San Diego, California; Brussels, Belgium; and Singapore; and with offices in Pune, India and in Moscow. Supported by more than four hundred faculty members and staff, it works annually with more than twenty thousand leaders and two thousand organizations. In addition, twelve Network Associates around the world offer selected CCL programs and assessments.

Also by Bob Johansen

Get There Early

Sensing the Future to Compete in the Present

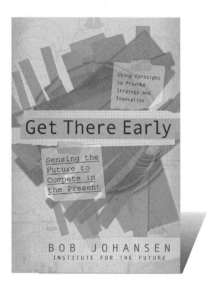

It's the ultimate paradox for leaders: you can't predict the future, but you must make sense of it in order to thrive. You need to sort out what's important, devise strategies based on your own point of view, and get there ahead of the crowd. Bob Johansen shares techniques refined by the Institute for the Future to help you navigate your organization's road to the future. Through fascinating examples from organizations such as Procter & Gamble, Disney, Apple, Reuters, UPS, and the Centers for Disease Control, he shows how these techniques enable you to find new markets, new customers, and new products ahead of your competitors. Using the institute's three-step Foresight to Insight to Action Cycle, you'll be able to establish a position before your late-arriving competitors even have a chance to organize.

Hardcover, 288 pages, ISBN 978-1-57675-440-5
PDF ebook, ISBN 978-1-57675-531-0

Berrett–Koehler Publishers, Inc.
www.bkconnection.com   800.929.2929

Berrett–Koehler
Publishers

A community dedicated to creating
a world that works for all

Visit Our Website: www.bkconnection.com

Read book excerpts, see author videos and Internet movies, read our authors' blogs, join discussion groups, download book apps, find out about the BK Affiliate Network, browse subject-area libraries of books, get special discounts, and more!

Subscribe to Our Free E-Newsletter, the *BK Communiqué*

Be the first to hear about new publications, special discount offers, exclusive articles, news about bestsellers, and more! Get on the list for our free e-newsletter by going to **www.bkconnection.com**.

Get Quantity Discounts

Berrett-Koehler books are available at quantity discounts for orders of ten or more copies. Please call us toll-free at (800) 929-2929 or email us at **bkp .orders@aidcvt.com**.

Join the BK Community

BKcommunity.com is a virtual meeting place where people from around the world can engage with kindred spirits to create a world that works for all. **BKcommunity.com** members may create their own profiles, blog, start and participate in forums and discussion groups, post photos and videos, answer surveys, announce and register for upcoming events, and chat with others online in real time. Please join the conversation!

Certified

Corporation
bcorporation.net